**REDISCOVER TH— ☑ P9-EAO-881
OF NATURE WIT—**

THE SCIENCE AND ART OF TRACKING
Tom Brown shares the wisdom of generations of animal trackers—revelations that awaken us to our own place in nature and in the world

THE TRACKER
Tom Brown's classic true story—the most powerful and magical high-spiritual adventure since *The Teachings of Don Juan*

DATE DUE

the ancien—

THE VISION
Tom Brown's profound, personal journey into an ancient mystical experience, the Vision Quest

THE QUEST
The acclaimed outdoorsman shows how we can save our planet

THE JOURNEY
A message of hope and harmony for our earth and our spirits—Tom Brown's vision for healing our world

GRANDFATHER
The incredible true story of a remarkable Native American and his lifelong search for peace and truth in nature

AWAKENING SPIRITS
For the first time, Tom Brown shares the unique meditation exercises used by students of his personal Tracker Classes

THE WAY OF THE SCOUT
Tom Brown's most empowering work—a collection of stories illustrating the advanced tracking skills taught to him by Grandfather

**AND THE BESTSELLING SERIES
OF TOM BROWN'S FIELD GUIDES**

Berkley Books by Tom Brown, Jr.

THE TRACKER

THE SEARCH

THE VISION

THE QUEST

THE JOURNEY

GRANDFATHER

AWAKENING SPIRITS

THE WAY OF THE SCOUT

THE SCIENCE AND ART OF TRACKING

TOM BROWN'S FIELD GUIDE TO NATURE AND SURVIVAL FOR
CHILDREN

TOM BROWN'S FIELD GUIDE TO THE FORGOTTEN WILDERNESS

TOM BROWN'S FIELD GUIDE TO CITY AND SUBURBAN SURVIVAL

TOM BROWN'S FIELD GUIDE TO NATURE OBSERVATIONS AND
TRACKING

TOM BROWN'S FIELD GUIDE TO WILDERNESS SURVIVAL

TOM BROWN'S FIELD GUIDE TO LIVING WITH THE EARTH

TOM BROWN'S GUIDE TO WILD EDIBLE AND MEDICINAL PLANTS

Most Berkley Books are available at special quantity discounts for bulk
purchases for sales promotions, premiums, fund-raising, or educational use.
Special books, or book excerpts, can also be created to fit specific needs.

For details, write: Special Markets, The Berkley Publishing Group, 375
Hudson Street, New York, New York 10014.

THE WAY
OF THE
SCOUT

TOM BROWN, JR.

Santa Fe Community
College Library
6401 Richards Ave.
Santa Fe, NM 87508

BERKLEY BOOKS, NEW YORK

If you purchased this book without a cover, you should be aware that this book is stolen property. It was reported as "unsold and destroyed" to the publisher, and neither the author nor the publisher has received any payment for this "stripped book."

THE WAY OF THE SCOUT

A Berkley Book / published by arrangement with the author

PRINTING HISTORY
Berkley trade paperback edition/ June 1995
Berkley mass-market edition / July 1997

All rights reserved.
Copyright © 1995 by Tom Brown, Jr.
Cover art by Julie Schulweis.
This book, or parts thereof, may not be reproduced
in any form without permission.
For information address: The Berkley Publishing Group,
a division of Penguin Putnam Inc.,
375 Hudson Street, New York, New York 10014.

The Penguin Putnam Inc. World Wide Web site address is
www.penguinputnam.com

ISBN: 0-425-15910-8

BERKLEY®
Berkley Books are published by The Berkley Publishing Group,
a division of Penguin Putnam Inc.,
375 Hudson Street, New York, New York 10014.
BERKLEY and the "B" design
are trademarks belonging to Penguin Putnam Inc.

PRINTED IN THE UNITED STATES OF AMERICA

10 9 8 7 6 5 4 3

CONTENTS

Santa Fe Community
College Library
6401 Richards Ave.
Santa Fe, NM 87508

INTRODUCTION

For those of you who are not familiar with my previous books, I would like to begin by giving you a brief introduction about my life and the man I call Grandfather. I grew up in a small town in southern New Jersey that was located on the eastern edge of what is called the Pine Barrens. The Pine Barrens is a unique area, to say the least, in that its subsoil is sand. Beach sand to be precise, for the area, millions of years ago, was the ocean floor. The forests are primarily made up of pitch pine, scrub oak, cedar, blueberry, and hundreds of other less abundant plants, many unique. It is a beautiful wilderness area in its

1

own right, but today it has changed terribly. When I was a child, this wilderness was vast and trackless, impenetrable in many places, with grand cedar swamps and tea-color waters. Now all has changed.

When I was just seven years old, I met an eighty-three-year-old Apache man named Stalking Wolf who, within a week, and for the rest of my life, I would call Grandfather. It was startling enough that an Apache would be in New Jersey; more startling was the relationship that developed between this old native American and a white boy. Fortunately for me and my insatiable appetite for wilderness and adventure, Grandfather chose to come here to the Pine Barrens to visit relatives. To me and my best friend Rick, who shared my passion for wilderness and ancient skills, Grandfather was the embodiment of all I've ever wanted to learn. He seemed to hold the answers to all the mysteries of creation, and the mastery of the ancient skills that had long since been forgotten.

Grandfather was raised not on a reservation but with his clan in the northern reaches of Mexico. His great-grandfather took care of him after his family was massacred. Grandfather's people shunned the ways of the white man, and permitted nothing in their camps made by anyone but themselves. Grandfather lived with his people until his early twenties, when he began to wander across both North and South America, searching to preserve the old ways and seeking spiritual truth. He became a master of tracking, survival, and awareness, and he lived the philosophy of the earth. For the nearly eleven years that I knew him, he lived the simplicity of pure survival, never using anything from society. He had only planned to spend a few weeks here in the Pine Barrens, but because of Rick and me he decided to spend the decade.

Through the years Grandfather taught us the skills of

pure survival, tracking, awareness, and the philosophy of living in harmony and balance with the Earth. But of all his teachings, these physical skills were just a small part. His full concentration was on the spiritual aspects of life, for it was Grandfather's passion to pass on the simplicity and truth of the spiritual realities before they were lost to time and obscurity. After all, the quest for spiritual truth and simplicity were his vision, that which he sought for his more than sixty-three years of wandering apart from his people. Yet Grandfather taught another element, with much the same passion that he had when teaching the spiritual and philosophical skills, and that was the way of the scout.

A few years after we had first met Grandfather, and after countless hours of practicing the skills of survival, tracking, awareness, and philosophy, Grandfather began to teach us the way of the scout. He began by telling us stories of the ancient scouts of his clan. He was very quick to point out that these were not the same kind of scouts that we hear about the U.S. Cavalry hiring to hunt down other native Americans. These scouts belonged to a secret medicine society within the clan. In fact it was so secret that no one outside of the society knew who were its members. Yet the scouts' main function was to be the eyes and ears of the clan. They would locate the game, direct the clan away from its enemies, decide where the clan would migrate and through what route, and otherwise keep the clan safe.

The scouts, beyond being secretive, were the best survivalists and trackers and the most highly aware individuals, most attuned to the earth and the spirit-that-moves-through-all-things. They were masters of escape, evasion, getting in and out of enemy encampments, setting man traps, stalking, and countless other skills. They took great pride in being able to leave camp with nothing and travel endlessly, through the toughest terrain and harshest weather conditions, and survive lavishly and undetectably. The scouts trained their own through an intense process that lasted more than ten years. To Rick and me the scouts were like gods, and we wanted to be scouts more than we wanted anything else in life. After all, Grandfather had begun his life first as a scout, before following his spiritual vision.

So that is how my own passion and quest to learn the way of the scout began. Of all the physical skills that Grandfather ever taught me, the scout philosophy was the most compelling and exciting, surpassed in my mind only by the spiritual teachings. What lies ahead is my journey into the realm of the scout, a journey that continues to this day.

CHAPTER 1

THE WAY OF THE SCOUT

Grandfather's teaching was always three-fold. He taught the practical skills of survival, tracking, awareness, and the philosophy of living with the earth. More so, he focused his teaching on the spiritual philosophies, which he considered the most important. In fact he spent most of his teaching time—perhaps ninety percent of it—conveying to us the skills and powers of the spiritual dimension. The purity of survival, tracking, and acute awareness were almost always delivered with intense spiritual overtones. Yet, a third part of his teaching seemed to bring together all of the rest, and that was the teaching of the scout skills and philosophy.

It became abundantly clear to us right from the onset that Grandfather would teach a skill in two different ways. For instance, he would show us a particular shelter for the classic survival situation, then after we had mastered that shelter he would go beyond and into the realm of the scout. He would add, ''Now if you want this shelter to become invisible on the landscape and thus to all eyes, then you must build it in this way.'' He would then demonstrate to us the way the shelter would be modified to fit the secretive aspect of scout life. He did this with all aspects of survival, stalking and movement, tracking, and awareness, using these classic skills as a starting point, then bringing them one step further and into the realm of the scout.

Survival living went far beyond the common ancient knowledge and skill. Grandfather took it to new heights of perfection and mastery. Rick and I learned high-speed and invisible survival techniques, so that hardly even a trained scout could find our camp, or evidence of our existence there after we had abandoned it and moved on. He demanded of us and we of ourselves that we be able to enter a survival situation purely, without any tools or clothing, naked, and survive lavishly no matter what the weather conditions or topography. We became scout purists, where everything came from the earth and was made by our own hands. As far as Grandfather was concerned, if we went into a survival situation with our clothing on then we were not living in survival, but camping.

Our tools came from the rocks and bones of the earth. Our foraging was like that of a deer, eating the vegetation when moving from one place to another, rarely stopping for a meal. We even used secretive traps and other hunting techniques the scouts had developed to remain invisible. Most of all we learned that there was no hardship or struggle in the wilderness, for the wilderness became our home. Everything was provided for us by the earth and we trusted the earth to take care of all our needs. Grandfather would continually tell us that if there was a struggle, or there was pain, in a survival situation then it simply meant that our skills were severely lacking. He would say, ''Only those with poor skills will find that survival is a battle, a struggle, and pain. It is only the 'children of the earth' that know the earth as home, for they have the skill to flourish.''

To the scout, the wilderness had to be his home. He had to live in perfect balance and harmony with creation and follow its laws. From his smokeless fires to his invisible shelters, everything had to blend into the flow of life so that there was no disruption in that flow. His skill had to keep him safe and secure in all elements and landscapes, where he would need for nothing. His self-sufficiency would give him the ultimate freedom to go as long and as far as he needed, without depending on anything but the earth. Until the scout attained and exceeded this level of skill and ease in living, he would stand out on the land and become a liability. Classic survival skills were not enough; they were just the beginning of that perfection and ultimate invisibility.

Tracking went far beyond our wildest dreams and expectations. At first we learned the basic techniques that all trackers of Grandfather's clan had done. We learned to read the various trails, runs, beds, lays, feeding areas, and numerous other signs. We then learned to follow tracks, and feel the animal moving through them. But then we learned the science and art form of tracking that was only known to the scouts. Up until this point in our tracking development, Rick and I had assumed that tracking was little more than following a set of lifeless depressions in the ground to get to an animal. We could certainly identify the animal, but beyond that we might only be able to define the animal's weight, what time he passed, and possibly a few other minor details. Also, we could only track effectively on soft ground. Gravel and forest litter were extremely difficult and time-consuming.

Eventually Grandfather began to teach us scout tracking. He defined the tracking that we had done as typical or novice tracking, but the tracking of the scout was defined as master tracking. Even at the onset, the difference became obvious. Grandfather told us that the earth was like an open book, filled with stories. These stories were written not only in the softest ground but also on every other type of soil even on rock. Our next step then was to transcend the typical tracker mentality and begin to become master trackers. To this day, the greatest tracking thrill of my life was when Grandfather first showed me how to read track "compressions" in impossible soils and on solid rock. That was when I began to look through the eyes of a master tracker and the earth never looked the same again.

Our tracking then became high-speed and there was no soil or rock environment where we would ever lose a trail or miss a track. It was at this time, just when I thought that tracking could not get any better or that there could be anything else to learn, that Grandfather introduced to us the magic of the "pressure releases." He said, "You must stop looking at the tracks as lifeless depressions in the ground. Instead, and you have noticed, inside of the track is a tiny landscape. There are hills, valleys, peaks, ridges, domes, pocks, and countless other little features. These features the scouts developed into a science, that which they call the 'pressure releases.' It is through these pressure releases that the scout can know everything about the animal or man that he is tracking. The scouts of my clan could identify and define over four thousand of these pressure releases, and I know of no peoples of the earth that have been able to do the same.''

I was awestruck as I listened. I had seen these ''pressure releases'' inside a track, but I never knew what they were, and I could not imagine that there were over four thousand of them. Grandfather continued, ''A man or an animal is propped off of the land and stabilized by his feet. Not only do the feet stabilize and balance the man or animal, but they adjust to its every move, even the tiniest movements. The feet then are in constant motion, balancing, shifting, reacting, and moving to compensate for all body movements and thus keep the body upright. It is this balancing and shifting that produces the pressure releases, and so, each pressure release has a function. If you can identify the pressure release you can then identify the function, and know the movement of the body that produced the pressure release. A track then is not just a window to the past, but to the animal's very soul.''

I asked Grandfather how fine a motion could be picked up in the pressure releases. He giggled at the shocked expression on my face when he told me that the pressure releases could tell if the eyes blinked, if the stomach was full or empty, any oncoming diseases, old injuries, swallowing, panting, speed, turning, emotion, intent, and the list went on and on and on. My look must have turned to skepticism, for suddenly Grandfather told Rick and me to stand up tall and straight and pay close attention to our feet. Once we were relaxed and fully conscious of our feet, he told us to swallow and see if we could feel the swallow move our feet. I was absolutely struck speechless such was my amazement. Not only had my feet moved, but I had felt them shift dramatically. He then asked us to take a deep breath and feel it in our feet, then to move the head slightly, and finally to lift a finger; all felt so clearly in our feet as they shifted in compensation.

We sat and listened to him explain the power of pressure releases to us throughout the rest of the day. Once, as he talked, Rick and I watched a rabbit moving far behind Grandfather, and we followed it with our eyes. We looked back at Grandfather and he smiled and said, ''Who knows that rabbit better? You who have seen the rabbit, or I who have not?'' He then motioned to us to follow him to the rabbit tracks. He glanced down and asked us if it was a male or a female, how old was the rabbit, was its stomach full or empty, was it fearful or relaxed, did it have any old injuries or afflictions, and countless other questions for which we had no answers. He then asked again, ''Who then knows this animal better? You see, Grandsons, awareness without tracking is incomplete. Tracking is the ultimate extension of awareness, it broadens, defines, and completes the philosophy of awareness. This is seeing through the eyes of the scout.''

So began our studies in the grand realm of pressure releases. We worked long and hard on this very detailed science. It consumed us with its magic, and we learned slowly but effectively. It became obvious why the scouts had developed tracking to such a splendid and detailed science. By just glancing at a track they would know everything about an animal or a man. They could read emotion, all the external physical movements, as well as penetrate the very core of the body. They could tell how aware someone was, how strong, whether he or she was angry, sad, happy, healthy. This kind of tracking actually became an invasion of privacy to a startling degree. After all, the scout could even tell if a track's maker had to urinate or not, and even to what degree one had to urinate. They could even tell if a bubble of air moved from one part of the stomach to another. This was the ultimate awareness without a doubt, and we were obsessed with learning its power.

We began to study people like we had studied the animals. We would watch people react to their environment and each other, recognizing their mood swings and then identifying those swings with the pressure releases. We would watch how they moved, what they observed, and what they didn't, then this too we would identify with the pressure releases. People's actions and reactions began to fascinate us. Everyone became a source of study, and we even used ourselves as ready subjects. We would be starving from a day without food, then track through the ground, eat a big meal, and track back alongside our original tracks. Thus laying side by side we could tell the differences and appearances in the pressure releases that marked a full and an empty belly. We did this when we were upset, happy, thoughtful, sick, injured, full, hungry, thirsty, and tired. We identified it first in ourselves and then confirmed it by studying others.

The pressure releases were and will always be a tremendous source of inspiration and wonder, and that which divides the common tracker from the master. Yet, our study of tracks did not end there. Grandfather would pick up a crushed cigarette butt and ask, "Right-or left-handed, male or female, degree of strength, mood, habits, and how long ago?" Question after question, till we found ourselves dedicating countless hours to the study of cigarette butts, cans, spent shotgun shells, tire marks, door handles, and anything else that people would come in contact with, discard on the landscape, disturb, or otherwise use. From them we learned to read far more than we at first could ever imagine. Every detail was scrutinized, analyzed, experimented with, and understood.

Grandfather taught us to expand our awareness and

tracking beyond even that level. He would stand beside a tree, point to a missing limb and ask, "How long ago was this done? What did it and how? What direction did the cutter come from? Was his axe or saw dull or sharp, was he right- or left-handed, what degree of strength did he have?" Grandfather told us that we should always hold one question in our minds at all times: What is this telling me? It did not matter if the landscape was disturbed or undisturbed by man; for him, all landscapes, all things had a deeper hidden meaning. All around us were secrets that had to be unraveled, mysteries that had to be understood, and countless questions that had to be answered. Thus we were always searching, seeking, and asking questions of the environment, whether of nature or of man.

Grandfather also took awareness to its highest, almost unimaginable level of mastery. Grandfather considered awareness to be the doorway to the world of spirit, thus the most powerful tool of the scout. He first began to teach us this expansion of awareness through the scout philosophy of the "concentric rings." He first began our study by saying, "If you were to take a stone and throw it into a quiet pond, the surface would be disturbed by its plunge. Where the stone strikes the water, there is the initial splash. Then, from the source of that splash come concentric rings, which move out far and wide, eventually reaching the most distant banks. Nature is not unlike this pond. When something moves in nature, it too sends forth concentric rings.

"However, unlike the quiet pond, the surface of nature is always moving. It has a background, a symphony of sound and motion. Whenever this symphony expands and grows markedly louder and movement increases, this is a concentric ring. So too, when there is a hush in the symphony this also is a concentric ring. If a fox moves in the distant bush, that is the initial splash. The birds set forth an alarm call, there is movement of other animals, and other alarm calls. The animals outside of this initial disturbance react to that disturbance also, like a concentric ring, and then animals outside of that ring react to that same ring and create another. A trained scout knows these rings, these disruptions and voices of nature, so that he can know something is moving far outside of his physical senses.''

As the pressure releases expanded tracking to a science and gave the scout exact identification of that which he tracked, the concentric rings moved a scout's awareness level far outside of his physical senses. Together they were two of the most vital tools to the scout. As with everything else we did, Grandfather was not satisfied in teaching us only the common awareness techniques that were known by his clan, for he demanded of us the awareness level of the scout. He taught us techniques that took us beyond the effects of using wide-angle and varied vision. We learned acute sensory awareness, which would push our physical senses to their maximum potential. Our senses were pushed so hard that they would actually hurt from overuse. It was only by building up our sensory stamina that eventually we could transcend the pain.

Yet, with all that Grandfather taught us in the realms of sensory awareness, we knew there had to be more, much more. Grandfather's ability transcended all physical awareness, and we knew that he had to be using something beyond what he was teaching to us. So too could we see in him not only a grand communication with nature and creation, but a dynamic communication with the world of spirit. Without it being said, we knew that whatever Grandfather was holding back from us was the key to the grander awareness that he so often spoke of. Looking back now, I can understand clearly why Grandfather was holding back, for he wanted us to fully master the skills in the physical before we began to study the skills of the spiritual. It was this spiritual aspect of scout life that was his most important skill.

Grandfather first began to teach us the spiritual aspects of scout life soon after he introduced us to the wisdom of the pressure releases. Though we had been involved in learning spiritual things since the day I had met Grandfather, these spiritual teachings were not necessarily used for the scout life. The spiritual teachings up to this time were for esoteric applications. What we needed were spiritual techniques that would aid in the life-style of the scout: to help him through his missions, and transcend the flesh in times of need. Generally the basic spiritual teachings of Grandfather required that one have a grander purpose beyond the self, but we suspected that the spiritual teachings applicable to scout life could be used any time, not just in times of dire need or when the world beyond the flesh beckoned.

As with everything else Grandfather had shown us in tracking, survival, and awareness, instead of teaching us something new, he would expand on what we all ready knew. We learned to apply our communications with the spirit-that-moves-through-all-things, and with the spirit world, to the scout life. We could use these spiritual communications to go beyond the limitations of the flesh and of common awareness, and reach to the limitless universe. We modified the ''sacred silence,'' which is the way of transcending the flesh and moving to the world of spirit, and used it while living the life of the scout. We intensified ''inner vision,'' which is the voice of the spirit world found within us, and we learned to move continuously in the ''oneness'' between the flesh and spirit.

We found after the first year of Grandfather's teaching that this balancing yielded an equality, thus the scout was an equality—equal parts flesh and spirit. It became obvious that to operate only in the flesh would be a liability, and one could never hope to achieve the powers of the scout through only the physical practices. Without the spiritual abilities, there could be no scout, and we could not do most of what being a scout required. More often than not the spiritual skills were stressed even more than the physical skills, and we found that many of the physical skills would not work without a deep spiritual understanding and proficiency. As with everything else, without the spirit, there was nothing. Life would then be so shallow.

Like everything else we did in expanding into the consciousness of the scout, we improved our stalking and movement to a point of invisibility. We learned movement techniques to blend with the ebb and flow of the symphony of life, so that we moved with the wilderness and out of context with man's reality. The "fox walk" we had once learned was not good enough for the scout. Certainly the fox walk, the primary walk of all peoples that lived close to the earth, was quieting, but the scout walk created an aura of invisibility. We thus learned to move like a shadow, creating no disturbances, for each step blessed the earth like a prayer. The "scout walk" moved us into a world of stealth and secrecy, where we moved outside the context not only of man's time, but also of animal time.

Stalking we also pushed beyond our personal concepts of what we thought the stalk to be. It became the ultimate movement, a deep meditation, in which we moved with the spirit of nature, deftly slipping across landscapes where hardly a cat could stalk. The scout's stalk was not just the art of moving silently and without abrupt motion. It was the expansion of movement into the silent realms of the spirit and the magnification of the mind. It was movement that fit into that place where men and animals were blinded to. We learned that the scout stalked in the area that animals and man did not know to exist, a place far outside the realms of common perception and understanding. Scout stalking was the ability to move in the realm between flesh and spirit.

Along with raising our stalking and movement skills, we learned the art form of camouflage. We learned to use the elements of the earth to make our bodies blend perfectly with the environment in which we stalked or waited. We painted and dappled with ash, charcoal, various soils and subsoils, clay, and numerous other elements, streaking our bodies or buckskins into an artistic blend of invisibility. Here too the camouflage transcended its physical applications of camouflaging agents, and moved into the spiritual realities. We learned not only to camouflage our bodies, but also to camouflage our minds and spirits, moving into the place of invisibility. We became so adept at camouflage that neither animal nor man could detect us even if they looked directly at us.

We brought all of the elements of movement, stalking, and camouflage into the startling consciousness of invisibility. We practiced these skills on the most aware animals, knowing if we could stalk and ultimately touch these animals, then the animal called man would be unbelievably easy. Like all the rest of the scout skills, movement, stalking, and camouflage could not be obtained fully on a physical level. The grand spiritual element had to be fused with every aspect of the skill. Without that spiritual level there could be no invisibility. A key element to camouflage was the ability to know intimately that which we stalked; for each entity, man or animal, had its own individual area of weakness, and it was in that area we would move.

While studying tracking and pressure releases, we also studied people intensely. We had to learn every quirk, not just the ways that are general to most people, but each little idiosyncrasy. We learned to look for people's patterns and ruts, what they observed and what they did not. We watched their actions and reactions, and learned to identify their level of awareness as well as their blind spots. We learned how people would look yet not see, how they became so focused on the flesh and out of touch with the reality of the earth and spirit. We watched people lust after the gods of safety, security, and comfort, and we could see how to use this passion against them. Grandfather pushed us hard, so that eventually there was no one that we could not stalk. There was no situation that we could not get in and out of easily. Our observations and analysis of people became a violation of privacy, nearly like reading someone's mind through their tracks, their actions, and their reactions to life around them.

Our training certainly took us far beyond the common skills of survival, tracking, and awareness, but the scouts were privy to countless other skills. According to Grandfather, these scout skills, like the pressure releases, were known and practiced only by the scouts. To the other members of a scout's tribe and clan, they were unknown. These were the skills that would take the scout into realms beyond comprehension. They were a discipline, a way of life, that would lead the scout to mastery of his art. These were the skills and concepts that most intrigued Rick and me, for they were not common knowledge. This obscurity added a great sense of magic and wonder to our practice, impassioning us to mastery.

On this higher level of scout skills, body control was

first on the list. Grandfather taught us that unless we could control our bodies through the mind, we would never master the scout art form. Body control enabled the scout to go beyond situations that would kill all other people. We learned to control our heartbeat and metabolism, raising and lowering them with just a thought. We learned to transcend thirst, cold, injury, and pain. By our second year we could enter frigid waters and command our bodies to sweat profusely, such was the power of our metabolism when uplifted by the mind's command. We learned to accelerate healing time, travel incredible distances with no rest, and otherwise push our bodies to do things we at first did not believe could be done.

Along with our mastery of body control, we did a daily workout routine. We could be sure, no matter what the time of year or the weather, that every day we were with Grandfather there would be a heavy workout schedule. He also expected us to work out even when we were not with him. Strength and agility were foremost to the scout. We dragged heavy logs for miles, climbed trees with huge sandstone boulders strapped to our waists, swam for hours towing logs behind us, and did a primitive weight-lifting routine using heavy logs and rocks in place of barbells. We ran constantly, moved through the forest from treetop to treetop, and pushed ourselves in the torrid heat of summer and the frigid temperatures of winter. Grandfather told us that we should do our workouts in the elements where our bodies must be used. To do a workout in the gym might cause our bodies to cramp or falter in climatic extremes.

Grandfather also taught us the "wolverine" fighting techniques of the scouts, combined with the use of fighting weapons such as the short lance, fighting sticks, and knives. We learned to release the "animal within," which is the primal mind and body. The "animal," unlike the normal human consciousness, knows no limitations or restrictions, just action and reaction, where the primal self directs the body. Where thought is concerned, there is always restriction and slow reaction. Yet, with all this demanding fitness routine, the fighting techniques, and the releasing of the animal within, the scout was anything but warlike. The scout code was that of the peacemaker, always the last to pick up the lance. We were taught to walk away from a fight even if it meant humiliating ourselves. Peace was the way of the scout.

Scouts did not allow hatred, prejudice, or anger to become ruler of their lives. They knew that these things were extreme "bad medicine" and would hinder clear thinking and pure action. The scout always held himself above such pettiness and instead would only allow love to direct his life. The scout learned tolerance, compassion, and love, even for his fiercest enemy. The martial and demanding physical fitness routines were not so much for war, but to build a scout's self-confidence and discipline. Grandfather hardly ever mentioned the war or fighting application, but it was a comfort for us to know that it was there if the extreme need ever arose.

Grandfather put major stress on the various strategies of the scout. We learned escape and evasion techniques, how to throw bloodhounds off our trail, how to erase our tracks, backtrack, raid camps, avoid traps and trip wires, and otherwise outwit our enemy. These techniques and strategies were driven into our heads year after year, until we had an unbelievably vast arsenal of scout tactics at our command. Along with these countless strategies came countless man traps. During my years with Grandfather I learned 232 primitive, very effective and deadly traps. Out of these 103 were man traps designed by the scouts. They are an unbelievable assortment of trip wires, deadfalls, pit traps, drop traps, spiked traps, whip traps, and many others, each designed to detain, injure, or kill someone if necessary. We loved trying out the various traps on each other. Rick and I would try to trap one another on any occasion, even at times in our own homes.

Nothing, however, was more exciting than the greatest scout weapon of all, that of psychological warfare. I believe that psychological warfare was brought to an art form and science by the scouts. These were mental tactics devised to confuse, frighten, anger, terrify, and otherwise bewilder the enemy. The effects were long-lasting, to say the least. In fact, I'm sure that there are people still confused or frightened today from psychological warfare I played on them thirty years ago. This, more than anything else, Grandfather took great delight in both teaching us and using on us. It was all so devious, designed to hit people at the most vulnerable part of their consciousness. Yet, here again, Grandfather would never permit us to take psychological warfare to its limits. That would only happen in cases of extreme need.

The last but most important rule of the scout was secrecy. Not only secrecy in our raids and missions but also in our everyday lives. Like the scouts of old, we had to lead a dual life. Our scout life and all that we did we never mentioned at home, at school, or even to those people closest to us. To open up in this way would only compromise our mission and life-style as scouts. Yet it was fun to lead this dual life, in much the same way that the ancient Ninjas lived. We played dumb all the time, especially when we heard people discussing sightings of the Jersey Devil or other stories that originated from the aftermath of one of our raids. As far as Rick and I were concerned, the scout life was the only life, a life filled with adventure, excitement, and rapture. Though we did not go out on our first raid alone until we had practiced strenuously for more than three years, even the practice and grueling workouts were adventure in themselves.

CHAPTER 2

The Party

This day began much like any other day in our Pine Barrens camp. Nothing about it gave us a clue that it was to become one of the most important days of our lives. Rick and I were practicing our scout skills by the stream. We both stood on a log that was nearly twenty-five feet above the water, spanning our swimming area. We had been going about our mock battle since dawn, and for nearly two hours, we could not drive each other off the log. We had used the three-quarter lances, the short fighting sticks, and now had reverted to combat without weapons. Still, as tired as we were, neither of us would give in and call it quits. It was exasperating in a way, because no matter what fighting tactic we used, the other always had a countermove. It was frustrating and draining, to say the least. I knew from past experience that the battle would not end until one of us gave in and quit. Oftentimes, a full day and night would pass before either of us would reach this point. Then it would have to be by mutual agreement. If just one gave up, he would be subject to ridicule from the other until the next fight on the log.

Both of us knew, without saying a word, that this would be one of those long days on the log. Neither Rick nor I wanted to give in and do something else. When I ventured the possibility of quitting, Rick countered with ridicule, and vice versa. We were clearly at a stalemate, both physically and mentally. Thus the battle continued to rage on the log. Jabs, blocks, screams, and kicks flew. Energy peaked and waned with the frenzy of the joust. Moments of silent reprieve, in which we glared at each other, suddenly would shatter into a frenzy of motion and energy. Nothing I tried could make Rick fall from the log. The power of the dual also took its toll mentally and emotionally. We had to remain absolutely focused on what we were doing. Any distraction would surely mean a defeat.

Distractions would come in many forms. It could come as frustration over the battle itself, or it could come as fatigue. The distraction I feared most, however, was anger. To give in to anger would only cause loss of control, loss of focus, and ultimately defeat. So the battle raged on, not only on a physical level, which was demanding enough, but even more on the mental and emotional levels. I knew very well that I could not allow myself to be beaten by any distraction, whether it came from Rick or from other sources. My exhaustion was not then only on the physical level but on all levels. For the hypervigilance necessary to ward off any and all distractions was draining me even more than any physical fatigue was. It became foremost in my mind. Nonetheless I was little prepared for the distraction that would ultimately knock me from the log.

Out of what seemed to be nowhere a mud ball splattered against Rick's forehead, causing him to reel back in shock and disbelief. Both of us immediately stopped the battle and began to search the landscape beneath us, combing the stream bank with our eyes. We knew very well that Grandfather had thrown the mud ball and that would mean that our lofty perch would not be of much advantage in finding him. We looked for a long time but nothing broke the natural rhythm of the woods. The sight of Rick with the splatter of black mud across his head caused me to burst into laughter. No sooner did I open my mouth to catch a breath of air than a mud ball hit me on the chin and splattered into my mouth. Rick began to laugh at me hysterically and almost lost his balance as I tried to repeatedly spit the mud from my mouth. I also began laughing again.

Suddenly Rick and I heard Grandfather's voice break into our laughter and we froze in shock. He said, "You call yourself scouts! Ha! Scouts do not become so removed from the land that they become unaware of that which surrounds them. They are never so focused that they fail to notice the flow of life around them and through them. The land, the universe is their power, which is cut off when the focus becomes so absolute and suffocating. To focus everything on the task at hand is to try, and trying negates itself. What a scout does is to use an expanded focus, where the task is but a small part of the whole picture. To expand in this way is to tap into the spirit-that-moves-through-all-things; thus you begin to know your opponent's next move before he even makes it, because he is part of the spirit.

You would also not have failed to notice that this old man had climbed up the very tree that supports the log on which you stand.''

All of this time Rick and I had been searching the landscape trying to locate Grandfather's position as we listened to his words. Upon hearing him say that he was in the tree above, we both looked up in shocked amazement. Our physical reaction to the shock was so powerful that it knocked us right off the log as though physically pushed off by some unseen hand. We came out of the water gasping for air as we craned our necks to look way back up at Grandfather. He was in one of the trees that supported our fighting log, not six feet above where our heads had been when we stood on the log. He was not camouflaged in any way, in fact he could be easily seen. Without a word, he jumped from the tree, giggling all the way down. He even emerged from the water laughing.

I was humiliated. Grandfather had been right. I had focused fully on the battle and cut myself off from the land. I had not only failed to notice Grandfather climbing up the tree, but even after he threw the mud and began talking, I had no idea where he was. I was so convinced that he had to be on the ground that I never ventured the thought that he could be above me. For some reason my mind held no possibility he could have been up in the tree, so I foolishly discounted that. It was bad enough, humiliating enough that I had failed to notice him climbing the tree behind me, but not to know where he was when he spoke really humbled me. Grandfather laughed all the way to the shore, turned back to us, and said that he would meet us back up at camp. We could hear him chuckling to himself all the way up the trail. We were left in a cloud of moody silence. Being humbled and humiliated to a point where we fell from the log caused me to beat myself up internally. Granted, Grandfather was stealthy to say the least, but to pass behind us so easily, especially with our experience, really forced me to question my own abilities. I guess in a way I was feeling a little cocky about my skills and abilities, but Grandfather's game certainly shocked me back to reality. It taught me a valuable lesson: to not assume anything and to expect everything, even the most unlikely or impossible scenarios. It did not give me much consolation to know that learning something valuable from a failure only turns it to success. I was too absorbed with self-pity and with dusting off my now-deflated pride.

Rick broke the silence and said, "He called us scouts." I reeled around abruptly, taken by surprise by Rick's statement. I thought about what Grandfather had said to us while we were on the log. He did not say that we were like scouts, he said that we were scouts. I knew Grandfather well enough to know that, even though his command of the English language was broken at best, he chose his words very carefully. There was no doubt in my mind as to what he had said, there was just doubt in whether he meant it in that way or not. I looked coldly at Rick, still upset from my emotional beating, and said, "Maybe he meant we were like scouts, rather than really calling us scouts." That struck up an argument between us almost immediately. Rick was sure that Grandfather called us scouts and I was sure that Grandfather did not mean it that way.

The argument got us nowhere and we knew from past experience that to pursue it any further would only get us into a bigger fight. We just agreed to let it drop and not mention it to Grandfather until he called us scouts again, then we could ask him. That way we would not suffer the embarrassment and disappointment if I was right and Rick was wrong. We were certain that if Grandfather had meant what he said then he would surely say it again. We slowly climbed out of the water and lay in the sun for a long time drying off. It was such a paradoxical feeling. Neither of us wanted to rush back to camp and face Grandfather, such was the intensity of our humiliation. But on the other hand, we desperately wanted to get there to see if he would call us scouts again. For a while the feeling of not wanting to go was stronger than the need to go.

Finally after a long break we headed back up to camp, still reluctant to face Grandfather. Though he would never ridicule us, I still was conscious of the fact that I might have let him down in some way. After all, he had put so much time into teaching us the way of the scout, only to have me make such a stupid mistake. It had to have upset him. Yet my heart pounded with anticipation for what he might say about us being scouts. We strolled into camp as if nothing out of the ordinary had happened, trying to camouflage our embarrassment and nervousness. Grandfather motioned for us to sit down, yet he did not sit with us. Instead he finished up the wrapping on a hide scraper he had been working on.

Rick and I sat in silent apprehension awaiting Grandfather to sit down with us. I imagined that he was taking his time and ignoring us on purpose, which only added to my apprehension and nervousness. Grandfather finally came over to us and sat down. He looked at us both with a big satisfied smile on his face. He did not look upset in the least but rather very pleased. He finally spoke, saying, "You see, Grandsons, you must never be so focused on anything that you do, no matter how intense, that you cut yourself off from the earth and the spirit-that-moves-through-all-things. By focusing everything on the task at hand you cut off the flow of energy and awareness from the earth to you and thus you remove much of your potential power. So too do you lose the expanse of your awareness and overlook so much else that lies beyond the task. You do not get a grand and clear picture of the event, just an obscurity."

"But Grandfather," I said, "haven't you told us many times that we lacked focus in something we were doing and that focus would produce the most powerful results?"

Grandfather then said, "Yes, you must always focus, but not to the point of exclusion of everything else. What you must learn here is an expanded focus where the task is but the central part of a greater picture, a grander consciousness. By doing so you hold the task in the center of your vision and your mind, but also let your mind expand to everything else around you. When you can achieve this expansion in focus you will find that you gain the energy of the universe and the task becomes effortless. That way, too, by allowing the spirit-that-moves-through-all-things to flow through you, you become part of the consciousness of the task."

A prolonged moment of silence followed Grandfather's words as he waited for us to understand what he was saying. He then continued, "To simplify what I am saying about the wisdom of expanded focus, let's say you are facing a problem or an opponent in battle, or even stalking someone or something. By expanding to the spirit you not only become fused with the consciousness of the land but also with the consciousness of your opponent or the problem itself. Thus you will know your opponent's thoughts, actions, and reactions, even before they happen. But by being focused on just your opponent or the problem at hand, your cut yourself off from all other possibilities, all other power. The task or the battle then is fought on a purely physical level and the physical, as you know, is very limiting. Whereas the spirit knows no limitation. Remember that to narrow your vision and thus your mind is to be open only to the realities of the physical body and mind. To widen your vision and thus your mind, you expand to the consciousness of the spiritual body and spiritual mind, which includes the consciousness of the universe.''

I felt dazed by the flow of information coming from Grandfather. It seemed too much to assimilate right away and I needed time to think. More so I needed to put into practice the things that he was saying and experiment with them. At this point I had no viable questions that would make any real sense. At least not until I had the experience to back up the questions.

Without saying another word about the concept of expanded focus, Grandfather said, ''There is a party out on the maze area. Several vehicles and many people are now camped there and will be for a while. There is already much destruction from them and it would be good for you to scout them tonight. Possibly some fear will sober them up and make them realize they should not destroy. Remember, though, that it is not their fault that they are wrapped in the ignorance of destruction, for they know no other way. Teach them, then.''

My heart leapt pounding into my throat. A scout mission was something Rick and I always looked forward to in the grandest way. It put us on the edge of life, of intensity, and excitement. Every time Grandfather had taken us on a scout mission before, I had become enraptured by the whole event. This I knew would be such a time. I then asked Grandfather where and when we would meet him. He smiled at me confidently and said, ''I will not be going. It is time that you both go out on your own and do what I have taught you.'' My mouth fell open as Grandfather walked away to leave us to wallow in our shock. I felt so excited that I wanted to throw up. I could not believe that Grandfather was going to let us go out alone. It was like some sort of graduation day. I looked at Rick, smiling to a point of pain. Tears filled our eyes.

We spent the better part of the afternoon planning our mission. Actually it was more celebrating than planning, for we could not shake the tremendous elation we felt from having our own scouting mission. However, as day moved closer to evening we began to take a more sobered approach to devising what we were going to do. We knew that to get there and back before sunrise the next day, we would have to leave camp before sundown—and sundown was close, not leaving much time to plan. Fortunately, we knew the area well and it did not take us long to plan our major mission, minor secondary approaches, several escape routes, rendezvous points, and to map out all the potentially dangerous and safe areas. As always we left room for last-minute adaptations to our plans, for we could not be sure of all factors involving the camp. As always, we would leave the final decision as to which plan to execute once we were in the area.

Rick and I spent the last part of the day preparing ourselves personally for the mission. We ate just a little, but drank quite a lot of water. There was but one place we could get water on the way there but it would prevent access. We knew that we could get to the spring under almost any circumstances, but we didn't want to take any chances. Before we camouflaged our bodies we both went in our sweat lodge, ridding our bodies of most human odors, just in case the campers had a dog. The charcoal and mud that we used for camouflaging our bodies to invisibility would also take care of any lingering scent. We were ready to go just as the sun was beginning to set. Though in the best-case scenario we could complete the scouting in less than four hours, we wanted time on our side. We could not allow ourselves to rush, for rushing produces mistakes.

We sat down with Grandfather for a few moments before we left. In a way, we were following tradition, in that the scouts would always consult with an elder before going out on a mission. Grandfather smiled at us with his approval. I could tell that he could feel the excitement and see the sparkle of unbridled wildness in our eyes, as it made him giggle. I guess that he must have remembered how he felt on his first scouting party. He eyed us up and down, then motioned us to turn around as he inspected our camouflage application. As was usual, he had picked up a piece of charcoal to take care of any spot that we might have missed, but he didn't have to use it at all. He shrugged knowingly as he tossed the charcoal back to the edge of the fire. I felt the rush of excited pride surge through me as he cast the charcoal down.

Now having passed Grandfather's close inspection, we stood before him, waiting for him to tell us to go. He said, "Remember the lesson you learned on the log today. At all times, but especially those times when you are faced with a problem, expand your focus and become the power of earth and spirit. Remember, fear, like rage, gets you out of control. When you lose control you lose everything. Expand your focus then in the face of fear, rage, or any other distraction and you will transcend that distraction." With those words, Grandfather fell silent, smiled, and motioned us to go. My heart leaped into my throat and excitement electrified every fiber of my existence as I slipped from camp and deftly headed out in the direction of the maze.

It was dusk by the time we reached the edge of our camp. The journey that would normally take us but fifteen minutes now had taken us the better part of an hour. The extra time did not concern us, for we had planned for it to take at least that long. After all, we could not use the trails but instead took the most impenetrable way through the brush. The first rule of a scout mission was to avoid all trails, especially those that a man could easily walk. So too by taking the wildest route we would be going the least expected way and leaving the most difficult tracks to follow if we were ever chased. It would also leave the natural flow of tracks around camp undisturbed, so that even a good tracker could not tell that anyone had left the camp.

The remainder of the journey to the outer part of the maze went without incident. Though we had an easy time of it, we would not allow complacency to set in. We expected the worst and trusted nothing to chance. Even as we approached the maze, knowing that the party was on the other side of the swamp and thus we were very protected by cover, we began to exercise even more caution. I knew that this first mission was some kind of test, whether Grandfather defined it as such or not. To me it was a personal test and I did not want anything to go wrong. I wanted it to be perfect and I knew that Rick wanted it to be the same way. Thus there was no argument between us, just silent agreement, and we both moved as one.

Ever so carefully we made the long journey through the swamp. Even though it was only about two hundred yards across, we still wanted to stay to the thickest tangles and make sure we left no discernible tracks or traces of our route in. The last several yards onto the outer edge of the camp took the longest time yet. Even though a huge fire danced light and shadows across the night and the blaring car radio and people's drunken laughter would have covered any sound we might make, we did not want to take any chances. I knew that dogs listen beyond all commotion and sound to other stray noises of the night. Though we did not know for sure if the camp had a dog or not, we did not want to assume anything. Our ears strained beyond the noise for anything that might give us a clue to the deep secrets of the camp. We slipped silently through the thick underbrush on our bellies, as silently as snakes, edging closer to the outer perimeter of brush.

Rick arrived at the edge of the brush first. I could see his head silhouetted by the campfire. Even though his position was obvious to me, I knew that looking from the opposite direction of the firelight would reveal nothing. Even if one of the campers looked close, he would never see Rick. I slowly edged nearer to Rick and then alongside. Through the scant final cover of leaves I could see the party clearly. There were two Willys Jeep wagons, two other street cars, and an old pickup truck. Rick and I did not know that much about cars as did other boys our age, but that lack of knowledge seemed trivial. We only concerned ourselves with vehicles that could easily go back into the woods, like Jeeps. The loud music came from the one car that had its convertible top down, and two people inside kept changing the radio station.

The vehicles were parked in a loose semicircle, headlights facing off to the right of where we lay. We had immediately taken this into consideration as soon as we saw the way the cars were parked. We did not want to be lying in the line of the headlights if someone suddenly decided to leave. So too did we not want to be behind or too far to the sides of the cars for they might roll over us when they turned around and certainly the headlights would fall upon our positions. The place we had chosen seemed to be the best. We were very safe from the cars and had a clear view of the party. I could almost feel my body sinking into the ground as I realized we had chosen the best overall position. Even more relieving was that we saw no sign of a dog. We then settled in to watch the camp carefully for a while, scrutinizing every pattern of movement, watching how aware the people were, and mentally planning what we were going to do.

I counted twelve people sitting around the fire on logs or blankets. Two more were in the convertible and one was in the bed of the pickup truck talking to another who stood alongside. There was an equal number of boys and girls, somewhere around late high school or early college age. As always, we could pick out the alpha male and female almost immediately. They were sitting in the best possible place by the fire. It seemed that the others were always looking their way to get some sort of approval. The alpha man seemed to be a little older than everyone else. He was also clearly in charge of the beer, which lay in a huge ice cooler behind him. Our suspicions were confirmed when he yelled at the couple in the convertible to leave the radio alone. The guy in the back of the pickup truck also confirmed the demands of the alpha man, indicating to us that he must be the beta man, or second in unspoken command.

As the party began to increase in intensity, more beer was being consumed, more and more of the couples were embracing in love, and intermittently bouts of laughter or horseplay would break out. Rick and I began to edge back into the swamp to plan the final part of the mission. Through a series of hand signals and touching each other's mouths so we could understand the mouthed words in the dark, we agreed on a plan. Rick would go into camp first and I would lie watching. That way I could warn him with an animal sound if he unknowingly got himself into a potentially dangerous situation. I crept back into my original position for observation while Rick slipped around to the brush nearest to the closest car. I had to look hard to see him lying there, so close to the front wheel that he could have easily touched it. I could feel his presence more than

see him, such was the perfection of his camouflage and
stealth.

Suddenly one of the guys got up from the campfire and
began to walk to the car where Rick was lying. I gave the
chirp of a cricket and Rick froze motionless on the ground.
The guy walked right over to where Rick lay and I held
my breath, feeling my heart pounding in my chest. He
walked past without the slightest hesitation and opened the
door. The puddle of light from the interior of the car
flooded the ground and brush where Rick lay, but he was
so well camouflaged that even I had to strain my eyes to
see him. Suddenly the door slammed and just as unexpectedly the man began to walk right toward where I lay at the
edge of the brush. He stopped just inches away from my
nose and I could tell from the movement of his feet that he
shot a quick glance back toward the fire to see if anyone
was looking.

I could feel the warm urine hitting my back, and the
surprise mixed with anger made it almost impossible to
remain motionless. The sound of a zipper was followed by
the sound of footfalls walking away. The only sensation
was my heart beating in my chest, the stench of urine, and
my boiling anger. At this point I wanted desperately to go
into the swamp, wash off, and then camouflage up again,
but I could not leave Rick without a sentinel. I resumed
watching Rick as he now slipped past the car, staying to
the shadows as he slithered up to the back of the nearest
blanket. A pile of food bags and other debris was now his
only cover. A rush of exhilaration washed through me, and
I forgot all about my predicament.

Just as Rick got inches from the bags, a hand reached
up from the other side of the pile and began groping. It
grabbed a can and then disappeared to the other side again.
A girl's voice called from behind the bags to the alpha

male, asking him for a can opener. The alpha male tossed the can opener her way, but the throw was long and hit the ground just inches from Rick's nose. The girl sat up, turned around, parted the bags, and firelight suddenly filled what was once deep shadows. Rick was clearly in view, frozen as if part of the ground. The gal never saw him but picked up the can opener and opened the can of beer. She fumbled around in one of the bags, which again caused the area behind to fall into deep shadows. I could feel my own great relief and I can only imagine what Rick must have felt.

After the gal had taken a long sip of the beer, she placed it at her side on the ground and disappeared behind the cover of the bags once again, probably to snuggle with her boyfriend. I could clearly see the outline of the beer can silhouetted in the firelight. Then, as if it was more of a mirage than reality, I watched Rick's hand slip slowly and deftly up to the beer. In a flash so fast I shook my head in disbelief, the beer can had disappeared. Rick slipped back into the brush and out of my sight. Time seemed to stand still as I awaited his return. I began to grow uneasy as I saw the girl's hand reach to where the beer can had been and aimlessly grope around. She then sat up with a start, pulled one of the bags aside and began searching for her beer. She yelled at the guy next to her, accusing him of drinking her beer. Suddenly I felt Rick's hand touch my foot and I slipped back toward him and away from the growing argument at camp.

We could barely hold back our laughter as Rick poured the can of cold beer out onto the ground. I could see a big smile, almost a laugh, appear on his face as he pointed to my back and held his nose. My anger returned full blast, but it was followed by the sensation of having succeeded. I slid into the water, washed off, and then camouflaged myself again. Then making sure that the commotion and arguments we had left behind had ceased, we went back to our original positions. This time Rick took up the sentinel position and it was my turn to raid the camp. As I slipped away from Rick I knew that it would be a little more difficult this time. Even if it had not been discussed, the missing beer can would have raised some suspicion. Even mild suspicion among the group could make things tough.

I decided to go around the camp and approach from the side opposite to where Rick had taken the can, just in case the girl was still concerned. It took me a long time to get through the swamp and into position, but once I emerged from the protective brush I found the going quite easy. My route brought me alongside the old Willys station wagon, which now provided excellent cover. This vehicle had been parked so close to the brush that it created an excellent tunnel that I could use to get to the edge of the party. As soon as I got even with the front tire, I could see the large cooler before me, just a few feet from the vehicle's bumper. I shivered to think that I was about to stalk up on the alpha male of the group. If I ever messed up I would be beaten up for sure. I had to fight back the fear that was causing me to think about retreating and going to an easier target.

As I edged closer I could clearly see the shine of the can opener in the firelight, lying on top of the cooler. In a shiver of excitement, I decided to take the can opener. I knew that once I took it, I would have a limited amount of time to get back to the brush before it was discovered missing. I also had to plan a different route back, away from the vehicles, in case people began to go through them looking for other can openers. As I edged closer to the cooler I could clearly see the edge of the brush where Rick lay, and that made me feel a little more at ease. However, I was not sure that he knew where I was, or if he did, that he could see me. Very cautiously and in one slow and flowing motion I removed the can opener from the cooler. I took it in such a way that I would remain undetected even if someone were looking.

In the same motion of taking the can opener I began slipping away into the brush that was directly behind the blanket that lay next to the alpha male. This made the journey easier in one sense, because the guy who had urinated on me and his girlfriend were not on the blanket. It also made it more difficult, because I had no idea where they were. I decided to head directly into the thicket behind the second blanket. That way I would not be caught in the open if the can opener was discovered missing earlier than I anticipated. Even though the route I chose was longer than the original route I had planned, I would immediately be safe. The crawl on my belly seemed to take an eternity, and the swamp seemed like it was miles away. The safety of the swamp was very compelling, but I could not allow myself the luxury of rushing.

Just as I was nearing the outer edge of the swamp, I was startled by a groaning that seemed to be coming from behind a tall bush. I then heard whispers and soft giggling and I knew that it had to be the guy who urinated on me and his girlfriend. Curiosity and the rush of adventure got the better of me and I changed my course to the direction of the noises. As I belly stalked through the thick brush I could see a small clearing just a few feet in front of me. I could also see the couple wrapped naked in a passionate embrace, oblivious to everything around them. I began to retreat and go back to my planned route when my arm brushed against something soft and out of place here. Carefully feeling with my hand I discovered to my delight that it was the couple's clothing. I remembered vividly being urinated on and without a second thought I took their clothing. I knew that it would not be long before a real frenzy and commotion would break out throughout the camp.

Just as I slipped back into the brush that bordered the swamp, I heard the alpha male ask for the can opener. What followed was a blur of activity and screaming. The last tangible thing I can remember is the alpha man yelling, "Where the hell is my can opener?" From that point on I was too interested in getting deep into the swamp to pay much attention to what was being said or done at the party. I determined to get to Rick before all hell broke loose. Even though he was hidden well, now he was more vulnerable than me. I hoped that he had seen me take the can opener and would be well on his way to the rendezvous point that we had selected. However, I did not think they would suspect that anyone outside of the party would have taken the opener, at least not yet. At least not until the two lovers found that their clothes had been taken.

I found Rick at the rendezvous point, just as we had planned if anything happened. We could clearly hear the arguments at the camp growing louder. There was definitely some shoving going on and heated accusations, from what we could hear. I knew that they did not yet suspect outsiders. Pushing our limits, we went back to the edge of the camp to watch the antics. Though we should have gotten out of there, I really wanted to see what was going on. Looking back now, I can see how foolish that decision was. I just wanted to witness firsthand the ramifications of the psychological warfare of the scout. It's one thing to hear about it secondhand but quite another to witness the scout's handiwork. Anyway, even if they did suspect outsiders, the thick impenetrable swamp would be the last place they would look.

We were greeted with the sounds of uncontrolled laughter as we reached the perimeter brush. There, standing just outside the firelight, was the guy who had urinated on me earlier that night. He was stark naked except for the shoe he held over his crotch. He begged the group for his clothes back, or at least a blanket. Everyone was laughing at his requests and he was becoming more and more upset with anger. For the life of me I have no idea what drove me to do what I did next. I guess part of me wanted to perpetuate the myth that someone inside the group was responsible for the missing can opener and clothing. In the midst of the commotion I slipped from the brush and to the back of the pickup truck. I carefully lifted the clothing and placed it on the tailgate, so as not to alarm the beta male who was standing in the truck bed looking over the hood at the group.

Just as I deposited the clothing and retracted, I heard the grind of his pivoting feet and the ensuing footfalls heading to the back of the truck. I crouched motionless under the tailgate, more from instinct rather than decision. The beta man jumped from the tailgate of the pickup truck and let out a yell to the group. People began to gather around the back of the truck. All I could see was their legs all around me. My only escape, if any, would be to take the dangerous belly crawl to the front of the truck, hoping that no one would suddenly decide to drive off. Just as this was going through my mind, some article of clothing dropped from the beta man's hand and onto the ground, just a foot from where I crouched. He bent to pick it up. I held my breath as his face came within inches of mine, so close in fact that I could feel his hot breath. He never saw me.

The gathering of people now began to move to the front of the truck. Arguments broke out over who had taken the clothing. One last pair of legs paused, lifted the tailgate, and then slammed it shut, leaving me now totally exposed. The beta man grabbed his beer from the bed of the truck while standing right beside me, then followed the procession to the front of the truck. I wanted badly to let out a sigh of relief as I slithered back into the scant brush beside the truck. As I got back to the original sentry position I found, to my horror, that Rick was not there. I looked out across the camp and beyond the arguing people, only to see the can opener in the process of being placed back on the cooler. It was like being struck by lightning when suddenly the alpha male turned and walked to the cooler.

No sooner had Rick set down the can opener than the alpha man picked it up and in a fit of anger turned to the group and screamed, "Who the f——is playing games?" He continued screaming in a loud voice, "If I ever find the a——hole responsible for this I'll beat him to death!" I could see Rick's legs disappearing into the swamp directly behind where the alpha man stood. Just as he was out of sight one of the gals, probably seeing some sort of slow slithering movement from the lower part of Rick's legs, screamed "Snake!" Every eye shot toward the swamp, but Rick could no longer be seen. Not a leaf moved, not a sound came, not even from the group. They just all stared in horror. The girl broke out again in a shriek, saying, "Don't you all see it? It was huge, ugly, and slimy. My God, what is wrong with your eyes?"

Everyone appeared to be looking at the brush even harder. My heart pounded so hard that I thought someone would definitely hear it and come my way. The gal then said, "What are ya, a mess of chickens? Big bad men, afraid of a little snake. Will you kill the damn thing or I'm going home." With those words most of the guys ran over to the place where they had seen Rick's legs. One grabbed the axe on the way and another grabbed a shovel. I could feel my gut coil, ready to jump out and scream as soon as the axe was lifted. The guys kicked around the outer brush for a while but found nothing. I chuckled to myself, now knowing that Rick was safe and probably at the rendezvous point. It was funny, I thought, how these tough guys would not venture outside the firelight or into the brush at all. I could sense their fear.

It did not take me long to return to the rendezvous point and find Rick. We glanced at each other, dying inside for the want of rejoicing, laughter, and conversation, but we could not chance any gesture other than the hand signal to end the mission. We began the slow and careful journey to the other side of the swamp. The sound of arguments still filled the night and we could see from the light reflected on the upper trees that the group had built the campfire much bigger. Probably to chase away the bogeyman, I thought. We were so quiet and I was so intent on listening to the sounds of the party that I bumped smack into the butt end of a raccoon that was feeding by the edge of a small spring. He turned with the fiercest snarling growl that I had ever heard and, fortunately for me, he turned and fled into the deep brush, crashing and snarling as he went.

His fierceness echoed through the night and the party fell silent. Suddenly I heard the voice of the alpha male shout, a car door slam, the bolt of a rifle click shut, and the voice yell again, "I'll get that bastard!" A shot rang out and I could hear the bullet ricochet not a yard above my head. Bits of bark and wood rained down upon me. I froze, terrorized, desperately wanting to run. It took all I had to fight back the distraction of the fear as shot after shot rang out and splintered the canopy of vegetation above me. The last shot ricocheted off a high limb and hit right between where Rick and I lay. A shower of cold mud fragments from the impact freckled us. All then was silent for a long time. I could smell the scent of spent gunpowder drifting in the still air and the cold chill of fear sent shivers down my spine.

I remembered what Grandfather had said about expanding my focus, especially in time of crisis. It took a great deal for me to control the fear and pass it from me, clearing the way for the expansion I sought. Suddenly I could sense the fear in the camp. Though there was no sound, I could feel that the people were packing up and talking in hoarse whispers, laced with anxiety. Rick and I began moving forward almost simultaneously, and I somehow knew that he too was in the state of expanded focus. Our instincts had been right, confirmed now by one engine after another starting up. We could see the flicker and dance of headlights reflecting off the upper branches as the vehicles jockied around and headed out to the main trail. As the sound of the last car disappeared in the distance, I could feel my body relaxing deeply. I was mentally and physically exhausted yet I could still hold on to the power of the expansion.

During the entire trip back to camp Rick and I made no attempt at communication, at least not on a physical level. Somehow there was no need. We had tapped into something far beyond any communication that we had ever known before. I knew exactly what Rick was doing, thinking, or reacting to without any hand signals, sounds, or motion. It was like we had become one organism of one mind, moving as if of one body. Somehow, through it all, we had learned to communicate with each other the same way the ancient scouts had once communicated. Through the expansion of focus, not only were we able to communicate with the camp, but also with each other, in a way that was even more powerful than words. I was so amazed over this intense form of communication and all I had done this night that my eyes filled with tears. I could hear Rick sniffle far up ahead.

We reached camp just as the sky was beginning to

lighten. Both Rick and I were far too exhausted to even talk. All our communicating had been without words on the way back to camp. As I lay down I thought about what I had learned, and I realized that it would take me a very long time to sort out all of the hidden lessons. Mostly I reveled in the intensity of the night, so different from the mundane things that people generally do. I had walked the edge of intensity and come alive. I knew at that moment that I would never seek the gods of safety, security, and comfort that society so zealously worships. Not for me. Safety, security, and comfort were euphemisms for death as far as I was concerned. I wanted, from this point in my life on, to seek intensity and to walk the edge of adventure. I wanted to live the life of a scout.

CHAPTER 3

THE BOAT

During all the time and training we had dedicated to learning scout methods so far, Grandfather had rarely mentioned the use of water, that is, the use of water to the advantage of the scout. I had heard that many Apache people in the past had a suspicion toward deep water, feeling that it might be a place of evil spirits, but I also knew that Grandfather had transcended his own religion. So too had I seen him enter the deepest water, swimming and diving deep, without any apparent concern. So his not mentioning water could not be for any religious reason. Rick and I began to suspect that the Scouts' use of

water must be a more advanced technique, and that was why Grandfather had not yet taught us anything about it. Anytime we broached the subject, we were virtually ignored or put off.

Grandfather had shown us some techniques dealing with water. We had learned the various stalking, swimming, diving, and camouflaging techniques used in and around water, especially for survival and observing animals, but we suspected that Grandfather had been leaving much out. We felt, given what we had already learned about the scout skills, that there must be more, much more in the water skills. After all, the scout was supposed to travel in the most difficult terrain so as to remain unobserved. Given the deep swamps and small streams of the Pine Barrens, a water route would be an ideal cover and easy way to approach any camp. And the swamps and streams were bordered with such thick brush that most people would not try to enter them except for the areas of easy access or known swimming holes.

Then one day, unexpectedly, all the silence and secrecy surrounding the scouts' use of the water changed. Rick and I had been alone in our camp for the better part of the weekend while Grandfather had been out on one of his long, mysterious journeys into the deeper recesses of the Pine Barrens. We were growing concerned that we might not see him at all that weekend, since it was getting close to the time we would have to break camp and leave for home. We waited around camp nearly all morning and by midafternoon we had no choice but to pack up camp. Once we finished breaking camp, we decided to go down to the stream and have a swim. Even though we were not yet out of school for the summer, and it was still early June, the day had been torridly hot, and the work of breaking camp made it seem sweltering. A swim would certainly revive us before the long trek out of the woods. Both of us were quite upset and a little angry that we had not seen Grandfather since early Friday night.

The long swim was certainly refreshing and helped us forget the annoyance of having to go home and face school in the morning. Yet it only intensified our concern that we had not seen Grandfather. Rick and I swam for a long time, until we were chilled to the bone. We then lay on the bank and basked in the warm sun. I felt so at peace. Life just could not be any better. The wilderness had become my home, my freedom, and here I wanted for nothing. Here was only purity, where I had a purpose and a vision, a place of deep spiritual reality, free from the mindless rushing of society. On days like these, as I lay in the sun, I could not think of anything more perfect in life. Rick and I must have lain for nearly an hour, just talking of our lives and reveling in the beauty that surrounded us.

Suddenly the clump of moss that I had lain my head against moved. I jumped to my feet, trying to stifle a scream. At first I thought that it might be a huge snapping turtle that had pushed under the bank of the stream and was working its way up through the noises that made up the bank. Rick and I moved cautiously closer to the clump, stick in hand to prod the clump and dislodge the snapping turtle. I cautiously gave it a push with my stick but it didn't move. Again and again I poked at it but there still was no response. I moved closer and began to part the mosses with my hands. There was a weird gurgle and a blinding flash of water, mud, and moss came right toward my face, knocking me to the ground. I thrashed and screamed, trying to get free of this unknown beast that had attacked me. I was so panic-stricken that it took me a while to realize that the mud-splattered animal that had attacked me was Grandfather.

Grandfather's uncontrolled laughter seemed to echo through the entire Pine Barrens and I felt humiliated, although not so humiliated when I saw that Rick had taken refuge atop a nearby tree. He too had been frightened by the attack. I was ashamed because not only had I overlooked a clump of moss that had never been there before, but I had seen no tracks to give away Grandfather's position. As Grandfather reentered the water to wash off the mud, he consoled me by telling me that I could not have known that he was there, even with my skill, for it was the way of the scout. As soon as Grandfather said scout, I felt better, for I knew the capabilities of the scouts to escape detection even where there was no cover. I could feel the rush of excitement surge through me as he told me that he would begin teaching me the way of the water the next time I came into camp. As I turned to thank him, he was gone. Not even a swirl of water was left to mark where he stood.

Rick and I stood staring at the water in utter shock over his quick disappearance. We searched up- and downstream, but Grandfather had virtually vanished. All the way home we could talk of nothing else but what had happened at the stream and how easily Grandfather had disappeared. My excitement built all week, especially as the weekend drew nearer. I would have gone to Grandfather's camp after school each day as I usually did, but this was Grandfather's week to go to south Jersey to visit some elderly friends and I knew that he would not be there. Rick and I satisfied ourselves by staying around the woods near my house and talking about what we would learn this upcoming weekend. The prospect of being able to do what Grandfather had done thrilled me to a point where I could think of nothing else. The last night before we left for Grandfather's camp was virtually sleepless, such was my excitement.

We arrived at Grandfather's camp as quickly as we could after school, practically running the whole way there. When we arrived at camp, Grandfather was nowhere to be found. We were desperate to find him, convinced we would burst from all the anticipation. We rushed around looking for him, first at the sacred area, then at the latrine, and finally at the swimming hole. We looked upstream and down, calling his name, but got no response. We looked out across the water once again and gasped with surprise when we suddenly saw him standing in the center of the swimming hole. There was no way he could have held his breath that long. It was as if he'd been born from the very water. He had materialized as deftly as a soft mist, then suddenly he was gone again.

Rick and I immediately plunged into the water, more than eager to play this impromptu game of water hide-and-seek. We searched for a long time without any success. It was as if he had become the water once again. Exasperated and cold, we did a final search of the banks up and down the stream, but there were no tracks indicating that Grandfather had left the river. It was sunset when we finally gave up and headed back to camp. Yet the cold of the evening did not bother us at all. We were too fired up with excitement over what Grandfather had done. When we got closer to camp we could smell the smoke of a campfire and we knew that Grandfather had to be there. What we couldn't figure out was how he had slipped by us without us seeing him, or leaving tracks in the muddy banks.

We found Grandfather sitting quietly by the fire, as if he had been there forever. We hovered around him firing question after question at him without letup. Finally he put up his hand, a clear sign that meant to sit down and be quiet. As soon as we were sitting quietly, he spoke.

"To learn the way of the scout and the place of water,"

he said, you first must become part of the consciousness of water. "You must first understand that it is the blood of our Earth Mother, the same blood that courses through your veins. Once entering the water you must blend your mind with that of the water, thus becoming part of the water and ultimately becoming invisible while wrapped in its mind. In the water you must feel safe and free of fear, though you must learn also to respect its power and obey its laws. You must learn to move with the water, for to disobey its laws and move against its power is to perish."

Rick and I were more than familiar with the power of water and its rules demanding our respect, but I could tell that Grandfather wanted us to go deeper into its philosophy and consciousness than we ever had before. We knew that the waters of the world were connected into one huge network. The lifeblood of the earth. So too did we know that we were connected by that same blood and part of its power, for it surged through our hearts and minds. But Grandfather was urging us to something more profound, something that would blend us into the mind of the water so that we would disappear. How this was to be accomplished, I had no idea. Grandfather told us that we would leave before first light and head for the upper reaches of Cedar Creek.

As dawn's first light appeared, we could see the small creek before us, reflecting the ever-lightening sky. Even though the stream was not very wide, its tannic water looked deep and dark. The current was not so strong that we could not swim upstream if we had to, but it would carry us easily along. Without hesitation, Grandfather entered the waters and beckoned us to do the same. Even though we were a little tired from the hike there, Grandfather did not linger. We suspected that we were going to travel quite some distance and that is why Grandfather wanted an early start. We had floated down streams many times before, but somehow we knew that this was going to be different, such was Grandfather's attitude. We were both excited and cautious over what might lie ahead this day.

We floated endlessly, without saying a word to each other. I did try once to ask Grandfather a question, but he waved it off and went back to his silence. Rick and I were having a tough time of it trying to keep clear of the heavy brush along the stream's edge and to avoid the fallen logs and wooden spikes of old branches. More often than not we failed to negotiate the flow of the stream and ended up crashing into a thick tangle of brush along the stream's edge. We got scratched and hung up, much like flies caught up in spiders' webs, only these webs would cut and poke us. The current would send us crashing into a submerged log, at times knocking the wind out of us or momentarily impaling us on a sharp branch. Grandfather on the other hand seemed to float quickly and quietly along without incident. He seemed to sense where the submerged snags were and how to hold his body to compensate for the current, thus easily slipping by the tangles of brush along the stream's edge.

After nearly two full hours of being impaled, battered, and tangled in sharp brush, Rick and I gave in to the stream's energy and began to move freely, silently, and quickly. The stream and Grandfather had somehow taught us a great lesson without uttering a single word. We quickly began to catch up with Grandfather; giving up our struggle completely, we became part of the stream. Though I did not know why, I seemed to be able to sense where all the invisible underwater obstructions were located long before I arrived at them. I could begin to sense something deep within my body reacting to the consciousness and whims of the stream, to a point where my body reached far beyond the parameters of my flesh and became the flesh of the stream.

By noon, we had reached the great Barnegat Bay and there on the thick banks of the estuary we rested in the hot sun. Though we were chilled when we came out of the water, we were not as cold as I might have expected to be after such a long swim. We did not use any body control at all, and that was quite difficult to believe because even though the day was warm, it was still mid-June and the creek waters were a bit on the cold side. As I thought back to the early part of the morning when Rick and I were being caught by the brush and snags, I remembered that we had been very cold. Yet when we had given in to the power and mind of the stream, we not only stopped crashing into things, but the cold was also gone. Somehow, we not only learned how to travel easily in the water by becoming part of its power, but that same power had kept us warm.

As I lay in the sun thinking, Grandfather spoke to us for the first time since we had left camp. He said, "It was the water that was your teacher this day, not I, for I could never have taught you these lessons of becoming part of the water mind. You learned long ago not to struggle against nature in a survival situation, but to become part of its power and laws, thus easily flourishing where most men would only find pain, struggle, and death. Now you have learned the same lesson in the water, which is also part of the conscious earth. You have learned to move within its power so that your flesh has become the flesh of the water, your mind that of water. You have accepted and understood the connection between your blood and that of the earth and in so doing have learned to flow with the water so that there are no obstructions and no cold. Like the water, you have learned to flow around things without injury and have learned to move with and in the flesh and mind of the water. It too has become your home, your blood, and your mind.''

Without another word, Grandfather slipped back into the water and allowed the current to carry him to the bay. When we hit the waters of the bay we could now taste the salinity of the brackish water and feel the warmer shallow waters. We drifted with the tide toward Barnegat Inlet, floating easily without struggle. A few miles down we pulled out again, this time by a smaller creek. We could see the Barnegat Lighthouse way in the distance and we knew we were at the mouth of the creek that eventually led back to our camp. As we again sat on the bank resting, Grandfather said, ''We will now travel upstream to the camp. Here too lies before you another lesson in the magic of the waters. No longer will the currents of life carry you but you must move against them. Moving again in such a way that there is no restriction or struggle.'' Grandfather then slipped back into the water and headed upstream. As easily as he had moved with the current he now moved against it.

Rick and I began to swim against the current. It was more of a struggle than we could imagine. Even though we could easily touch the bottom, the oncoming current, the obstructions, and the thick muddy areas beat us up physically and mentally. Now instead of being of one mind with the stream, we were fighting it again. Somehow Grandfather had gotten a considerable distance ahead of us, apparently without struggle. It appeared to us that he was actually going with the current rather than against its power. Late in the afternoon we were at the midway point, and we hauled ourselves out of the water to where Grandfather was sitting waiting for us. He had that smile on his face, unruffled and relaxed, depicting an air of not having struggled at all. Rick and I, on the other hand, were cold, exhausted, bruised, and cut.

We sat for a long time without saying a word. I contemplated going the final distance to camp overland, rather than face the water again. "You have forgotten your lesson of the morning," Grandfather said. "Just because the current now goes against you, you have lost the power of the water's mind. You struggle and fight instead of moving with the waters. You have chosen the fight and now you try to match your power to that of the water. A battle you cannot win."

"But how can I not struggle, moving against the current?" I asked. Grandfather only smiled at me knowingly then motioned for us to follow him back into the water and to stay close.

The cold chill of reentering the water bit deep into my flesh, but I fought it back. We began to follow Grandfather closely. His motions were like those of a well-choreographed water dance, a flowing ballet, where he moved effortlessly. He weaved back and forth, riding whirlpools, slipping through backwaters on the inside parts of bends in the stream, and dancing across submerged logs without a struggle. He used the power of the waters to move him. Soon too we were caught up in this water dance. Our minds cleared and once again became part of the water's mind. Our bodies reached out and fused with its power so that we moved as easily as Grandfather did. Soon there was no struggle and no cold. We were again part of the water.

I led as we approached the swim area of camp. Instead of being cold, we were quite warm and in no hurry to get back to our shelters and prepare dinner. Instead, we sat on the bank of our swim area basking in the final rays of sunset. Rick and I talked about all we had learned. It was frustrating because we could not easily articulate the lessons of the water. Grandfather finally spoke, saying, "You have learned once again the power of the water's mind and to make your mind one with that power. You found that traveling up- or downstream there still is no struggle once you know the way of the water and do not fight its power. Certainly there are powerful rivers and streams where going against the raging current would be a futile battle, but even in that power there can be found a way. Only by becoming one with the consciousness of the water and using its power, rather than fighting against it, will you know the invisibility of the scout in water."

For the next several weeks Grandfather took us on similar journeys. We explored large and small creeks, slithered through thick, mucky swamps, played in the coves and open areas of the bay, and even ventured far out into the raging storm surf of the ocean. The more we practiced the more our minds became that of the power of water. We became the water, so that there was no longer any struggle, just the dance of flow, mixed with mind and body to become one with the water. In the end, there was hardly any new stream or waterway that Grandfather took us to that we could not immediately become. Just by touching any strange body of water we instantly knew its secrets and respected its awesome power. We were on our way to the water dance of the scout, that which would open up a whole new world to us.

Once Grandfather was satisfied with the way we moved with water in general, he began to show us the finer and more technical approaches. Our lessons began when Grandfather told us to watch the herons and egrets feeding in the shallows. We knew that this was the beginning of our advanced water stalking and movement techniques, for it was the herons that had taught the ancient ones how to hold their bodies when stalking. Now, the herons were not only teaching us how to hold our bodies, but how to move in water, and how to silently walk on the bottom without stirring up sediment. We watched herons and egrets for many days, spending sometimes from sunup to sundown along the rivers or in the estuaries watching every movement of these birds. They were certainly masters of the water. Once Grandfather was satisfied that we fully understood what the herons had to teach, we moved to our first lessons.

First came the lessons and laws of water drops. We were taught to stalk through the water and exit the water perpendicular to its surface. That way the water would wick down our bodies without a telltale dripping that would alert even the most unaware animals. A droplet of water hitting the surface or ground would be an alarm signal to danger. That tiny sound of one single drip would send animals bolting for cover. Thus for hours we would practice slowly moving through water, and exiting water without the sound of one single drop. It would take us the better part of half an hour to come from a fully submerged position all the way to a standing position on the stream bank. Often our hair and bodies would be perfectly dry before our feet had even left the water.

Then came the lessons of concentric rings. We had to move through the water, enter and exit water, without leaving one single concentric ring of movement. Like the alarming effects of the sound of a single drop of water, a single concentric ring could send animals running away from water. Even our breathing had to be controlled and slowed in such a way that it would cause no concentric rings. Unlike stalking on dry land, water stalking not only encompassed the art of deftly slow and silent movement, but also the element of water and how it reacts to dripping and concentric rings. Here again, we had to enter and exit still water without moving its surface. Even the basic step of the land stalk had to be modified to that of the heron walk so that there was not only silence but no sediment plumes from the bottom to give away our position.

We also learned how to move up- and downstream in all kinds of water without stirring up the bottom, making a sound, or throwing a concentric ring. Upstream we stalked, downstream we stalk-floated, and in still water we did a little of each. What we had learned so long ago about water stalking for survival and observation purposes paled in comparison to the science and art form of the scout water stalk. We also learned to move equally as well in swamp and mud conditions without a sound. Then finally we learned to use the waterways as camouflage, using the snags, banks, and brush to our advantage, becoming nearly invisible. Then, once all of this was understood and mastered, we learned to stalk underwater, holding our breath through the use of body control, far longer than we could ever imagine. It ultimately made no difference to us if it was a sunny day, locked into the grip of a violent storm, or the blackest of nights. We knew how to easily handle all situations equally well.

During our practice times, Grandfather encouraged us to stalk the animals of the rivers and streams. To test our skills against the most aware animals and succeed would hone our techniques to a fine edge. After all, if one could easily stalk and touch a fox quietly drinking by a stream bank, then to stalk man in the same element would be easy. After all, modern man was basically unaware. Rick and I began stalking right up to feeding ducks and tickling their bellies, touching the feet of feeding herons, lifting fish from the water with our hands, and generally becoming a nuisance to any animal that happened to be by the water while we were playing. We laughed at the antics of our local wildlife population around the waters of camp. They had become a bit neurotic when approaching the water, but nonetheless seemed happy to join in the game.

Then came the day of what we remember as being the first part of our two-part final exam. It began early one morning when Grandfather spotted two deer drinking at a spring on the other side of the cedar swamp. He did not say a word to us but only pointed and we knew what he wanted us to do. Nothing less than to stalk and ultimately touch them. At first it did not seem a difficult task, for we had done this several times before, but the landscape was such that it would really push our skills to the limits. We would have to slither through the mucky swamp, enter a small stream that was filled with all manner of snags and tangles, slip up to the spring, and touch the deer. Time was a factor, for the deer would not be drinking there for very long.

Without a word, Rick and I entered the swamp on our bellies, slowly and cautiously slipping through the warm, thick mud like snakes. As we negotiated the route, we took care not to allow the mud to create a suction with our bodies, while making sure we stuck to deep cover whenever possible. Though it seemed to take forever, the initial part of our stalk probably only lasted about ten minutes, but it still had been tough at times getting through some of the thicker areas, especially over the fallen cedar logs with their sharp spikes. Here in the mud we made a few mistakes, but these we could afford because we were quite some distance from the deer and there was no way we could have spooked them. To an outside observer it would look perfect, as if nothing had gone wrong. But to us, we had nearly failed the initial test whether we spooked the deer or not.

We slipped into the stream from a low, muddy bank, taking care not to create any ripples or concentric rings. Here the stream moved very slowly so we had to exercise great care, for the slightest mistake here would spook the deer. We no longer had the luxury of distance nor had we any cover of wind or other natural sounds. Stalking, drifting, and picking our way up through the tangle of vegetation that choked the stream was trying indeed. Not only was the task nearly impossible, but we had to work under the scrutinizing eye of Grandfather and that put the most pressure of all upon us. Nearly twenty full minutes had passed since we had begun the stalk and even though we were only a few feet away from the deer they looked as if they were growing disinterested in drinking.

A little more than a foot from where the closest deer stood we came to a huge fallen cedar log that blocked our path. There was no way we could get over it in such a short period of time. Besides, the effort required to slide up and over the log would only succeed in alerting the deer to our presence. Any ripple of flesh or trembling of muscles would undoubtedly catch their attention. Without thinking, I grabbed Rick by the ankles and motioned to him that I would push him up and over the log. That way he would not have to exert any effort and my struggle would be masked by the log. I didn't care if I touched them, all I wanted was for one of us to touch the deer.

The final approach went beautifully. Rick easily slid over the log like a length of limp garden hose. There was absolutely no movement. Even my straining to push Rick's limp body over the log didn't create a ripple or tremble the water. Suddenly there was an explosion of mud, water, and debris as Rick was yanked from my grasp. I could hear Rick scream with delight from the other side of the log. I scrambled out of the water to watch the deer bound off in bewilderment. Rick lay laughing so hard he almost sucked in mud. Excitedly he told me that he had slipped his hand through the deer's leg and grabbed hold of its thigh. Not only did he touch him, but he'd grabbed him, and the deer lunging to safety yanked Rick several feet. I worried at first that the deer might be hurt in some way, but seeing him walk off in the distance with no indication of injury, except to his pride, came as a relief. We heard Grandfather's triumphant war whoop come thundering through the swamp and we rejoiced in Rick's success.

We picked our way out of the swamp to where Grandfather stood, absolutely beaming with delight over what we had done. To my amazement he walked right past Rick to me, congratulating me on what I had done. Bewildered at the attention, I explained to Grandfather that Rick had touched the deer, not I. He should be the one getting the praise. Grandfather smiled and said, "You have demonstrated the greatest wisdom of all. You put your brother before you, even at the cost of your success. That is truly the way of the scout, for the scout puts his brother and his people before himself. A scout would sacrifice his all for his people. You have learned this truth through the wisdom of your own heart and I am proud of you." He then turned to Rick and gave him a big hug and said, "I know that you would have done the same thing for Tom if the circumstances had been reversed. I am proud of both of you."

We rested at camp for the better part of the afternoon, reveling in our success. Grandfather seemed to dance around camp, humming to himself, and seeming very satisfied with our ability. It was so rare to see Grandfather show any emotion over something we had done. His antics certainly took us by surprise. Then as the sun was disappearing on the horizon, Grandfather pointed downstream and told us that a camp of fishermen was not far away. He didn't have to say another word. We knew that Grandfather wanted us to scout the camp that night on our own. Our hearts pounded with excitement for we knew that this was the second part of our test of water.

As soon as the sun disappeared over the horizon Rick and I slipped deftly into the stream. We were well camouflaged, sporting our paints mixed with scented tallow mixed with lichen and moss coloration to give us a dark mottled green color that would not wash off in the water. The scented tallow, made from rendered fat for waterproofing, would also hide our scent from any animal that might otherwise catch our scent and send out an alarm call. We drifted silently and efficiently downstream, never creating a ripple, and easily flowing by all manner of snags and brush. Again our bodies became that of the stream, knowing what lay along, beneath, and above us without knowing how we knew. We became so much a part of the stream's consciousness that we became invisible. Even though Rick was only a few feet in front of me and the night was lavishly lit by a nearly full moon, I had difficulty seeing him, such was his flow, stealth, and camouflage.

Within an hour we were at the shore of a small fishing camp. Two older men sat around a campfire, and voices from one of the two large tents indicated possibly two others. As we lay at the bank, we watched the camp, gathering in every detail before we made our assault. We counted shoes, boots, fishing poles, tackle boxes, lawn chairs, hanging clothing, and other equipment that even the keenest observer would overlook. We fingered the tracks along the stream bank, confirming our belief that there were three men and a woman. The other man and woman that were in the tent were much younger than the two men sitting by the fire, according to their tracks. So too was there a dog in camp, lying by one of the men's feet, content beside the warmth of the fire.

Their actions and other details we gathered about the

people in camp told us that these were not any ordinary weekend fishermen and campers. These people seemed a little more aware and in tune with the forest; so too was their dog. He would raise his head and listen intently to the surrounding darkness at every squeak of a mouse or hushed crackle of brush. We knew instantly that we could take no chances with this camp. The dog was something we did not expect, but it upped the odds in the camp's favor. Several times one man or the other, locked deeply into conversation, would walk down to the stream to retrieve a bottle of soda or beer. We knew that the older man was the dog's owner, for each time he walked to the stream the dog would follow and lap the water only a few inches from my head. The first time the dog came to the water I froze, nearly in a panic, for he drank so close to my face that I could feel the splashes thrown from his lapping tongue. Yet the dog never took notice. My camouflage was working very well.

Finally the men began to turn in and we knew that our chance would soon arrive to scout the camp. Unfortunately the dog did not enter the tent with the men but lay just outside the door. We waited in the water for what seemed a lifetime, for the dog to eventually go to sleep. Slipping out of the water we silently moved through camp like shadows. We stalked the camp exactly as if we were stalking a deer or a fox, for the presence of the dog made anything less a liability. In good scout fashion we wanted to leave something in camp or do something to make our presence known, but of course we did not want to do any damage. After all, these people were not our enemies. So we set about switching the tackle in tackle boxes, swapping reels and poles, and hanging clothing and waders high up in trees. All of this took the better part of the night.

Finally as the first light of dawn was beginning to glow on the distant horizon we slipped back into the water, erasing our few tracks from the muddy bank. Heading back upstream a bit we found a place where we could climb out of the water and into a low-hanging tree that afforded us a fairly good view of the camp. Just as we got settled in the tree the younger man and woman emerged from the tent, greeted by the dog who was eagerly wagging his tail. At first they did not notice that boots and clothing hung from trees like strange Christmas ornaments, but soon the woman let out a very audible gasp. The two began to laugh and talk loudly and we could hear them blaming the hanging clothing and switched tackle boxes on the other two men, who emerged from their tent bewildered and denying everything. The last thing we heard as we slipped back into the water was the young man telling the others that no one could have done that with the dog in the camp, so it had to be one of them. Rick and I smiled at each other knowing that this would only produce years of confusion and speculation on their part. A good game of scout psychological warfare well done.

We took much longer to get back to our camp than we had to reach theirs. We did not want to break any of the scout rules and we knew that coming back from a scouting mission should be done with ever more caution than going to a mission. So too we did not take the stream on the return trip, obeying the rule of not going and coming by the same way. Tracks and all other evidence we erased as we traveled the inner streams and mud flats that paralleled our original route of travel. Finally we arrived back at camp to find Grandfather sitting in camp next to the fire. His attitude looked very solemn and his eyes seemed to look right through us as we walked up. Without a word, he handed us a silver bowl. To our amazement, it was the same dog bowl we had seen at the fishermen's camp.

Our hearts sank, for not only had we failed to see that

the dog's bowl had disappeared during our foray in camp, but we had failed to notice that Grandfather had been in the camp at the same time. Grandfather seemed then to be more mildly amused than disgusted. He finally spoke, saying, "The fishermen's camp was your fixation point, to the exclusion of everything else. It was the way of the scout to assume nothing. At any time, other scouts from other tribes could be out and about, even scouting the same place. Your awareness should reach beyond your goal, for as you scout, you may be scouted. It is not enough to beat the awareness of common man, but to become invisible to other scouts. You must scout like you are scouting scouts, which takes even more stealth and wisdom than stalking the most aware animal. It seems that you are learning the expanded focus lesson all over again. Just because there was no real danger does not mean that you narrow your awareness."

We were heartbroken. Our triumph had been dashed to pieces and we sat in the silence of our failure and embarrassment. Grandfather continued speaking. "This is the only way I could have taught you this. All of the voices in the world could not teach you to approach all places as if you were stalking a scout camp. I too learned this same lesson in this same way. You too have failed as I once failed, but now your failure is a success, for you have learned." With that Grandfather laughed wholeheartedly and we too laughed as we discussed what we had done to the camp. The failure to notice Grandfather was set aside and we all reveled in the success. I knew in my heart that I would not make such a mistake again. Again I learned the lesson of being beaten by my own complacency and arrogance.

Even though we had laughed off the incident at the fishermen's camp, both Rick and I were troubled by the failure. It festered in us and grew more intense with each passing day. We vowed to show Grandfather that we could be a full success on a water mission before the end of the summer. We wanted to make him as proud and happy with us as he had been when Rick was yanked forward by the deer. Though we did not know what our grand water mission would be, we searched for opportunities. Those that we did find would not have been that great of a test. What we were looking for was something that would test our skill. Something that at first appearance would seem impossible. We were so obsessed with our vow of perfection on a water scouting mission that we practiced our water skills almost to the exclusion of everything else.

As summer neared the Fourth of July weekend, Rick, while shopping with his mother, overheard some other shoppers talking of a boating rendezvous and overnight tie-up on the Toms River. A good scout never takes time off. He is always watching, always listening, and always aware of things in a far deeper way than most people could ever imagine. Pretending to be shopping, Rick followed the boat shoppers through the store, catching bits of conversation and watching what they were buying. Not only could Rick tell that it was going to be a big overnight party consisting of several huge yachts, but he found out exactly where it was going to be. It was typical during the Fourth of July celebration and fireworks for boats to raft alongside each other and party for several days. Rick knew that this would be the big one for us. We finally found the challenge we were looking for.

Rick and I knew two of the boats that would be rafting together because Rick had overheard the shoppers mention the names. We did not want to go and scout them out beforehand, however, not only because it might raise suspicion but because we wanted to face the mission without fully knowing what we were getting into. This would make it more difficult, which was what we wanted, a true test of our skill. We did scout the stream and river cove where the boats would be tying up, deciding the route we would take there and back. Even though the party was two full days away, we needed all that time to plan. Every detail of our scout mission we reviewed time and time again, like a well-choreographed dance. We had plan A, plan B, and plan C, as well as several emergency backup plans. We did not want to overlook anything, no matter how small and obscure the detail. We even went out of the way to tell Grandfather of our plans, in case he wanted to test us like he had at the fishermen's camp. Not knowing whether he was there or not would really be a test.

Rick and I watched the boats tie together from our vantage point well across the river. Even though it was not yet noon, six boats had already moored together, and from the way they'd placed bumpers on the outside of the boats, we knew they expected more. We could not stay and watch, for we had to leave soon after noon. Our approach would be from the far side of the river from a small stream that spilled into the cove where the boats were anchored. It would take us several hours to get around the river to our entry point and we wanted to leave plenty of time. We did not want to head directly across the river from our vantage point, for the river was crowded with boat traffic and during the fireworks display it would even be more crowded. It would make a great return route when the river slept, but not at the height of this frenzy.

Even before the sun set, we were at the stream we would take to the cove. We had to start well back from the cove because of various houses and developments that lay between us and the river. The best way past would be a water route. Our only problem there was that the homes along the river and the cove all had boat docks and bulk-heading. Not much natural cover, at least not the kind we were used to. However, we had practiced in these types of unnatural conditions for the past few days and felt comfortable with the challenge. We put on our camouflage, erased our tracks, and entered the stream, even before the sun was close to the horizon. We knew that the fireworks display would begin just after full dark and we wanted to be at the cove at this time. The distraction of the fireworks would make our open-water swim across the cove much easier.

Our early entry time into the water would pose its problems. It meant that it would still be light when we passed by the houses on the stream and only dusk when we encountered the river houses. We had to make damn sure that we stuck to cover as much as possible. Many of these houses had dogs, and one mistake would only send the neighborhood into a barking frenzy. No doubt, if seen or caught by anyone, we would be hard put to explain the camouflage and our skulking around the docks. Yet, despite the fact that it was light for the first part of our journey, we drifted the little stream without a second thought. To us, the daylight was just another challenge to test our skills to the maximum, and we welcomed that challenge. After all, if we were to someday be scouts, we would have to be able to operate under all kinds of conditions.

The first part of our journey went far better than expected. We quietly floated along the stream with just one close call. We had to sink deep into the shoreline brush as a canoe passed us by. But the occupants of the canoe never even glanced our way. However, the canoe taught us a lesson, for we only heard it at the last minute. We had been far too caught up in what was ahead of us, and not paying attention to what was behind. We had broken a primary rule of the scout. We had assumed that nothing would be coming up from behind since the stream was so small and nearly impenetrable. We learned again to assume nothing and expect anything, for assuming could have become our failure. The canoe incident was all we needed to break free of the complacency and put our nervous systems on full alert.

It was not even sunset when we encountered the first house on the stream. We were ahead of schedule and that was both good and bad. Good because it gave us plenty of time to get around any difficult situation that lay ahead, but bad because it was still full light. To make matters worse, a large family picnic was going on in the backyard, right on the stream bank. We froze motionless in the upstream brush to get a better look at what was happening and decide how we were going to get past. It became obvious that we had to call into play the first rule of scout camouflage— that is, to camouflage into the most open areas. The action of the people at the party confirmed our belief, for each time one of the parties looked out over the water they looked to the distant bank. We quickly and quietly slipped by them just a few feet below the bank, a few feet from where they sat having their picnic.

We had no problem slipping by the next few stream bank houses. At the last house before the development began we did have an adrenaline-rushing encounter. Just as we were moving slowly by an old dock and makeshift bulk-heading, an older man walked to the edge of the dock, pausing just a few feet above our heads. We froze motion-less, fearing that the man had spotted us. Rick saw the man simply scanning the distant bank, then up and down the river, never realizing that we were around. At one point he even looked into the stream just a few yards from us, but still did not have a clue that we were there. Finally, after what seemed to be an eternity, the man moved off and headed back into his house. We relaxed and continued our journey only after we heard the door slam behind him.

Getting through the development houses where the stream emptied into a small lagoon was far easier than we'd anticipated. Very few people were around and not even the dogs stirred. We stayed between the maze of tied motor boats, small sailboats, and other watercraft, emerging at the mouth of the cove just at sunset. We were right on schedule and would wait until full dark and the fireworks display before making the open-water drift to the flotilla of boats, anchored only one hundred yards from where we were. We drifted to the last dock and worked our way under, then pulled ourselves out of the water and onto the beams that supported the dock. There we could wait for dark while drying out and warming up after our long float.

Not even the feeding ducks drifting in and out from under the dock were aware of our presence. We lay still as mannequins, blending with the wood rafters. Our camouflage held fast and made us even more invisible, to the point that several birds landed on us, pausing on their way to their nests neatly tucked under the dock. Someone came down to feed the ducks bread and we could see through the cracks that it was a small child. Still we didn't move. Then just as the sun disappeared, the child's family came down to the dock. We could hear them setting up lawn chairs and spreading blankets. We heard the lid of a cooler and the fizzle of bottles just opened. The family was settling in for the fireworks display and that would only make our trip away from the dock more difficult.

We could not afford to wait out the full dark, for now we had to contend with a disruption in our plans. We slowly and carefully lowered ourselves from the beams and entered the water. Instead of moving out straight from the dock, we headed farther along the shore of the cove among remnants of old pilings, dock outcroppings, and heavy brush. It was a place where once a magnificent mansion had stood. There the debris would afford us natural cover so that we could begin our journey to the boats unobserved by the family on the dock. Just as the first display of fireworks exploded in the sky, Rick and I had reached the last piling of the old dock, which put us now only fifty yards from the boats. Though it was not as open and brazen as our planned approach, it was a good second choice, especially given the circumstances.

We had planned our approach to the anchored flotilla of boats so that we would be coming up from behind the people as they watched the fireworks display. The slow swimming drift across the open water and to the first boat went without incident. The boats were anchored and tied together so that people could easily travel from one to the other without stepping very far. This was good for them but better for us, in that we could easily get between the boats without being seen. As expected, everyone's eyes were looking high in the sky in the direction opposite from where we approached. It was all too easy, yet we knew enough not to let down our guard. There was no way that we were going to assume anything. We treated this flotilla of people just as we would a scout encampment.

Rick and I moved closer to the bow of the first boat. That way, if someone looked over the side, they would not be able to see directly down to the water. As we held on to the side of the boat, resting and intermittently giving each other hand signals, a stream of water poured over the side of the boat. I almost jumped and stirred the water, wondering for a moment what had caused the stream of water. It didn't take me long to realize that someone had left the crowd and was relieving himself over the side. The sound of a zipper followed, so too the hiss of a cigarette butt hitting the water, and soon followed by an empty beer bottle thrown nearby. Rick and I glared at each other, so enraged that I wanted to climb right onto the boat and throw the guy in.

Still fully engrossed in our rage, Rick and I moved to the very bow of the boat to get a good look at what lay ahead. We could see seven boats in all, with the two largest anchored in the center side by side. We estimated that the larger of the two had to be over fifty feet long. Drifting from one bow to the next, we began to make our way to the largest boat, which seemed to be the one with the most activity. As we moved we found ourselves surrounded by all manner of debris that had been cast overboard. Rick began to collect as much as he could carry and still hold his head above the water. Fortunately a small tender boat was tethered to one of the larger anchor lines and we began to use that boat as a garbage can. In just barely ten minutes of cautious collecting the little tender was nearly half full of garbage. Beer bottles, wrappers, cigarette butts, and countless other kinds of debris made up the bulk of the garbage. All thrown carelessly overboard.

As the fireworks display came to an abrupt but spectacular end, the party on the boats got into full swing. Loud music poured from the boats and people wandered about, some staggering under the effects of alcohol. With the crowd's dispersion our chances of getting caught increased, so Rick and I took refuge between the two larger boats. They were moored so closely together that there was no way anyone could see clearly between them. As we lay there resting and thinking about what we were going to do next, I caught sight of one of the people leaning over the railing and looking in our direction vacantly. I immediately recognized him as one of the older fishermen from the fishing camp we had raided. He didn't seem the type to me to litter so freely.

As soon as the fisherman moved from the railing, Rick gave me the "to shore" motion of his hands, and without question I followed him. We reached the shore quickly and concealed ourselves in the brush. I asked Rick why we left and he told me that there was too much activity going on for us to try to board the boats. He felt that it would be better if we warmed up, got some rest, and waited until the boat people went to bed. I agreed with him wholeheartedly. Though we hadn't really planned on boarding the boats, it now seemed like a good idea, even though technically our scouting mission was complete. It also gave us more than enough time to plan what we were going to do to leave our mark.

As we heard the last of the boat music being turned off and saw the final few lights extinguished, we slipped back into the water again. My heart pounded because we were pushing the edge of our skill. We knew that at least two of the boats had dogs aboard and we saw several sleeping bags laid out on the bows. So too did we know that dawn was not far away and we had to get to the distant shore well before first light. The lateness of the hour, our fatigue, and the cold hardly made a difference to us now, such was the adrenaline flow. Our mission was going to be tough and nerve-wracking but well worth the effort, such would be the outcome of our new master plan.

We reached the bow of the first boat again and immediately began collecting the garbage that remained around the boats. Within a short time we had filled the little tender boat to a point of nearly overflowing. Unhooking the boat, we cautiously and slowly maneuvered it around the boats and to the rear of the second-largest boat. We chose that boat because it afforded the easiest access over its railing.

Rick and I slowly pulled ourselves up over opposite sides of the stern so as not to rock the boat to one side. Each tiny movement that was out of the ordinary seemed like an earthquake to me at this point. By the time we were fully over the back rail and onto the deck we were nearly completely dry. My heart pounded so loudly in my chest that I feared someone would easily hear me.

Rick and I set about our chore of scout psychological warfare. We carefully opened the engine compartments and removed the distributor wires from both engines. Rick then climbed into the small boat and began handing me garbage which I carefully placed into the engine compartments. We then closed the hatches and went on with our work. Cautiously we swapped the flags on the two larger boats, hanging along with them a clutter of assorted debris, equipment, and various articles of clothing. By the time we had finished, the boats appeared more like a clothesline for garbage than boats. We began to do the same to the other boats, pulling their distributor wires and then hanging them from various parts of the boat. We even pushed our limits with the people sleeping on deck, cautiously stealing and hiding their clothing.

Then for the final act, Rick slipped into the water and began to tie all the anchor lines together, entangling them very badly. I began to untie all the boats so that they began to drift apart. Then as I deftly danced from boat to boat, I took all the keys I could find and tied them onto a length of string. Then slowly slipping into the water I found Rick as he completed his job of entangling the anchor lines. I held up my string of keys then pointed to the anchor line. Without a motion or the stirring of water, I submerged into the blackness, following one of the anchor lines to the entangled anchor. There I tied on the string of keys securely.

This way there would be no doubt in the boat people's minds that they'd been raided during the night.

Rick and I drifted away from the boats, across the channel, and to the distant shore. Going now mostly by land, we did not stop or talk until we reached camp. Dawn was just breaking as we sat down to relax before turning in for some much-needed sleep. Between the physical exhaustion, the cold water, and the constant adrenaline rush, we were beyond being drained. The scout mission now over, we felt our bodies and minds beginning to collapse in on themselves. We were far too tired to speak much or to revel in what we had done. I knew for certain as I fell asleep that there would be no doubt in the boat people's minds that they had been raided. I also wondered what the fisherman would now think about all of this. Kind of a déjà vu experience, no doubt.

I was awakened sometime later by raucous laughter. Both Rick and I climbed out of our shelter, wondering what all the noise was about. Grandfather stood before us and said, "You missed the show. I took a walk to the river this morning and saw a cluster of tangled boats. People were screaming at each other, clothing was being taken down, some men were diving the anchor lines and cussing, dogs were barking, and there were more fireworks on the water than were in the sky last night! You should have seen it! But you two wouldn't know anything about it, would you?" He laughed to himself again as he walked off toward the stream. Rick and I smiled at each other, the grin of success.

CHAPTER 4

THE FACTORY

Rick and I had been going out on various scouting missions for over a year. Each mission we undertook would push our skills of stealth, camouflage, stalking, evasion, and scout psychological warfare even further than the one before. Grandfather even seemed pleased with our progress. In each mission I tried something different, something that would test me and challenge me to go to a higher level of intensity. If given a choice of taking the easy way or the hard way, I would always choose the most difficult. After a while I would never take the safe approach to anything, even when the situation became intense or dangerous. My philosophy was the same for the scout skills as it was for everything else I did. I wanted to push the limits and deliberately make things difficult. After all, if I always took the easy way I would stagnate, but by pushing the limits I was always growing. Basically this was the same philosophy Grandfather held for himself.

As far as I was concerned, I was most alive when I was in wilderness, and even more so when I was pushing my limits and walking the edge of the scout experience. Rick and I relished every opportunity we had to go out on a scouting mission, whether it was to scout a party or just to watch a hunter getting into his blind. To me the greatest times were when I had to face some sort of dangerous situation, like a camp dog, a frightened camper with a gun, or even a drug deal taking place along the back roads of the Pine Barrens. We even sought out those who were savvy in the woods, and had spent much of their lives in a wilderness environment. Every time we put ourselves up against these outdoorsmen we triumphed and proved Grandfather right. Grandfather had always said that there was no one who could come close to the skill of the scout just by doing well in the wilderness. We confirmed what he said time and time again. Many times we would even go out on daylight raids just to push our skills and up the odds of being detected.

After so many scout missions or ''raids'' as we began to call them, we found it more and more difficult to push our skills. We had a hard time finding challenges. We had single-handedly nearly cleared out our area of the Pine Barrens of destructive party-goers, illegal dumping, and illegal tree cutting. It seemed that no one really wanted to go into our section of the woods anymore. Stories abounded about the Jersey Devil and other demons, which we succeeded in creating and perpetuating. Using the scout's command of psychological war-

fare, we would get covered in mud and then stand just outside
a campfire light until someone saw us. As soon as we were
seen we would deftly disappear into nothingness. That would
send a camp into a panic. We would be seen as many times as
it took to clear out a camp in uncontrolled terror. We even did
it in neighborhoods bordering the woods. I loved it any time I
heard anyone describe the demons of the woods.

However, we never bothered anyone that was serious
and committed to the wilderness. If we found a camp where
the people were there to enjoy the solitude and splendor of
the wilderness, we left them alone. Our targets were those
who would destroy the woods by illegally cutting trees,
littering, dumping toxic chemicals, or starting forest fires.
These were our enemies, but it did not take long to drive
them from the temples of creation. We began to look at
ourselves not only as scouts but also as guardians of the
wilderness. We would tolerate no abuse. The Pine Barrens
were fragile and vulnerable to man's stupidity, and someone had to protect them.

Grandfather gave us several basic rules that we were
never to break. First was that we were never to be seen or
identified in any way. To be seen was one of the worse
things that could befall a scout. Even more important to
Grandfather was the law that we do not destroy anything
or hurt anyone. Whether the destruction or hurt came as
a direct or an indirect encounter with us made little difference. Grandfather very often said, "It is not those
people who destroy the earth that you should hate, but hate
instead their actions. They know no better. Fight their ignorance, and teaching them the way of wilderness will become your greatest weapon." So often we wanted to
destroy equipment and drive people from the woods with
physical violence, but my heart would never allow it to

become my reality. Yet so many times I came so close and I must admit that it was a struggle not to strike out. My biggest test of control would come when Rick and I began to reach beyond our area of the Pine Barrens and into the larger, more destructive realms of man.

For many years Rick and I had heard of a local chemical company that was dumping toxic chemicals and even raw sewage into the river that ran past my house. Many of my friends had become sick from swimming in the river and yet no one seemed to be doing anything about the problem. As far as we knew, there were no laws against such dumping. Even if there were laws it would be hard to prove that the chemical company was dumping into the river. After all, the facility was off-limits to the general public and guarded around the clock. It was even impossible to get close to the chemical plant via the river. Fences blocked access to the back of the plant, where the valves and pipes used to dump the chemicals and sewage into the river could be found. We knew that they were legally allowed to dump some things into the river, but we also knew that they were mixing it with things that they were not allowed to dump.

The problem became obvious anytime we floated the river. Until the point of the chemical company, the river was a dark tea color as was true of all waters of the Pine Barrens, but as soon as it reached the chemical company it turned a turbid black color. Also at this point the river began to smell of sewage and other caustic, almost antiseptic, chemical odors. Several times, especially when we floated the river at night, our skin would become red and sore, feeling like we had been sunburned. Once in a while either Rick or I would end up with blisters later in the day. Yet this only happened at night and rarely during daylight hours. So too would it be intermittent, and never seem to follow any pattern. This led us to suspect that the plant was dumping its illegal substances and sewage after dark and late at night so that no one would detect their presence. By daybreak the color of the river would nearly return to normal, or at least normal for that part of the river on down to the ocean.

We could only assume what was really going on. The random caustic change in the water, the smell of sewage, and the late hour that it happened made us realize that not only was there illegal dumping but someone was going to great pains to cover it up. We also knew that very few people, even in government, would be willing to investigate the problem further. After all, the chemical company was one of the larger employers in the area and no one wanted to jeopardize any jobs. So too, some of the officers of the company were involved in local politics and they had far too much influence as far as we were concerned. As we saw it, there was a major cover-up by both the company and some of the local government, as well as fear of losing jobs. The chemical company was just too big, powerful, and rich for anyone to confront. No one seemed to want to do anything, though there were many hushed complaints.

Rick and I had just returned from one of our raids, in which we had successfully and easily scared a group of poachers out of our area of the Pine Barrens. Even though these men were armed with high-power rifles, spotlights, and rifle scopes, we had terrorized them with such effective fierceness that in their panic they almost shot each other. The mission had gone so easily that we were not even excited about the results. We treated it more as commonplace, just another night of easy work. This is when Rick first broached the subject of getting into the chemical plant to see what we could do about the pollution problem. He got no argument from me. I saw it as a splendid opportunity to push beyond my limits and create a new and intense challenge. I took no convincing at all to agree to the raid. In fact I thought it was the best thing I had heard in months.

Because of the intensity of the challenge, the intermittent chemical dumping, and the near-inaccessibility of the guarded compound, Rick and I took the better part of the week in planning the raid. Here we were not dealing with just campers and partyers, but with armed guards, the local laws of criminal trespass, and most probably the police, if we were ever caught. We knew that it would also probably take several raids to accomplish what we wanted. After all, the intermittent chemical dumping would pose the biggest problem. We might not get into the compound on the same night that they would be dumping, but have to go back time after time until we caught them in the act. Another problem was the frequency of the necessary raids. Each time we entered the compound we would run an even greater risk of being caught, for just one mistake on a previous raid might alert them to our trespass. This would only put them on alert and up the possibility of our getting caught.

We broached the subject with Grandfather, but he remained uncommitted. Other than to say that we must make the decision on our own, he made us promise to follow the laws of the scout. We must not destroy property or hurt anyone. Grandfather looked very concerned, however, and I suspect that he feared for our safety. Yet, paradoxically, I felt that he thought it would be a much-needed step in developing our scout skills further. I was very concerned about Grandfather's attitude. I wondered so often if he thought that the mission we had chosen to undertake was too far beyond our skill level, or that we might somehow be hurt either physically or emotionally. I also wondered if he really trusted my temper and aggression in such a situation. After all, I was brutal in my approach to people who would destroy the wilderness and had a hard time containing my rage. With the monumental intensity of this destruction, it could become the most intense internal battle of my life.

Even though Rick and I were very familiar with the river that passed the chemical company and the fences that surrounded the perimeter of the pipes and dumping station, we still scouted it several more times. We knew from past experience that things and situations can change overnight and it had been a while since we had explored that part of the river. Most of our scouting explorations were in the early evening. Most people would not be around at that time and I knew that most dumping did not occur until well past midnight. We were as careful as usual not to leave any tracks or other signs that anyone had been around. Even these preliminary scouting missions were treated like full-fledged raids. We could not afford at this early stage of the planning to arouse even the slightest suspicion.

Once we knew what we were up against we could plan the entire mission and several alternatives. We knew that the first full mission would be to get past the outer fence, across the gravel field, and to the inner fence. We knew that this fence was at least ten feet high with tightly rolled barbed wire across the top. We also knew that a guard would frequently pass there, stop at some kind of concrete outbuilding, also surrounded by a fence, and check the door. From the outer perimeter fence we had only been able to see the inner fences and buildings. Just barely visible from behind was a series of tangled pipes and wheel valves. We could tell that the area was infrequently used and off-limits to the factory employees. A small road ran from the factory and terminated at another gated fence several hundred yards away from the little brick building. We only knew this because we could see that portion of the fence from the upper part of the river.

Normally we would have chosen a route into the compound near the fence separating the factory from the small brick building, but we had no idea what lay between the gate and that building. Our view was obscured at best and oftentimes we heard some kind of machinery running. We had no other choice than to plan our route through the gravel fields, which would leave us entirely in the open. Going that route was dangerous, but not as dangerous as the unknown portion of the trail that we could not see. If we did take the chance and go to what looked to be the easier route we could possibly run into workers, another gravel field, or worse yet, a guard dog. It was mostly the fear of a highly trained guard dog that caused us not to take that route. We had seen dog tracks in the gravel beds, but had never seen a dog. Yet we had heard barking coming from the hidden area between the building and factory on several occasions.

We not only had to plan the raid, but we had to plan several raids. After all, we could not be sure what night or nights the dumping may take place. It could even be a random occurrence, where the dumping did not take place every week, but every time the holding tanks were full. So too might the dumping occur during rainstorms or when the river was high, thus further masking the dumping by having the heavy currents carry away the chemical and sewage evidence faster. We assumed nothing, for we had no idea what we were going to do when we got into the compound. After all, people there were probably not going to scare off easily, and any scare would only be temporary. The overwhelming variables made planning difficult and raised the risk factor markedly. Every possible precaution had to be taken and every possible variable, no matter how obscure, had to be analyzed.

We could be reasonably sure that no dumping of any sort would occur on the weekends of the summer. Far too many people would be swimming and boating in the lower river, increasing the likelihood that the pollution would be spotted. It could happen on a rainy weekend, but even then the company would be pushing its luck. The weekends would also be downtime for the company and any workers there at the time would be more of a skeleton crew than the general work force. Though we assumed nothing but expected everything, the weekend seemed our best chance for scouting the inner compound area. Once we became familiar with the compound we could plan a more dramatic raid and thus make the final decision on what we wanted to do. Also, from the inner compound we could possibly find better and more obscure routes in.

I particularly liked the fact that we would have to travel across the gravel beds, which afforded little or no cover. After all, it was scout consciousness to do the unexpected, and no one would ever expect someone to sneak into the compound in the wide open. Any guard would be looking in the heavy brush and thickets. Even if anyone glanced across the gravel field they would not look directly at the field itself but around the fenced perimeter. With good camouflage to fit the terrain, even a trained guard would nearly have to step on us before he could see us. As far as I was concerned it was the best route of travel and Rick agreed. My only concern, of course, would be some sort of guard dog. But we would minimize that when we descented our bodies. Here again the guard dog would have to step on us to detect that we were there.

The following Saturday night became our proposed target date for two reasons. First, it was forecast to be a very hot and humid weekend; which would mean that plenty of people would be using the river. Second, Saturday was right in the middle of the weekend. If they had to dump on the weekend it would be on a Friday or Sunday night. Saturday would be far too risky for the company to chance. I would suspect that even on a rainy Saturday night it would be chancing too much, considering all the die-hard fishermen who would use the river rain or shine. Even though it was only Wednesday evening when we made the decision to go into the compound, we still felt a little rushed in our planning. We wanted as much time as possible to get everything perfect.

When Friday afternoon rolled around, Rick and I left Grandfather's camp and headed to our upriver camp, which was located several miles above the chemical company. The nice thing about using this camp as our staging area was that we already had well-camouflaged scout-pit shelters in place there. Our plan would be to drift down the river to the company fence, then exit back into the river and float downstream. A few miles down from the fence we would intersect the mouth of the stream that ran through Grandfather's camp. We would travel upstream from there and be back in camp before sunup. There were no roads along this route and most trails were inaccessible by even four-wheel drive. Using the water would also make it impossible for any dogs to follow our scent. Anyway, the river would be an unexpected route, especially at night. So too were there many swamps that would afford us numerous escape routes along the way.

We found it very difficult to get to sleep that night. We were just too excited and worried over the oncoming raid. Yet I forced myself to stay in the scout pit longer and later than I would have normally gotten up. I just wanted to make sure I was well rested for the raid. For the most part, all of Saturday morning and much of the afternoon we spent lounging around. The waiting was one of the most difficult parts of any raid and this was one of the most difficult I can remember. I did not mind waiting for long periods of time once I was on a raid, but the waiting time beforehand became unbearable. Fortunately the afternoon went by a little more quickly than the morning, for we made ourselves busy by playing some primitive games. Also we spent part of the afternoon thoroughly camouflaging in our camp area better than we ever had before. We wanted no worries or regrets due to a sloppy job.

About an hour before sunset we began to camouflage our bodies. First we washed using a natural soap and then rubbed charcoal all over our bodies. Even though much of it would wash off during our trip down the river, there would still be enough left to give us a good base for finishing touches when we exited the water. We left even before the sun had touched the horizon, and floated silently along the bank, moving always to keep ourselves close to the camouflage of brush. We used the same deal of caution we would have if the compound were right around the river bend and people were along the banks. I had not felt that kind of intensity in an initial part of a mission in a very long time. The rush of excitement was overwhelming and I reveled in its intensity. I vowed at that moment to always seek that kind of intensity in every scout mission I ever undertook.

It was only about half an hour after dark when we began to hit the swamp area that lay just upstream of the compound. It was there that we had planned to pull out of the water and get to high ground where we could warm up and wait for the night to grow late. The reason we left so early was that we did not know what we would encounter along the initial water route that might eat up valuable time. So too could we listen intently to the sounds of the distant factory and climb one of the taller trees to get a look at the well-lit compound area. From the lofty lookout of the tree we could easily track any vehicle headlights heading to or from the compound. Though we could not see the compound because of the distant trees, we could see the flickering of headlights playing against the constant illumination of the compound.

This period of waiting was not bad at all, for time slipped away unnoticed. Though we would not talk, even in the thick protected and impenetrable recesses of the swamp, we went over our plans time and again using sign language. This is what really ate up the time and totally occupied our consciousness. After a few hours we headed back into the water and toward the upstream area of the compound. It hardly seemed like a long break at all. Yet I am glad that we had it, especially being so close to the outer compound. It not only gave us time to relax and review the plan but also the much-needed rest before the long and relentless night that lay ahead. It also succeeded in uplifting the anticipation and excitement level to a higher plane.

As soon as we reached the outer part of the fence we paused there in the water for a long time, listening, watching, and reaching out with our feelings. Something inside me told me not to move yet, though I did not know from where it came. I could tell from the position that Rick had chosen to rest in that he too felt the same sense of it not yet being time to move. It's so ironic how the intensity of the scout experience can bring out the best of inner vision. Within moments of our first sensations of having to wait, we heard the sound of a heavy, metallic door closing, followed by distant footfalls, then a vehicle door closing, the engine starting, and the fading sound of the vehicle driving off. Yet we still had the Inner Vision sensation of having to wait. Though it did not make much sense, we knew from experience that we had to obey that feeling without question. Soon there was another sound of a big door closing and another scenario of a second vehicle driving off. Inner Vision now said that it was time to move.

We moved to where the gravel bed spilled out from under the fence and created its own river bank. Mixed with the gravel were clumps of clay of the same color as the gravel itself. Taking care to remove the clay from its bed only below the waterline we rubbed it into our flesh, effectively camouflaging ourselves so as to disappear into the gravel. Once finished, we left the gravel bank area, taking care to walk in the water so as to leave no tracks, and back to a long grass area that led to the corner of the fence. There we waited until the damp clay had thoroughly dried on our bodies. We did not want to leave any discoloration on the grasses to alert anyone of our route into the compound. Grandfather always told us to assume that everyone was a master tracker. Though we knew that this was not the case, we still felt that this was the only safe assumption.

Once we got to the fence we headed into the thicket and to a large tree that grew several feet outside of the fence. The chemical company had effectively cut back all vegetation near the fence and the tree would be the only way over; otherwise we would be forced to climb the fence, which was something we did not want to do. Climbing the fence would only leave more tracks and traces of our point of entry. We climbed the tree silently, slipped out onto the thickest limb that hung over the fence, and with our added weight it lowered us slowly to the ground inside the compound. We planned our landing so that our feet would touch down on the area that held the largest patch of gravel rocks. That would barely show our prints at all and most

people would overlook such an area. We hoped that the
combination of earlier charcoal application and the scent of
the river and clay would effectively camouflage our scent
to most dogs.

We paused for a long time at our entry place, straining
our senses as we searched for anything that might be contrary to the flow of the night. We could now clearly see the
inner compound fence and the brick building inside. All
was quiet, except for the chorus of insects and sounds of
other animals outside the fence. Once we were nearly certain that all was the natural order, we lay flat on our bellies
and began to inch our way toward the compound using a
faster version of the scout crawl. Even if someone looked
our way they would still not be able to detect our movement. We headed toward a small, low patch of vegetation
just outside the inner compound's fence. We chose the distant vegetation as a second staging area because not only
would it conceal us but it was also the only vegetation in
the compound. Or at least the only vegetation we could see
at this point.

As we inched our way past the midway point in the
gravel field we could see the distant dark outline of a blacktop road that led to the gate of the inner compound. It was
something unexpected in a way, because we could not see
this roadway from the river or even from the vantage point
of the outer perimeter fence. The fact that the roadway was
paved rather than just gravel told us immediately that it
was very frequently used. As we worked our way nearer to
the road's edge we could clearly see that the driveway
apron leading into the small brick building was used not
only by the guard's vehicle but by several other vehicles—
and several times a day, such were the wear patterns along
its sides. This could probably be seen even without the aid
of the floodlights that lit the entire compound.

Just as we were about to begin crossing the blacktop road, we heard the distant sound of a sliding gate, the sound of a vehicle moving forward, and then the gate closing again. We were caught in the open with not even the scantiest of cover. There was no way we could even move to the other side, for the lights of the oncoming vehicle shone directly upon us. We had no other choice than to flatten ourselves, remain motionless, and pray that our gravel camouflage was enough. Worse yet we were located at the major bend in the road where the lights would sweep us full blast when the vehicle made the final turn to approach the parking apron. It had been such a long time since I had felt so damn vulnerable during a scout raid. I hoped that all Grandfather had taught me about scout invisibility would hold up under such an astringent test. My confidence was shaken as the vehicle approached; all I could think about was the eventual route of my panicked escape if I were seen.

Actually it was a comforting thought that psychologically, according to scout law, our position was the best possible. First, we were entirely in the open, which meant that the guard would not be looking for anything there. In the guard's mind it would be impossible for anyone to hide there. Second, the guard would be looking above where we lay and toward the fence, as the fence would be the place of entry and afford the heaviest camouflage. Just as I was thinking about the factors in our favor, the vehicle passed without showing any signs of slowing or otherwise indicating that the driver felt something was wrong. I watched as the car stopped at the parking apron thirty yards away. I could clearly see that the vehicle was the same make and model as the local police cars, even sporting flashing lights on top. At first I thought it might be the police but in the light I could clearly see the company emblem stenciled on the trunk.

The driver exited the car and tossed a cigarette on the ground, not even taking the time to crush it with his foot. Without hesitating or looking around, he opened the back door and out jumped a German shepherd dog. My heart jumped in my chest. It was of great consolation that the dog, upon jumping down from the back seat, did a long, elegant back stretch and went directly over to the fence to urinate. He showed no signs of being aware at all, which led me to suspect that he was untrained in police work. The stretch also indicated that the dog must have been in the car for a long time and probably asleep during the drive. So too was the driver of the car totally unaware. He did not look around the compound but first at the dog and then at the gate leading through the inner fence. There was no doubt in my mind that this guard, despite the neat appearance of his uniform, had very little training and had worked himself into an unaware rut from job redundancy.

We watched as the guard unlocked the fence and walked into the inner compound, followed by the dog. Instead of following the roadway, he walked directly to the corner of the building where he paused to urinate, still not looking beyond what he was doing. The dog wandered about aimlessly as it waited for him to finish. From there the guard went to the huge steel door, took out a key and unlocked it with a distinctive click that we could clearly hear. The darkness of the room soon flared with a bright flickering flash when he turned on the fluorescent lights. The lights were so intense that they flooded the outer apron and even illuminated our position. The guard and the dog disappeared inside, apparently walking to the back of the building. The purpose in their walk indicated that they were about to take care of some sort of work.

Rick and I used the opportunity to deftly move toward the building in a low crouch, taking care not to come too close to the fence, where we might leave scent that the dog would pick up. We went directly to the scant brush cover alongside the fence and there settled in, camouflaging ourselves as we nestled down on our bellies. From our position we had a clear view of the layout of the building and what was taking place. We could easily see that the building contained several small valves that led into one huge valve, all connected by pipes of various size and color. We could also see the guard at the back of the room, apparently writing in a book and looking at his watch midway through the writing. Apparently he was signing in that he had checked out the place. The dog stood wearily by his side, apparently not liking the late hour and broken sleep. The whole process took quite a long time, as the guard did not appear to be in much of a hurry.

The guard then left the building and closed the door, never checking to see if it had latched. He then walked to the gate and repeated the process, closing the padlock but never checking to see if it had truly locked. At this point the guard's feet were only a few inches from my face; he was still totally unaware of our position. The dog sauntered over to the low brush in which we lay and with a token sniff lifted his leg and urinated. Unfortunately he urinated directly onto Rick's hand and forearm. The guard called him from the now-open back door and the dog walked over and jumped inside. The dog gave not the slightest indication that he even remotely suspected something was wrong. Neither did the guard as he entered the car and drove away.

As we listened to the sound of the distant gate closing and the slowly disappearing sound of the engine, Rick and I silently breathed a sigh of relief. We lay there a long time straining our senses into the night as we tried to detect any other sound of someone else coming or something still out of the ordinary. Satisfied that we were reasonably safe, we set out to explore the back end of the building outside the inner compound. Out back was nothing more than a tangle of pipes of all different sizes, leading eventually to a concrete embankment where they entered and disappeared. Apparently these led to the holding tanks that we could see in the distance, clustered just behind the main plant. It was obvious to us that the brick house, with all of its valves, was the place where they controlled the flow of the chemicals into the river.

We explored then the road that led from the inner compound to the outer gate and eventually into the back equipment storage area of the factory. There in the distance we could see some heavy machinery and other nondescript piles of pipe and other equipment. The road leading from the gate to the block house was buffered on both sides by wide gravel strips, also cleared of vegetation. This was also where the fence of the outer compound entered the thick woods, obscuring our view of it from the river, and no wonder. Here the thick woods came almost fully to the fence and this would afford one of the safest entry routes we had yet seen. Trouble was that I wondered if this vulnerable place would cause the guard to become alert, at least for that portion of his beat.

Upon closer inspection of the woods outside this section of the fence we found that it was nearly all swamp and heavily tangled thicket. Again, no guard would ever expect anyone to attempt to enter the compound via this route. Thus this possible entrance would be even more overlooked by the guard than any other place. There was no doubt in my mind that this would be our next route into the compound. The remainder of the time we just explored the fence of the inner compound. I almost laughed out loud when I discovered that the back of the fence had such a huge hole cut in it that I could crawl through on hands and knees. Apparently the hole had been cut for a larger pipe that had subsequently been replaced by a smaller one. The crew never bothered to close the gap between the new pipe and the fence. As far as I was concerned, the inner fence was only for show, which indicated that the guards and management did not expect anyone to sneak into the compound.

As we belly-crawled across the outer gravel compound on our way out, the guard came again. His lights again flashed directly over us but there was no hesitation in his travel. Given the interval since the first visit we assumed that the guard must be ordered to come here every hour or so. The dog's urinating again indicated he must not have been let out of the car since the last trip. This led me to believe that this guard must have the job of patrolling the areas outside the factory, and this valve house, as we began to call it, was one of his many stops and probably the longest. In fact, we wondered if he even got out of the car at all during his patrol other than at this compound. His walk and subsequent stretching were those of a man who had spent a great deal of time in a car.

Once the patrol car left, we slipped out of the compound using a slightly different and more obscure route. We entered the water and were easily back at camp and in our huts hours before dawn. I was upset because the raid had been no challenge at all. The closest we came to a challenge was when the headlights danced across us as we lay in the open and when the dog urinated on Rick's hand. As far as I was concerned, if we were to get any excitement at all on the next part of this raid we would have to push our limits by getting right up to the company itself. Possibly right into the equipment storage area and maybe right into the building. All else would be of little value as far as pressing our skills was concerned. However, I really wanted to do something to let the company know that someone knew that they were dumping in the river.

After a good night's sleep, Rick and I set immediately to planning our next raid. We did not want to wait a long time because the circumstances could change. I worried little that anyone would have picked up our trail from the night before, thus putting the guards on alert, as we were far too careful. Under different circumstances, in which we suspected that they might be wise to our raid, we would have waited a long period of time before the second raid. That way things would cool down and a buffer of time would allow the guards to get back into their rut of complacency again. In this case it would be better to get back there as soon as we could. That was one of the things I loved best about planning a scout raid. Not only did you have to plan for the physical logistics, but you also had to work through the psychology, as well as so many other variables. As always, you could not plan for everything and you had to expect anything.

We decided to go on our next raid the following Wednesday night because it seemed the most likely time to dump the chemicals. The long-range weather forecast called for intermittent rains. Especially after so many weeks without rain, this would almost force the company to dump. As far as we were concerned, we could not think of a more inviting set of circumstances. Not only would it be possible to catch them in the act of dumping, but it would further press our limits. Especially if we went beyond the compound and into the equipment storage and parking area. There might also be a different guard; since it was the weekend when we encountered the last one, the shifts might have changed and there could possibly be someone new.

Thus we could not rely on the same guards with the same habits. With so many variables there was a greater risk and thus greater intensity. We could push beyond our limits.

As Wednesday afternoon rolled around, we left Grandfather's camp after going through the usual procedure of camouflaging. It was our plan this time, just to break any routine, to move upstream to the compound, enter between the back gate and the valve house, and retreat through the thick swamps. The swamps would take us upriver of the camp stream and we could float the final mile or so back to camp. In this way, even if they were looking for us, we would have so broken our routine that it would give us the advantage. A scout never takes the same route twice and we had more than accomplished that goal. Yet given all our confidence and the overwhelming and easy success of the last mission, Rick and I took greater care in planning the next. There was now so much that could go wrong that we could take no chances, especially because this time we were going to leave a lasting impression at the factory.

The moment we left camp we were on full alert, even more so than the first time we had gone out to raid the compound. Again, we wanted no sloppiness that would lead to regrets, and we wanted no chance encounters with anyone who might become a witness later on. Everyone at this point was a potential hazard. The trip to the river from camp and the long journey up the river went without incident. In fact it went too easily. Even when an evening canoe party passed us, they had no clue that we were hidden in the water along the banks. I had this overwhelming feeling to get right up behind the last canoe and follow in its wake for a while, but I could not afford to waste the energy. Anyway, these canoeists looked to be out to enjoy the paddle and were not like some of the beer-guzzling canoeists I had encountered in the past.

We had chosen a pull-out site slightly downriver from the compound. Except for the few moments we'd had to wait for the canoes to pass we were right on schedule and had plenty of time to relax and warm up before starting the most intense part of our mission. As usual, we spent the time going over the plan using sign language, scouting the area from the tall trees at the edge of the swamp, and just generally reaching out with our feelings. However, this wait, unlike the last one, seemed endless and overwhelming, such was our excitement and anticipation of the events that lay ahead. Several times I had to pull myself out of the rapture and euphoria of excitement and remind myself that I had a job to do here and now. That job was as important as any other step of the raid. Complacency or ineffectiveness now would only become disastrous later on. Excitement and anticipation at this point became a distraction that I had to transcend.

As soon as Rick and I felt the time was right, confirmed by our inner vision, we slipped back into the water, through the swamp, and to the fence that lay between the valve house and main gate, as quickly and deftly as imaginable. We knew even before we approached the fence that things had changed dramatically. We could hear the commotion of voices and see the movement of several people around the valve house. Several cars were parked there and other cars were traveling in and out of the compound randomly. We could also hear the crackle of radios as people communicated with each other. This time there were two patrol cars. One was parked on the curve of the blacktop road and the other by the outer fence near the river. The one guard by the blacktop was scanning the perimeter fences and the other guard was watching the water. We knew now that the stakes were very high.

What troubled us was that these guards appeared highly

aware, although their awareness was relative. To us they might as well have been living in a vacuum. However, they were much more aware than the guard that we had encountered on our first raid. We recognized one of the dogs that was with the guard by the river as the dog from the other night, but the guard nearest the valve house had another dog locked in the back of the patrol car. This dog just kept looking out the partially opened windows, snarling viciously at passersby. This dog, we knew without a doubt, would pose the biggest potential danger out of everyone and everything there. Fortunately, given the apparent viciousness of the dog, I did not suspect that the guard would readily let him out of the car. He looked mean and would probably go for one of the workers before he even suspected us.

From the actions of everyone there, especially from the vigilance of the guards, we knew that this was going to be one of the nights that they were going to dump. The body language of the group suggested a covert operation and they all knew the illegality of its consequence. The number of people and their actions were such that we had no other recourse than to wait until things died down before we could cross the fence. Though if I really wanted to press the limits I could have taken a different route and gotten right up to the inner compound with very little likelihood of being seen. Those who were watching were either involved in observing or working on the valves or watching the river. Rarely did anyone look back toward the factory and in our direction. Even then they looked but did not see.

As the night grew later, various cars began to filter out of the compound. After a while even the guard with the vicious dog left the area. I suspect that they felt a false sense of security from the late hour and subsequently let down their guard. Finally only the guard by the river was left and one man inside the valve house. This was when we saw how stupid we'd been not to realize that the guard by the river was in fact the same guard from the night before. We had falsely assumed him to be a different guard because his actions were so radically different and he appeared to be quite aware and professional. That facade he set aside when the other guard left, for now the guard by the river reverted to the same habits he'd had the night before. It had all been a show, thus leading us to believe that he was a different guard. We breathed a silent sigh of relief, knowing that this guard would not pose much of a problem.

We began to move in, inching toward the back side of the inner compound on our bellies. By the time we reached the point where the pipes crossed under the fence and into the brick valve house, the guard by the river was leaning on the fence having a cigarette and his dog was laying curled up near his feet, apparently asleep. We edged our way between the fence and the pipes, slipping now fully inside the compound. I could tell from the vibration of the pipes and the faint sound of running water that they were in the process of dumping. I assumed that the man inside the brick house was controlling the dumping, though we still could not see him. An anger that bordered on an uncontrolled rage welled up inside of me and took me by surprise. It is the personality of a scout not to get sidetracked by emotion, for emotion will cause failure. Yet I couldn't help myself. I just wanted to go into the valve house, tie up the man, and throw him into the polluted water. I wanted him to drink it, the same way all the plants and animals downstream were having to drink that poison.

It took me a while to compose myself and get back into the unemotional consciousness of the scout. Holding on to that hatred and rage would definitely cause the raid to fail.

As we neared the place where the pipes entered the building, we found a loose opening between the bricks and the smaller cluster of pipes. From there we could clearly see most of the inner valve room. There, dressed in a white lab coat, holding a clipboard and periodically glancing at his watch, was the man in control of the dumping. He stood next to the largest wheel valve, apparently waiting for the flow to stop. Like all of the others, he was totally unaware of the things around him. All his concerns were toward the valve and his watch, to the exclusion of everything else.

It became a real struggle for me as I lay there and watched him through the crack. I was torn between hating him and pitying him. I knew that the dumping was not fully his fault. He was just doing his job, and as long as he made money it did not make much of a difference to him what he had to do for it. After all, he could not see the far-reaching destruction that he was causing or the things that he was hurting. I guess he knew it was illegal, but since he could see no apparent damage, it was not a bother to him. His ignorance made me sick. I wondered to myself if he had any kids and if so if they swam in the river. I doubted it immediately. He no doubt made a lot of money and his children probably swam in the protection of their family pool or at the local country club, far removed from the poisons of the river that the rest of us had to swim in.

Rick and I began to work our way around to the corner of the building and over to the edge of the fence, where the clump of brush we had hidden in during the first raid was located. Though the brush did not come through the fence and into the inner compound, we knew that if we lay up against the fence we would be camouflaged by the backdrop of brush and deep shadows. This would also put us right up against the gate and afford us a clear view of what was going on inside the valve house. Technically it would have been a risky hiding position under different circumstances, but given the personality of the inept guard and the lack of suspicion on their part, it was a good choice. It did not take us long to get there and to blend with the shadows to a point of invisibility. There was no way they could have seen us even if they looked directly at us.

Just as we got into place we heard the patrol car start up and at the same time the sound of the valve being turned. It was obvious that the dumping process was now finished. However, we could not tell if it was because the tanks were empty or because the light misty drizzle that had been falling most of the night had now stopped. The patrol car stopped just a few feet from where we lay and we could hear the guard get out. It was a relief not to hear the sound of the second door closing, which meant that he'd left the dog in the car. Within moments the sound of clicking heels approached us, paused at the fence for a moment as the obvious grinding sound of a cigarette being crushed out followed, and then the clicking walk continued past us. We could see the guard, now in plain view, enter the valve house and begin talking to the other man.

I slowly poked my head out of the bushes and looked back to the patrol car. The dog was nowhere in sight, apparently lying down on the backseat. At that moment I felt a slight tug on my loincloth and looked at Rick. He held a large, odd-shaped pebble in his hand and pointed to it and then to the door. I had only a hunch what he was going to do, since our communication had to be sketchy at best, given the circumstances. Instinctively I knew that I had to assume the position of lookout so I went back to poking my head up through the uppermost portion of the shadows. Rick slipped away from the fence and began to head for the door. He stayed low and quiet, keeping himself well inside the shadows so as to escape detection if the dog was looking. I could feel the blood surging in my temples, for this was pushing our limits far more than we had during the raid thus far. Rick had put himself in the most vulnerable position yet and if he were caught it would cause a domino effect and I would be caught too.

I still had no idea what Rick was going to do. He moved up behind the deepest shadow of the door and froze. The guard had chosen that moment to go back out to his car and retrieve his pack of cigarettes. Seconds felt like hours as he opened the door and lit a cigarette. We did not know if he was going to let the dog out, nor did we know where he was going to go from there. The door of the car closed again and he moved toward the valve house. Instead of walking back inside, he paused by the open door, intermittently inhaling the cigarette and talking to the man inside. Apparently inside the valve house was some sort of no-smoking area, such were the fumes that we could smell coming from the building. All this time Rick was frozen in the deep shadows directly on the other side of the door. I prayed that the guard would not close the door, for that would leave Rick standing directly in the light and fully exposed.

I was shocked to see Rick's hand slowly slip toward the edge of the door and do something to the latching mechanism. I had no idea what he was doing, but I was enraged because he was severely jeopardizing our safety. Just as Rick was retracting his hand, the light inside the building went out, and the man in the white lab coat walked outside and joined the guard. If they shut the door before Rick could get away, the bright lights of the courtyard would certainly fall upon him and leave him standing in full view. To my horror, the guard grabbed the door and began to close it. I held my breath as the door slammed shut, leaving Rick standing against the wall in plain sight. The guard then turned to talk to the technician, yet he never looked beyond the technician's face. If he had, he would have seen Rick.

Abruptly they both turned toward the patrol car. I could hear one door open and close and then another. The engine began to crank to a start. The shock of terror raced through me, for I knew that when they turned on the headlights they would shine directly on Rick. I looked toward Rick just as the headlights came on, but Rick was gone. I breathed a deep and audible sigh of relief as soon as the patrol car's engine faded in the distance. I heard a light giggle come from the edge of the building, apparently Rick was also relieved and satisfied. Though I should not have let down my guard even for an instant, I got up and walked directly over to Rick, patting him on the back as if to congratulate him. Yet I knew that he had taken a horrible chance.

Rick grabbed me by the arm and pulled me around the side of the building, out into the full light of the courtyard, to the steel door. I had no idea what he was going to do. Without a sign he placed his hand on the door and opened it. It suddenly became obvious to me what Rick had done with the stone. He knew from the last raid that the guard did not check the door to see if it was locked, the stone would hold the lock open, and the guard would never know that the latch had not tripped. This would allow us easy entry after everyone left the area. Though at this point we had no real plan to do anything inside the building, I decided that we might as well take a look inside. Possibly that could give us some sort of clue as to what to do on a future raid.

We could not chance putting on the building's lights even though no one was around. Instead, I held the door slightly ajar, allowing the outside floodlights to partially illuminate the interior. Rick began to walk back toward the table at the back of the room, where we had seen the guard write something during the last raid. I looked around the interior at the maze of tangled pipes of various sizes. I could barely see Rick pick something up off the desk and begin to write. In a panic I moved toward Rick to stop him and as soon as I let go of the door it slammed shut. I groped around the edge of the door to find the handle, but the only handle the door had was a heavy metal bar. I pushed at the door but it wouldn't budge. The door had not only slammed shut but it had locked, and there was no way to open the door from the inside.

I cannot remember the last time I felt so vulnerable and frightened. I actually trembled. My mind seemed to swoon with fear, to a point where I could not think clearly. The blackness only intensified my feelings of vulnerability. Suddenly Rick's voice whispering in my ear startled me. He told me that he was going to turn on the light for a moment and that we should take a quick look around for a way out. He found the light by the door, and though he only left the light on for a moment, I saw instantly that there was no way out and no workable handle on the door. We were trapped. Our only hope was to wait for the guard to return on his nightly rounds and hopefully escape as he opened the door. Even though that plan seemed good I knew it could be deadly. If the guard saw us and got frightened then we ran the risk he would shoot us in his panic. Yet that seemed to be our only hope other than to give ourselves up. That would be a disgrace. As far as I was concerned I would rather be shot than to give up.

As time passed, the fear began to dissipate and I began to think clearly again. I began to weigh all the variables, human nature, the added concern of the dog, and the advantage we had thus far of no one knowing or suspecting that anything was wrong. Rick's plan was good, but it had too many critical areas that could cause trouble. What I needed was some sort of diversion. Suddenly it occurred to me. I whispered to Rick to trust me, and moved him to the edge of the doorjamb, pressing him up against the wall, and told him to stay put until he saw me move. He started to question me but I cut him off. It was growing late and I knew that the guard would be back to make his rounds. I had to hurry for this would be the only chance we had.

I climbed atop the highest pipe that I could feel and began to grope at the ceiling, searching for the light. I knew about where the light was located but I could not get directly to it. Just as I touched the heavy wire bars protecting the light, I heard the faint slam of a car door outside the building. I eased my fingers through the mesh and slowly unscrewed the bulb a few turns. Just as I dropped to the floor I could hear the turn of a key in the door. I raced to take up position next to Rick, trying desperately to control my breathing. The door opened wide and the floodlights from outside the building poured in, nearly blinding us. I heard the guard attempt to turn on the light switch, clicking it several times without success. He cursed to himself and suddenly a flashlight beam appeared across the floor. Rick and I pressed closer to the wall.

The guard walked by us and directly to the table at the far end of the building. We slipped outside, around the corner of the building, and into the safety of the shadows. I did not want to venture to the fence, for I had seen the dog sniffing about the low brush as we left the building and to chance an escape at this point would only alert him. Suddenly the silence of the night was shattered by the guard's voice. It was distraught yet filled with anger, cursing at the top of his lungs. He raced out of the building and directly to his car, where he picked up the radio and began to scream into it. His dog was now beside him and away from the gate. We knew that it would be impossible to get out of the compound at this point. Certainly now that the guard was alert to something we would certainly be seen.

I pulled Rick to the back of the building, motioned to him to follow, and I climbed the outer pipes to the top of the building. The roof of the building was flat and we could hide up there until things cooled down. Choosing that alternative would be the best, for if they began looking for us they would assume that we had escaped the compound and would not suspect us of being on the roof. Anyway, to anyone other than a scout, there would seem to be no possible way someone could get up on the roof without a ladder or rope. We pressed flat against the center of the roof as the first of many vehicles rolled into the compound.

For at least the next hour we were surrounded by voices, flashlights, crackling radios, dogs barking, and a frenzy of activity. The few times I did look up I could see people searching the fence area with flashlights and the flashing red lights of other patrol cars coming and going from the compound. It was like we had stirred up an angry bees' nest, though I had no idea what had alerted them to our presence. At first I thought that the guard was only angry because there was no light, then I thought that there must be something mechanically wrong in the valve house, but when I saw all the people searching the fences, I knew beyond all doubt that they were looking for us. Yet I had no idea why. We made no mistakes. I even wondered if someone else had tried to get into the compound and alerted the guard. It baffled me.

The sky was beginning to lighten as the last patrol car left the compound and headed back to the factory. Without a word, Rick and I slipped off the building, over the fence, across the lower river, and through the swamp. We never tried to communicate, but rather concentrated fully on the task of getting back and leaving no traces. I could not figure out where we had gone wrong or how the guard had detected our presence. In the eyes of a scout we had failed our mission and I was emotionally beating myself up over the failure and near disaster. Finally, with the sun well into the sky, Rick and I reached the whisper zone. The whisper zone is the place where we were close enough to camp and safe enough that we could communicate in whispers, with little fear of being caught.

It was Rick who first broke the silence. He said, "You're not to blame. It's my fault they suspected we were there."

Confused over his statement, I asked him what he meant, having no idea why he should be to blame. After all, we were a team. He lowered his head and sheepishly said, "It was because of what I had written in the guard book."

Shocked now, I asked him what he had written. He said, talking now like a naughty child, "We are watching you. You are polluting our river and we are gathering information to put you in jail. Photographs don't lie."

"Photographs don't lie!" I said, and immediately broke out into an uncontrolled laughter. Rick also began to laugh, now knowing that I wasn't angry at him. I was also relieved to know that we had not physically made a mistake, but rather made a poor choice in writing in the book. The written message would have been great if I had not let the door slam shut. In essence we were both to blame, but we got out, and got out perfectly.

Rick had delivered the ultimate in scout psychological warfare. In their minds they had been photographed and possibly there would be legal repercussions. I'm sure that they would not be dumping anytime soon if at all. And if they did try to dump again it would be one of the most agonizing things they would ever do in their lives. I wondered how safe they would now feel, knowing that the message was written in a guard book inside a locked building and inside a floodlit and guarded compound. Paranoia must be flourishing inside the walls of the company at this point, I thought. We had not only completed a great mission and escaped impending disaster, but succeeded in temporarily, at least, stopping the dumping. We could not ask for more of a mission. We had truly walked the edge of excitement and tested ourselves beyond even our wildest expectations.

CHAPTER 5

THE BASE

Until this point, Rick and I had always taken the time to plan every mission we went on. Even for those scouting raids that needed no planning at all, we tended to hang back and overplan everything. Yet Grandfather had told us many times that a scout was a creature of opportunity. A scout should always be on the alert for a potential mission. Oftentimes the mission must be acted upon immediately, otherwise the opportunity might vanish. In such a situation the scout would have to devise his plan as he went along. Here the scout would have to act on his instinct and his vast reservoir of knowledge and experi-

111

ence. These situations would push the scout's skills, his resourcefulness, and his ability to make the right decisions as he adapted to the ever-changing situation. It would also push the edge of his limits, for he could never be sure of the elements of an unknown area or situation.

So many times Rick and I would miss a tremendous opportunity for scouting because of the time we took to back off and plan the mission fully. Even though we had many successful scouting missions behind us, we were not yet confident enough to go blindly into a situation and rely solely on our instinct, experience, and skill. Planning the mission thoroughly would always give us the edge and add to our confidence, for there we could plan for nearly all possibilities, even those that seemed very improbable. However, this left out the sense of excitement and intensity that could not be fully lived when everything was so well planned. We knew this to be true, for we had the best times on scout raids when the unplanned or unexpected happened and we had to rely on our adaptability, quick thinking, instinct, and skill. A great example was being caught in the valve house, which will always remain the most vivid part of that raid.

Our overplanning even began to concern Grandfather to a point that he said something to us about it, taking us totally off guard. We had just come back from a mission that Grandfather had sent us out on earlier in the day. Someone was apparently dumping chemicals into the ground, not far from where we were camped. Somehow Grandfather sensed that he was back and he sent us out to find out who it was, get the license plate number, and possibly see if we could find out the origin of the chemicals he was dumping. We did not like the situation for many reasons. First of all it was in broad daylight, second, the request took us by surprise, and third and most important, it would give us no time whatsoever to plan.

We did make it easily to the edge of the clearing where the chemicals were being dumped. We knew exactly the spot because there was evidence that this area had been used as a chemical dump several times before. We could clearly see the truck way in the distance and a man standing alongside the truck directing a hose. We instantly backed off a good distance and began to plan how we were going to get to the truck, who was going to take down the license plate number, and who was going to find out what chemicals were being dumped. We fully planned the mission, the way in, the way out, and considered every other possible alternative if something went wrong. I don't know how long the whole process took us but when we finally started on the raid and got into position, the truck was gone. It became obvious to us right then and there that we had to become more spontaneous, no matter how much it pushed our skills or luck.

All the way back to camp we were wrapped in guilt and disappointment. If only we had gotten the license plate number of the truck we might have prevented future dumping. We might have succeeded in getting the man arrested. But now, future dumping was inevitable. Our planning obsession now made us responsible for everything this man destroyed in the future. Our slow response to the situation made us indirectly responsible for the destruction. I knew all too well that I had also let Grandfather down. He had trusted us with an important mission and we had failed him. There was no doubt in my mind as to why. Not only were we obsessed with planning, but our obsession was born of fear. Fear of getting caught. We always wanted things in our favor and were afraid to take a chance. Afraid that our skills had not yet developed to a point where we could trust them.

When we reached camp, it appeared deserted. Grandfather was nowhere to be found. This only added to our pain and sense of failure because we wanted to get our encounter with Grandfather over with. I know we had only sat there for a short time but it seemed like hours before Grandfather finally showed up. He walked toward us, a solemn look on his face. There was no doubt that he knew we had failed. Without a word he squatted on the ground and carefully drew out some symbols that did not make sense at first. As I looked at the symbols from all different angles I could not make out what they meant. They were entirely unlike anything I had ever seen Grandfather draw before and as far as I knew they did not even look like native American artwork. It then suddenly dawned on me that it was a license plate number.

I had been so convinced that the sand drawings must be of some symbolic origin that I had failed to notice that they were letters and numbers from the English alphabet. So too did I know that Grandfather could hardly even speak English, far less write it, yet here it was in front of me. It did not take me long to realize that it was the license plate number of the truck. Grandfather simply had looked at the symbols as any artwork and remembered the lines. I was humbled. Grandfather had been in and out of there without us knowing. He had beaten not only the awareness of the man dumping the chemicals but also our awareness. Yet it served us right. We had been so focused on planning our mission that again we had failed to be aware of everything else around us. Grandfather never mentioned that repeated mistake. It humbled us beyond all description.

Finally Grandfather spoke to us, with a loving and knowing impish grin, saying, "A scout must be able to move and react at a moment's notice. He must make instant decisions and begin to rely on instinct and skill more than on planning. As a scout grows in skill there becomes no need for any plan, for he transcends all plans and becomes the plan. Until a scout reaches this point he must always plan. I know it is now time that you no longer plan your missions. Instead, go out and push your skills, learn to react to each situation instantly, and adapt as need requires. That is the only way you can reach the final level of proficiency. That is the only way you can ever push your skills beyond what they now are. Otherwise you remain in the clutches of mediocrity and stagnation.''

We knew that Grandfather was right. In fact we had been talking about that very concept the day before. We realized that our skills were stagnating and the missions were lacking excitement and spontaneity. By overplanning we were acting more like machines, following in preplanned ruts, and removed completely from the need to think or react spontaneously. Not only had our skills become stagnant but also our minds' ability to adapt and react quickly. There was no doubt what we had to do, and right away. We had to seize every opportunity that came our way, and go after it without a plan. We made a vow that from this point on, whether there was enough time to plan or not, we would immediately go on the mission. Little did we know that the next time we were afforded a scouting opportunity it should have taken weeks to plan, such was the intensity of the situation.

It was one of those lazy summer mornings, hot and humid even before the sun rose fully into the sky. Rick and I were exploring a small swamp area far to the north of Grandfather's camp, relaxing and playing in the damp, cool inner sanctuary of the cedars. We had never before been to this particular area, yet we had known it was there because

so often we heard it mentioned by one of the old Piney
people that lived in the Pine Barrens. Supposedly this
swamp was fed by several pure springs and was one of the
only sources of water that could be found in that area.
Needless to say the animal population thereabouts was
abundant and afforded Rick and me an opportunity for limitless exploration and animal tracking. The tracking was so
concentrated and unique there that it was one of only a few
areas like it in the Pine Barrens.

We had arrived at the camp the night before and quickly
set up, eager to go out and explore at first light. All through
the night we had heard the sounds of countless animals,
and in the early morning light the swamp exploded with all
manner of bird sound. We knew this swamp was relatively
close to some sort of civilization, for through the night we
heard the deep rumbling of big engines. We guessed that
it had to be heavy equipment from a sand and gravel company, but as far as we knew there were none up in this
area. Yet we never gave it a second thought. The rumbling
was too far off and it was too late at night for that kind of
thing to catch our curiosity. It wasn't uncommon for sand
and gravel companies to work through the night, especially
if they had a deadline to meet. Yet this morning the sounds
had suddenly ceased, thus it passed from our minds as we
explored.

We began to make our way to the upper back end of
the swamp, pushing through the heaviest vegetation that
grew on the outer edge of the swamp's buffer zone. The
going was very tough, slow, and hot, such was the personality of the brush. If we went any faster than a stalk we
would surely be scarred up by sharp sticks and greenbrier.
We also didn't want to make our presence known and alarm
the animals, so we took extra care in going. Eventually the
brush got so thick and tight that we had to crawl on our

bellies to get through it. It was dark on the ground because of the thick lower canopy. Hardly a shaft of sunlight could be seen, but the area was laced with numerous animal runs that made the going a little easier.

Eventually this lower world became very quiet. There was not a sound of a bird except for a distant alarm call and we had not seen another animal for quite some time. Many of the more recent tracks showed that the animals had been running in a panic, and we began to grow uneasy. To cause that kind of disruption in the flow of nature it had to be either a feral dog pack or, more likely, man. We began to grow concerned that it may be poachers so we slowed our crawl even more, growing even more aware. The deeper we crawled into the brush the more we could sense that something was wrong. Eventually we could almost sense some kind of huge presence, though we could not define it at all. Curiosity got the better of us and we kept pushing on, taking the same care in our actions that we would have on a scout mission of exploration.

I heard Rick give the soft alarm chirp of a bird. As I looked up I saw him freezing motionless in front of a dark object. I deftly moved closer. Nestled in the brush, not a few inches in front of us, was a huge piece of iron of some sort. It looked like a blade plate on a bulldozer wheel but much larger and more aggressive. I reached up to touch it, unable to see beyond it through the thick curtain of brush. It looked surreal and out of place in the purity of all this greenery. Just as I grabbed hold of the blade a loud grinding sound started, followed suddenly by the most powerful roar of any engine I ever heard. The blade I held onto trembled then lurched forward out of my grasp. It all happened so quickly that there was no time to think. My reaction was to roll back into the brush and freeze, filled with panic.

Rick and I searched each other's expressions for answers. The metal had disappeared from sight but the tremendous engine still thundered a few feet away. Curiosity was stronger than good common sense and I moved forward and cautiously looked out from beneath the brush. I gazed up and let out an audible gasp that Rick could hear above the engine. He joined me and we lay frozen someplace between the state of panic and awe. There not a few yards ahead of us sat a huge armored tank, the turret slowly turning back and forth as it surveyed the horizon. A man was apparently seated somehow inside the tank with about a full third of his body exposed. To his side and mounted on a bracket was some sort of menacing machine gun. It looked like a picture we had seen in history class.

With another tremendous thundering roar, black smoke poured from the tank as it lurched forward, crushing all vegetation in its wake. Suddenly there was a pounding boom that hurt my ears. Smoke poured through the air and the tank was shoved back by the blast, while a flash of fire spewed out the barrel. An instant later the tank began to back up toward us, moving quickly and crushing vegetation and small trees. We crawled in a frenzy, retreating barely faster than the tank was moving. We did not stop moving until we hit the thick cathedral of cedars and deep muck, hoping that this would be too much for the tank. We did not know that it had stopped several yards before and was now moving forward, back to its original position. As we looked around, the engine fell silent and all we could hear were men's voices and the crackle of a radio.

My hearing was temporarily deadened by all the noise of the engine and the gunfire. I could not clearly understand what the men were saying or any communication coming over the radio. Rick and I were so shaken by the event that we could hardly move at all and it took me a while to come to my full senses. All I could clearly understand of the conversation was that some sort of argument was going on, though it did not sound heated. Slowly my hearing began to return and the shaking had fully stopped. Now I was more angry than anything else. I could not believe that I had been so stupid as to overlook such a huge concentric ring, indicating the presence of the tank and its crew. I had to learn the lesson time and again. Just because I didn't expect something to be there did not make it so. I had to learn to expect everything, even when I was not on a scout mission. This was a very blatant example of a very narrow focus that obliterated everything outside of what I was doing. The second thing I was angry about was the men's total disregard for nature. So many plants had just died, and no one seemed to care.

Rick and I glanced at each other knowingly. There was no doubt that Rick was thinking the same thing I was thinking. We were going on a scout mission. Just as the thought cleared my head, Rick was slipping away from where we sat, heading in the direction of the voices. I followed, with neither of us needing any confirmation as to what we were going to do. I knew that some kind of military base or fort was somewhere north of us but up until now I hadn't realized how close it really was. It was obvious that these men were involved in some sort of war game or training exercise and we just happened to stumble upon them. The intense thing about this situation was that this would become our first unplanned mission and we were dealing with people who were already on full alert. I could sense that this raid was going to test our skills.

We took great care in our approach of the tank. Not only had we read about what a tank was capable of and had seen bulldozers operate before, but now we had first-hand knowledge of their power, especially after being nearly run over by this one. We wanted to keep the biggest trees between us and the tank and so it took us a while to work our way around to where the largest and closest trees were located. That grove of trees would also prevent any shooting, for it would not allow the tank much of a clear shot. Even though I suspected that they might have been using blanks, I did not want to be anywhere near the muzzle blast. I'd seen the tremendous fiery flash a few minutes before and I did not want to be anywhere nearby. If the flash did not burn me then the blast would certainly damage my hearing.

As I crawled closer to the tank I began to grow very awed in the face of such indestructible power. After all, what good could one man, an unarmed scout, do against such a formidable weapon if in fact we were being chased by this thing in time of war. Modern weapons seemed the only thing that could be used against it, and in the pure consciousness and purpose of a scout to use such weapons would be out of the question. Yet despite this feeling of vulnerability, somewhere inside of me I knew that somehow the scout must have the advantage. After all, we had gotten to within just a few yards of this machine and its crew without being seen. I was suddenly determined to find out its weaknesses and how an ancient scout could defeat it without using modern weapons or warfare.

From our position just a few feet from the right track of the tank, we could clearly hear the men talking. Apparently this was not only practice, but some sort of war game. From the conversations of the crew and the crackling voice coming in over the radio, we could tell that there was some sort of bunker position about a mile away that they were trying to defend. We also found that this tank was far back from the action we could hear going on in the distance. From what we could gather it was lying in wait for enemy tanks to roll by or to repel a side attack on the bunker. I was very certain at this point that if this had been a real war and I had some sort of explosive charge I could easily plant it on the tank. I had also gathered a wealth of information, critical information, that the enemy could use.

I did not realize it at the time but somewhere inside of me something began to shift. Though it remained unspoken, I wanted to become part of this grand game and see what I could do. Looking at Rick I could tell instantly that he felt the same thing I did. Though we had no plan, nor did we know what we really wanted to accomplish, we would simply let things unfold and use the opportunities provided to push our skills and learn as much as we could about the military. Not only did I want to know about their machines but also about the men of the military. I wanted to see how aware they were, how good they were, and in the intensity of this mock battle they would have to be at their best. This would be an excellent testing arena.

The man who had been standing through the top hatch of the tank had disappeared inside for a moment. We could hear the crew talking, though now the voices were muffled by the tank's heavy steel shell. Unless there was a lookout somewhere watching the landscape, then at this point they were very vulnerable. I could not be sure when the man would reemerge from the tank so I dared not make any moves or adjust my position in any way. Within moments the man poked his head up through the hatch once again, but this time he came all the way out. He jumped down to the side of the turret and looked off into the distance. Apparently satisfied that there was no danger, he called down to someone inside that he would be right back. Reaching back into the tank he grabbed a roll of toilet paper, moved to the front of the tank, and got down. We could hear him walking off into the distance, someplace far behind us.

Rick suddenly grabbed my arm as a warning gesture

that he was going to move. I immediately took the lookout position, not knowing what he was planning to do. I divided my attention between looking at the turret, listening for the man who had gone off to relieve himself, and watching the horizon for other signs of military activity. Rick, without any hesitation, quickly climbed to the back of the tank, grabbed the long antennalike wire to which was attached some kind of military flag, bent it toward him, and cut the strings holding the flag with a small chip of flint. Just as quickly he was down off the tank and back by my side grinning from ear to ear. I was shocked by not only what he had done and the risk he had taken but how quickly he had accomplished his raid. I was so happy and excited for him, but also very envious, though I wouldn't show it.

Quickly, we retreated far back into the thickest brush, knowing that as soon as the man returned and found the flag missing they might come looking for us. No sooner had we settled in than we heard the man returning. We could only see the top of the tank and the turret from our position, but that was enough to see the show that followed. The man screamed down into the tank, demanding to know where the flag was. Another man's head emerged and looked around bewildered. He said in a disgusted voice that they had probably lost it back in the brush. There was no discussion that we could hear or see, but both men walked toward the back of the tank and jumped to the ground. We could hear them crashing through the crushed brush as they followed the tank's path back to its original position.

Then we heard a man yelling, "It's got to be here, damn it. If blue team stole our flag then we are going to have hell to pay. Look for the damn thing! Look for traces of a scouting party from blue team!" The sound of crashing brush followed for the better part of fifteen minutes, then all fell silent except for the sound of footfalls heading back to the tank. We could see the two climb aboard the tank and a third man joined them. They appeared to be talking to each other in normal voices then suddenly one of the men ordered the other two back into the tank in a loud and demanding voice. He resumed his position in the turret, the engines fired up, and the tank rolled off. We watched it travel only two hundred yards or so along the outside of the swamp and then back into the brush, assuming the same position as it had earlier.

Rick and I could not figure out what they were doing, but we were determined to find out. We traveled again into the inner recesses of the swamp and reemerged behind and on the opposite side of the tank than we had been before. I knew if they suspected that some kind of military scouting party had taken their flag then their attention would be drawn back to their original location. We did not want to be on that side of the tank though we were certain that they would overlook us. The new location also provided us with another large grove of trees for protection. No sooner had we taken up our new position than we clearly heard the men discussing what had happened. The tank commander, as we began to call him, told his men that they had to move because blue team would report their position to the planes or artillery. If they were to remain back where they had been they would probably get hit. It was bad enough that their element of surprise had been taken away. The radio crackled a command, and the tank roared and sped off through the woods in a straight line, crushing everything in its path.

The tank's actions not only told us that they had been ordered out of that position; its direct line of travel told us they were going to the battle. A more zigzag course would mean that they were running and trying to make a less easily hit target. There was no way we were going to follow anywhere near that tank, though it was heading right where we wanted to go. The tank would draw too much attention. So we followed it from far behind and to the side, sticking to the thickest cover. We expected anything and everything. We assumed nothing was safe, for there could be soldiers hidden in position or we might run into another sitting tank. This made the going slower, but we had all the time in the world as far as we were concerned. If the war games ended right then, we had accomplished much to be proud of.

We heard the tank far in the distance come to a roaring stop. We decided that it was best to work our way over to where it had gone; that way we could keep tabs on its position, and possibly overhear its crew's plans again. Throughout our mission we had crossed and recrossed many tank tracks, heavy boot prints, and all manner of other jeep and truck tracks. Most of the tracks were made the day before, with the only fresh track being that of the tank we were following. Here and there lay discarded ration cans, spent shells, and all manner of other garbage. It made me sick to think that not only were these games destroying the woods, but the men did not have the common decency or respect to keep from littering the area. As I stared down at a pile of garbage and a smoldering campfire I turned to Rick and said, "I'm going to steal every last flag I see."

We had finally worked our way in close enough to where the tank had stopped to get a good look. It was parked at the far end of a field. The men were outside the tank and standing on the ground just under the gun. In the field were three other tanks, two tank trucks engaged in fueling the tanks, and several other troop carriers. Men milled about, rifles were randomly resting throughout the area, and no one seemed to be on the lookout. Here were several permanent outhouses where some men stood on line to get in. We could immediately tell by the red and blue arm bands the soldiers wore that this was some kind of safe zone where both sides could relax from their game. Though we did not see it at first there was a huge tent mess hall at the far end of the field where men were eating.

We lay watching the area for a long time as men and machinery came and went. We tried to establish some sort of pattern in the camp but the only pattern was that when one group of men and machines moved out, another would move in right behind them. The rest consisted of the men eating, refueling, and visiting the latrines. Once finished, they seemed to lounge around waiting to get back to action. The men as a whole did not look very happy or interested in what they were doing, yet they did not appear to be exhausted. On the contrary, many looked too well fed and far too rested. An easy target at best. I was not impressed with anything I had seen thus far. I hoped that they would become more aware and aggressive once away from this camp, for right now they were no challenge at all. We decided to follow the next column out, hopefully to where the action was. That is, if there was any.

We followed the next column of men and machines out of the camp, staying well back and to the outside of their line of travel. We followed more by listening than by seeing, for we were forever falling behind and did not want to rush. It did not take us long to get to the playing field. Here the taller trees of the Pine Barrens gave way to a vast open area of small pines, scrub oak, and heaps of crushed vegetation. The earth was badly rutted and scarred, showing the signs of years of abusive war games. Tanks, trucks, and men moved all over this vast field. Gunfire, large and small, pounded all around, while billows of smoke, spent gunpowder, and dust filled the air. It took us a long time before we could determine fully what was going on, for it was such a frenzy of motion and noise.

Apparently at the far end of the field was some sort of encampment. A brick building surrounded by sandbags sat in the center of this camp. Sandbags and barbed wire marked perimeter after perimeter. Foxholes, trenches, and machine gun nests were throughout. Men ran here and there, guns fired heavily then suddenly fell silent, only to resume again moments later. We could see men wearing blue arm bands trying to move up on the camp, while men in red arm bands tried to defend it. It was obvious that the camp or fort had the upper hand, whether by plan or accident I did not know. No sooner would a small group of men get close to the outer sandbags of the fort than some guy with a white arm band would stand up and send them running back to where they started. We assumed that he had to be some sort of referee.

It took us nearly the entire afternoon to work our way around the huge field and into the forest behind the fort. Here on the forest side there was little activity, at least little compared to the frenzy going on out front in the open. Behind the fort a whole different kind of war was going on. Small patrols were working their way through the woods. The men were even more heavily camouflaged than those out in the field and they moved with a certain stealth and determination. From what we could see, these soldiers were a little older and more experienced. Definitely more aware of the land. This would finally give us a chance to really test our skills, or so we thought.

We could see from our position that sentries were posted around the back of the fort in various sandbag bunkers. There were also several raised platforms that afforded the spotters a clear view of the woods. The highest platform was located atop and to the back of the brick building. On this platform were a group of older men wearing white arm bands. It was obvious from their actions that they were in charge of this whole war game. No doubt the top brass. There was no doubt now that even though this war game appeared to be just one big battle, in reality two battles were going on: the frenzied battle out front and the quieter battle out back. For us, the opportunities seemed endless and exciting, giving us a wealth of scouting conditions under which we could work and test our skills. With each passing moment the excitement within me grew more intense.

As the sun began to set we made our first real move of the raid. Up until this time we were just observing and except for taking the tank's flag we had done no real raiding. It was clear that this battle was going to last well into the night, though at a greatly diminished scale. The men in the field were already preparing small camps outside the mock line of fire, yet the men in the forest kept on the move. We retreated to find the nearest source of mud, camouflaged to the point of invisibility, then returned to the woods behind the camp and waited for the sun to fully disappear on the horizon. Judging from the awareness of the men we had observed, there would have been no way they could have seen us even in full daylight, but we wanted to take no chances at all.

We moved toward the most open area we could find in the woods. The stalking men moved in the thickest brush, thus drawing the attention of the spotters and sentries toward that direction. Psychologically, only a trained scout would know to look in the open, coverless areas. To everyone else there would be no way in their minds that anyone could come from that direction. So too did our camouflage blend so well with the ground that even if a sentry did look our way they would see nothing. We knew that we could not only intercept the oncoming soldiers from our position but we would also have easy access to the sandbag perimeter of the outer compound. Though we had no plan at this point as to what, if anything, we were going to do, it was enough just to get close to these men and to stalk the compound.

Just at the far edge of the open area we encountered a soldier moving into position on his belly. By far he was the closest man to us on that side of the forest, and it was clear that he was trying to work his way up for a closer shot. No doubt a sniper of some sort. He was so intent on his forward travel that he never noticed that he came to within inches of Rick's face. As he passed me I noticed a broken twig in the shape of a hook around his trigger. Attached to the wooden hook was a length of thin natural cordage. At first I was shocked to see a military man with such a naturally made string. Then I suddenly realized that it was the string Rick always carried with him on missions. I looked back to catch Rick tying the other end of the long string onto the lower part of a small bush. He then signaled me to move off.

There was no hesitation on my part, for I knew that when the man discovered the string on his rifle he would begin looking around to see where it had come from. I assumed Rick had put it on the trigger to hold back the gun and cause the man to lose his grip. After all, he was close to the perimeter and one slight noise would cause his capture. I also assumed the rifle was on safety. After all, any modern hunter I knew of kept his safety on until he was ready to take his shot. What I did not bank on was that the man had already taken his gun off safety so that it would not be heard when he got close to the compound. The unexpected bang caused me to jump, but the man jumped higher still. Immediately some kind of machine gun fire opened up and the man stood up, cursing his head off, holding the gun in one hand and the string in the other.

A rather loud and authoritative voice boomed down from the upper tower after all the commotion ceased, saying, "You f—— ing idiot! If you are going to drag your f——ing rifle off safety then you best watch the debris you're crawling through. If that had been a live round you could have killed yourself. Now get up here, stupid! You're a prisoner." With that the man threw down the string, never taking notice of the broken stick tied to the end and apparently thinking that he had accidentally crawled through some old discarded string. It never occurred to him that the string's placement was a deliberate act. In his mind there must not have been any other possibility. I could understand so clearly now why Grandfather always stressed the expansion of focus and to suspect everything and anything. This man had been so focused on his objective that he missed everything else around him, even Rick's hand slowly emerging from the bushes and retrieving the string as he walked away.

Rick and I moved into a little deeper cover to communicate with each other using slight finger signals. It was obvious to us that the ridiculous glossy smudges of painted camouflage that the military people wore on their faces were no match for the camouflage we wore. As I watched the men moving up to the bunker I could not understand why any of the guards could not see them. Their camouflage was so unnatural that it literally glared from the underbrush, even in the waning light. In comparison, our camouflage was so detailed as to shadow, texture, and color of the earth that one would literally have to step right on us before they ever saw us. Our movements were without sound, slow and flowing, not the abrupt, trembling, and dragging sounds of the men pulling their bodies across the ground, or the abrasive crunching of their heavy, booted feet on the earth.

The differences between us and the trained soldiers were so blatantly obvious. I whispered a prayer of thanksgiving for all that Grandfather had taught us thus far, hoping that he would somehow feel the appreciation carried to him on the silent winds. Even those men who watched the woods from the bunkers seemed so unaware. Even though they were more aware than most folks, we could not understand how they could not see the approach of the oncoming men. The concentric rings of disturbances they threw, the movement of body and brush, the grinding of the earth, all screamed their location, yet no one noticed. Grandfather would have known that these men were in the woods even miles away from them, such was their unnatural impact on the land. I could understand so easily now how Geronimo had eluded thousands of cavalry men.

At full dark we moved again out into the open and far in front of the approaching men. In several places we encountered trip wires, probably set out by the men in the compound to warn them of approaching danger. These trips were attached to some sort of flare device and in one case, the end of the trip cord was attached to several empty cans. We giggled to ourselves as we cut the lines. After all, the compound had a severe advantage over the approaching men and we wanted to even up the odds. We especially did not like the arrogance and attitude of the man who had screamed at the sniper earlier. He seemed so pompous and confident. A break in his supposedly impenetrable barrier of men, guns, sandbags, and trip wires would really burst his bubble.

We slipped along the outer rim of sandbags, right into the very open, where there was nothing between us and the distant woods but sand and scant, short grass clumps. We had observed earlier that no one was guarding that portion of the wall, because no one could believe that anyone could come from that direction without being seen. Here a coil of barbed wire lay across the top of the high sandbags, but we slipped over the wall and under the barbed wire like water flowing over the ground. Even as we got inside the compound we could clearly see that this little corner had been forgotten in its fortifications. The few floodlights inside the area were directed outside the compound perimeter and into the thickest wooded areas, which kept our little entryway in full darkness.

We slithered along the ground to the next wall of sandbags. These were lower and did not have barbed wire across the top. We moved along the outside of this inner wall, slowly working our way to the little brick building in the center of the compound. Our advance suddenly stopped when we heard a strange noise coming from the other side of the inner wall. It did not take us long to realize that the sound was of light snoring. I peered over the wall to see a guard reclining against the wall, fast asleep with his rifle propped next to him. Without thinking I moved the gun away from him and slipped it over to our side of the wall and into the deepest shadow. If the men did get to the wall and began to storm the compound this soldier would not be able to find his rifle.

We kept moving along the outside of the inner wall, which would eventually lead to the outside of the little bunker house, and to the framework that held up the observation platform. Our belly crawl led us past several other men who were also reclining, relaxing, whispering, joking, or sleeping along the inside of the wall. Unfortunately for them their rifles were either placed flat on top of the sandbags pointing to the distant woods, or leaning against the wall far from them. It did not take us long to deftly collect all of these weapons and hide them on our side of the wall. The men were so caught up in what they were doing that they would never notice that their guns were missing. Even if they did, they would not yell out, for fear of being reprimanded for losing their rifles. Even if they did suspect something, they would blame it on one of their buddies. They were far too blinded by the security of this compound, and were relying on someone else to stay vigilant. Among scouts, everyone was vigilant and nothing was secure.

We finally reached the scaffolding of the high observation platform, which was anchored to the building itself. Just a few yards in front of us and away from the building was some sort of bunker, where a big gun was mounted on a tripod. We could see no one from our side of this little bunker, or machine gun nest, but the smell of cigarette smoke told us that the men of this bunker, like the others, were taking a break. We crawled up to the side of the bunker where, though cast in shadows, the spotlights at the edges of the platform silhouetted the gun and the belt of bullets. I watched Rick as he slipped up to the front of the gun, deftly moved his hand over the wall, and placed a small oak stick through the belt. As soon as the gun fired and the stick was pulled to the opening, the gun would jam. I could barely hold back a big smile as we moved up the rafters toward the platform above.

As we peered over the lower lip of the platform we could clearly see two men leaning against the railing, close to the outer corner. The floodlight nearby not only drew their attention out into the woods in front of the compound, but cast the rear portion into the deepest shadows. Even if the men were inclined to look back in our direction, their eyes would not adjust to the dark quickly enough. We lay atop the building, watching the men on the wooden observation platform for a long time, trying to observe any pattern in their movement. As they spoke in low whispers they would move their attention from the conversation at hand to the woods before them. Soon they stopped standing upright altogether and leaned on the railing, whispering, and gazing out into the floodlit area below them.

I tapped Rick gently, the sign that he should remain vigilant as I went out on a mission. I moved to the flagpole that was anchored on top of the building and began to untie the flags. Three flags in all were on the same staff. One big one bore some kind of military emblem that I could not make out, and two other flags had nothing on them at all. I could not easily tell what color they were because of the blackness of the night. I didn't care what color they were anyway. No sooner had I finished folding the flags than Rick tapped me on the shoulder and handed me a rifle. I was amazed. He pointed back to the two men on the observation platform and then at the gun. A shiver went through my spine. He then pointed to the flagpole and I knew what he wanted. While Rick saluted I raised the gun up the pole.

Our progress from the flagpole to the outer edge of the compound seemed to take an eternity. We knew that it would only be a matter of time before one of the guns was discovered missing and all hell might break loose. Once outside and along the edge of the brush line by the open area, however, we felt a bit more relaxed and eager to go back to work on our raid. Again we gave each other hand signals to indicate that we would split up and go out separately. This would really become intense, for we had never split up before during a mission. It meant that there would be no lookout, and without planning neither of us would know what the other one was doing. Yet a certain confidence and peace washed over me for I knew how well we had been trained, and if each of us took care of ourselves then there would be no real threat.

I had no idea what Rick had in mind when he reversed

course and began to crawl back to the front of the line. I began to grow worried that he might go back into the sandbag area, but at the same time I knew he would easily be able to pull off most anything. I retreated toward the back end of the woods, determined to crawl up from behind the advancing men and find some more opportunities. No sooner had I gotten to the edge of the woods, where it opened to low brush, than I heard snoring again. I lay low to the ground, silhouetting the horizon to the sky, and could clearly make out a soldier sitting up against a tree. He was facing away from the advancing men and the compound, apparently a rear guard of some sort, but this rear guard was deeply asleep. I decided that he would become my target.

I slipped ever so carefully and slowly behind him and to his rifle, which was held firmly across his lap. Very carefully I tied the large flag to the end of his rifle, taking care to make the tie as close to his arm as possible so that the weight of the flag would not pull down the gun. I then attached the other flag to his helmet, which lay on the ground beside him, and the last flag I tied to his rear belt loop. During the whole process the soldier never stirred, but slept like a baby as if he was in the security of his own home. As I slipped away, I spotted another soldier far up ahead lying flat in the underbrush. I could see his head moving up and down as he looked toward the sandbag camp. At least this one was not asleep and would pose a greater challenge. Without hesitation I slipped up behind him.

Several times he looked back over his shoulder and brushed his neck with his free hand to knock away mosquitoes. Stupid, I thought, for such a move would only make his position obvious. Grandfather had always said that the natural diet of survival would make us tasteless to insects, and, judging from the soldier's antics, he was right again. I could not remember the last time I had been bitten by anything. I now moved dangerously close, so close I had to fully control my breathing and heart rate with the sacred silence. Reaching out I carefully grasped his dangling bootlace, which had come undone sometime during his travels. I looped it through the lower laces of the other boot and tied them together. There would be enough slack in the lace to permit his grinding crawl to continue without restriction, but if he got up to run, without a doubt he would trip himself.

As I moved back from the man and fused with the shadows I knew that I was running out of time. Rick would surely be back at the primary rendezvous point by now. As I carefully got into position at the place we had chosen to meet, I saw that Rick was nowhere to be found. The area we had chosen was well concealed in thick impenetrable brush, but it afforded a grand view of the compound and the area of woods where the soldiers were advancing. I carefully scanned the field through the eyes of the scout, watching and listening for any tiny nuance that would give away Rick's position. I knew that he would choose the open route back to the rendezvous point so I narrowed my search to the barren sand that stretched before me. To my amazement Rick lay only a few yards from me in the sand, perfectly camouflaged. The only reason I could detect him was because he had become an abnormal contour to the land.

It bothered me that he was not moving to our rendezvous point, but instead lay flat, facing away from me and toward the compound. Suddenly his hand moved slightly up and back with a pulling motion. Almost instantly a gun fired from somewhere in the thicket. Then he moved the other hand in the same motion, which set off an explosion far ahead and a flare went flying skyward. Voices rang out, and I cringed back into the thicket as I heard Rick yell out,

"Charge!" I was shocked beyond belief by his actions, for they were contrary to the stealth and silence of the scout code. Yet at the same time I was shivering with delight at the whole mass of confusion that ensued. I would never have expected in my wildest dreams what transpired, as I was torn between watching Rick move to the safety of the rendezvous point and watching the monumental chaos that followed.

The men in the field began to stand and run toward the compound, firing their guns as they charged. The compound was a flurry of confused voices, shouting and running in all directions. There was a short burst of machine gun fire from the compound and then all of their guns fell silent. I could clearly see the antics of the men on the observation post as one searched for his gun and the other struggled frantically with a searchlight. Within moments the compound was overrun with the soldiers. As the celebrating died down a lone soldier could be seen running from the woods, flags waving in the wind, to the cheers of his group. The last thing I remember seeing is the leader on the observation platform looking toward the flagpole with his searchlight, only to find the hanging rifle. The men cheered louder and the leader appeared to be going into a state of delirium as he cussed out the man beside him. Rick and I slipped off into the brush and vanished into the night.

It was dawn when we reached Grandfather's camp, only to find him sitting there waiting for our return. Grandfather gave us the biggest grin I had seen him lavish on us in a long time. He sat us down and said, "Now you can understand the way of the scout. You have seen the training of the modern fighting man and now realize that they are out of place in the wilderness. By not knowing the voices of creation, by not being children of the earth, they do not know what it is to be a true warrior. They do not then possess the power of the earth and creation. These powers are what defeats them and makes the scout victorious. As did their forefathers, they depend on their modern weapons, clothing, camouflage, and battle plans. They know nothing of the concept of becoming an ally of the earth, but choose instead to fight the earth. Man cannot fight the earth and win, for he would be fighting himself. Thus these soldiers defeated themselves.

"Rick was not wrong to call out the battle cry. He did not reveal his position, nor was he seen. He used the power of human nature and thought to draw attention from himself. To this hour they know not from where the cry had come. Neither does the one who carried the flag to victory. You and I know that he will never tell anyone of how the flags came to pass. No one would believe him anyway. The psychological warfare you have created has sent in motion a confusion as to who did what. It has cast the victory into a sea of doubt. The leader now feels vulnerable and humiliated, the one who carried the flag now wallows in hollow victory, and everyone is suspicious of everyone else. You have created confusion and mistrust. The victory is not theirs, but yours." With those words, Grandfather handed to Rick and me some gold stars. I remembered these stars. They had been on a jacket that hung over the railing of the observation platform.

It did not shock us in the least that Grandfather knew the whole story, and had seen everything. We had grown to expect his presence during our missions and had accepted the fact that we would never see him. It was also his way of showing us without a doubt that there were still far greater levels of skill that we had to aspire to. It was humbling in a way, but also enlightening, for it kept us ever striving for excellence, for higher goals, so that we would not fall into the grasp of stagnation and mediocrity. Just knowing that Grandfather was out there, unseen by us, even in the light of all of our training, continually held us in awe.

CHAPTER 6

THE PATROL

The day following the raid on the war games, Rick and I were eager to return to the site of the battle and see what we could find. This would pose a grand challenge for us, in that every soldier involved in that battle the night before would be very suspicious and on constant alert, or so we thought. These circumstances would certainly be more demanding than the night before and would definitely increase our odds of being caught. After all, we thrived on this sort of excitement, and the previous night's raid was not much of a challenge at all. We wanted to push ourselves hard against the odds. So with no planning whatsoever we headed back in the direction of the battle, moving this time, however, by a totally different route.

Making the going a bit easier was the fact that we had already become familiar with the battle area and surrounding landscape. To get to the edge of that area was the least of our problems, since we would be approaching from the thickest area of the swamp and into the most open area of the battlefield. However, we would not allow our confidence and ease of movement to lull us into a false sense of security. We still expected anything and everything, for the lesson of running into the tank tread the day before had sobered us and remained an embarrassment. On our route through the swamp I imagined that any clump of vegetation that was out of place, any faint track in the ground, and any overhanging tree was a place of concealment for a waiting soldier. Even more than usual we took great pains to cover our tracks so that even we had difficulty seeing them.

As we got up to the edge of the swamp and to the clearing, we could clearly see the sandbag compound in the distance. The flag was flying again and we could see the movement of men within the compound's walls. The movement indicated some sort of changing of the guards was going on, and once in place the new guards looked out and around the area with intensity. We knew that they had been taught a valuable lesson the night before and this time they were not going to take any chances. The tower was now manned by five men, and the leader sported a pair of binoculars, which he frequently looked through. His body language was filled with anger and determination. The back of the compound, where the previous day's great tank war had taken place, was now totally abandoned. It was obvious to us that some sort of vendetta was about to occur.

There was no trace of any soldiers stalking the compound as on the previous day. The landscape around the area was completely deserted of people, such was the free movement of birds and other animals throughout. However, a major concentric ring contrary to the flow of life advertised to us a large group of men at the far end of the swamp's edge. We could not understand why the men in the compound did not take notice of the disturbance, but we learned long ago that what was painfully obvious to us was not the least bit obvious to everyone else. It was immediately apparent that the men who were supposed to be stalking the fort were the cause of the natural commotion. From the concentric rings we also knew that these men were not moving at all, though the people in the fort did not know this.

We decided, especially because it was still daylight, that our first consideration should be the men in the field. That way we might find out what was going on. We reentered the swamp and began to work our way around to its lower side. Though it was close to our original route of the night before it was still far enough away so as not to be an area of suspicion. As we got closer to the area of the men, we could clearly hear the sound of voices fluctuating between argument, discussion, and everyone trying to talk at once. From the sound of it there was very little leadership at all. Except for the intermittent request for someone to quiet down, no one really seemed to be in charge. I could not understand why the people in the sandbag fort could not hear them, but I supposed that they themselves were too busy barking orders and moving about. Silence was not one of these people's strong points.

Rick and I edged our way closer to the commotion, nearly confident that if we stood up and ran the men would never take notice, such was their commitment to the argument. We deftly crawled to the edge of the swamp where trees gave way to a little clearing in which the men sat in a loose circle. Most of the men faced away from the swamp and toward a man who sat on his helmet and stroked the ground randomly with a stick. The etchings on the ground looked like some sort of map that someone had drawn but now no one was using at all. Silence had fallen over the group and they all appeared to be somewhere between forlorn and confused. It was almost an attitude of having been defeated, or about to be. During this time of silence I noticed that one of the men had a red flag attached to his belt loop, the same flag I had tied on the night before. I could tell from the way he played with it that it had now become a ball and chain. Everyone seemed to be looking to him for advice.

Suddenly the man sitting next to the man with the red flag spoke up in a rather angry voice, saying, "Damn it! We proved ourselves last night. Why does S——head want us to do it all over again? We won fair and square, and what the f——do we get for it. Everyone else gets to go back to the barracks for the weekend."

Another man chimed in, saying, "That's because S——head and his a——holes lost and they don't think we can do it again. He's got to prove something. We kicked his butt and he can't admit that he lost. We beat his a—— and that makes him look bad to everyone. Now he's got to punish us and pump up his ego. I just feel sorry for his men."

The guy with the flag then joined in and said, "Yeah, he can blame his men for his defeat, but he can't explain how Sarge's gun got up on the pole right behind him."

"Why the f——don't you explain to us how you did it, then," another man interjected.

Now the flag man humbly looked to the ground and mumbled, "I did it once. I don't see why I have to do it again. I proved myself once, and now the guys in the tower are going to be lookin' for us. It wasn't easy the first time.'' He sheepishly looked around him for rebuttal, like a man with a secret to hide.

Suddenly the man that had been drawing on the ground stood abruptly and said, ''You gotta do it again. You could hardly make it through basic and you're the last one I would ever think could pull something off like this. I don't know, you got a guardian angel or something.''

The man only smiled and said, ''Sometimes.''

The other man retorted and commanded, ''Then you best get your f——ing guardian angel to do it again! Let's get to it!''

As he got up to walk away the man with the flag began to say something but the other man cut him off, saying, ''I don't want to hear it, a——hole. You wanted to be some sort of f—— ing hero, so now you can pay the price. If you make me look bad I'll be on your back all the way to the South China Sea. You'll wish you were dead.'' The other men muttered varied agreements to the leader's statement as they began to walk away. One man said, ''If it weren't for you, a——hole motherf——er, we'd be back in the barracks catching some R and R, but no, you had to be a f—— ing hero. You're going to make a guest appearance in a blanket party if you f——this up, a——hole.''

As the flag man stood to follow the group, he turned to pick up his gun. I could clearly see his face and eyes filled with tears, which he quickly tried to wipe away.

As he walked away, a sparrow chirped from a low bush and he nodded in acknowledgment. I could tell that the flag man did not want to be here and I could also tell, from his acknowledgment of the sparrow, that he loved the woods. I watched him looking around as he left, half studying the landscape, not for the enemy but for the peace that nature seemed to bring him. Yet he walked away like a man about to face a firing squad. I felt so very sorry for him. Like many people I knew in his position, he did not want to be here.

At that point I motioned to Rick to retreat back into the swamp where we could talk, and as soon as I was sure that we could not be heard I asked him what a blanket party was. Since Rick's father was once in the service Rick knew very well what it was. I could see the pain in Rick's face when he told me that a blanket party was when the other men in the barracks cover a sleeping man with a blanket then beat him up. I felt sick. Suddenly the soldier was not one of them but one of us, no longer a mock enemy, but possibly an ally. I did not know how but I was suddenly determined to help him, whether he knew it or not. I also wanted to humiliate not only the people of the fort again, but also the other men in his platoon. They deserved all the humiliation they could get as far as I was concerned. I could tell from the look on Rick's face that he wanted to do the same.

We followed the platoon from far behind, noting that the flag man was bringing up the rear. He too was quite a distance behind the rest of the group. Every once in a while one of the other men would look around and make an obscene gesture at him, or mouth obscenities silently, in such a way that he knew what they were saying. He rarely looked up but humbly stared at the ground as he walked so he did not have to face the ridicule up ahead. After a while we knew where the platoon was heading and took the opportunity to slip back into the depth of the swamp and fully camouflage our bodies. Until then our camouflage had been of the type that would fit thick brush, not open areas, and it was back to the open area that the platoon was heading.

After finishing our camouflage, taking even more care than the night before, we cut back through the swamp, knowing that we could move quickly and easily without being seen. It took us no time at all to pass the patrol, who were now moving slowly and cautiously even for them, and get out in front of them. We slipped into the brush by the trail and watched them while they passed by. They had no idea that our faces were less than an inch from the side of the trail. I could not believe the men were going to take the same route into the camp as they had used the night before. This no doubt would be one of the areas that the guards would watch the most. The only other areas they would not scrutinize would again be the most open areas. There was no doubt in my mind that they would be caught even before they reached the halfway point.

We watched the men move to the thick brush at the edge of the tree line where the forest opened up. There was no way they could be seen by the men at the fort in that cover, but once they emerged, that would be a different story. When the last man disappeared into the brush we realized, much to our horror, that the flag man was not with them.

We began to think of the flag man more as our child than as a military man. I began to worry about him when he did not come along the trail as had the other men. It grew later and later as we lay in wait for him, but he was not coming. Not even a faint concentric ring came from the natural flow of things that would indicate the flag man was coming along the trail. Already the men were beginning to move out of their cover and into the bushy field. Yet, none of these men showed any concern that the flag man had not shown up. It looked like they were eager to get things over with so that they could go back to the barracks. We grew restless and began to move back along the edge of the trail.

Even when we reached the last place we had seen him, he was nowhere to be found.

Within a few moments of scanning the area we found his tracks leading off the trail and toward the sandbagged fort. Distant concentric rings of nature indicated that he had reached the edge of the clearing, but the softness of the sounds told us that he was staying put. Somehow, by accident or by choice, the flag man had chosen the best way into the compound. However, his poor camouflage and his inability in the wilderness, though seemingly better than that of the other men, would prevent him reaching the edge of the compound. Even with the eventual full cover of darkness he wouldn't stand a chance. I knew that I had to get to him and somehow stop his progress, though I had no idea how. Just at the point that I was about to move toward him, the surge of concentric rings indicated that he was on the move again, fortunately back toward the tree line where we were sitting.

He came back to the high brush line, slipped through the brush with ease, and rejoined the trail. We could tell from his movements that he was no stranger to the woods or to hunting, but not to a point where it would do him any good. We watched him go over to a log, sit down, and place his head in his hands. We were not three feet from him and we could hear him sobbing. I watched Rick slip forward in the brush, quietly pick up the rifle, which was lying on the ground, and silently slip it back into the brush in which we lay. I was shocked at his action, but unable to tell him so. The flag man was already upset and this would only add to his agony and humiliate him more. I had no idea what Rick had in mind, but I somehow knew that it was not to hurt or humiliate the man any more than he already was.

The flag man looked up toward the sky with a deep

breath of determination. It was obvious to us that he had lost his nerve at the edge of the field and had retreated here to re-collect his composure. He began to talk to himself in a hoarse, determined whisper, saying, "I'm going to creep right up on those bastards and as soon as they see me I'm going to blast away. The other men will join me and know that I have guts. Then . . . No, you a——hole, you and the others will only get mowed down by machine guns. Maybe I'll wait till dark. That'll give me enough cover to get closer and make a difference." Just as I was thinking about how stupid the plan was, the flag man began to stand while reaching for his rifle. He groped for a moment without looking, then whipped around to find that the rifle was missing. Letting out a horrified gasp, he began frantically searching, hoarsely whispering, "Oh, God! No! Not this! Oh, God! Oh, God!"

Just as his voice began to crack with terror, I heard Rick speak in a voice unnaturally deep to try to camouflage his age, which was difficult or impossible. He said in a whisper, "Do not look around. We have your gun. Just take the trail a few yards up ahead and follow it deep into the swamp."

"Who the f——are you?" the flag man asked in a loud, bewildered voice, forgetting for a moment where he was.

Rick said rather matter-of-factly, "I'm your fairy godmother!"

I could tell from the warble in Rick's voice that he was trying to hold back laughter. Rick then said, in a more demanding way, "Now get to the trail and deep into the swamp."

Without hesitation, the man moved forward, found the trail with a little effort, and began to follow it into the swamp. I could tell that he was trying to remain as quiet as he could, and I watched him looking back in the direction where our voices had originally come from. I guess in his mind we must have still been there because he had heard no movement on our part.

He almost lost his balance and fell into the swamp when he looked around and saw Rick and me standing a few feet in front of him, holding his rifle and smiling. We both let out a laugh, while the flag man just stared at us in utter disbelief, mouth open, as he fumbled for words and his composure. "Who the hell are you?" He demanded. "Why, you're only f——ing kids. Give me my f——ing gun."

"Only kids?" I retorted. "The same kids that you almost stepped on moments ago. The same kids who took the flags, tied them to your gun and body, who tied your friend's shoes together, hid rifles, jammed guns, pissed off people, and won you the war."

"Yeah. We're the same kids that are going to get you out of trouble," Rick said confidently, now having the flag man's interest.

"But who the hell are you?" the man inquired again, this time more sheepishly.

I then said in a joking way, "Let's just say we are the government's secret weapon against the stupidity of war." That statement really got his interest and there were no more questions. He then pointed to the camouflage pattern on Rick's body and told us that it was the best he had ever seen. It made us invisible. I then told him that he must also become invisible the same way and without complaint Rick and I began to camouflage him up, right over his army fatigues. We then stripped all loose objects from his uniform so nothing would clank, rattle, or grate when he moved, and then did the same to the gun. All the while he never said a word, but just let us make him invisible. I felt that in some way he must have been in awe of the whole

procedure. It did not take us long to have him fully camouflaged as well as we were.

Though he did not say much during the whole process,
but rather looked on in amused amazement and respect, he
did tell us a little about himself. All I can remember now
was that he was from Texas and had been forced, because
of financial reasons, to join the military. He made it clear
that he did not want to be here or involved in any war. We
told him very little about ourselves other than just to say
that he had to keep our existence a secret. We in turn would
never tell anyone that he was not the victorious flag carrier
of the mock war. In fact, if he followed everything we did,
we would make him an awesome warrior in any war, real
or imagined. We made that solemn agreement between us,
and I could sense that it was from his heart. I could also
sense that he was eager to learn, such was his excitement.

We moved back out onto the trail to where we could
see the rest of his platoon. The Flag Man, as we now called
him, did not know how to communicate in hand signals,
except for the basics, so we had to break scout law and
whisper to him what was going on. We pointed out to him
that his advancing platoon was afraid to move any closer
to the compound and that from the body language of the
guards we knew they were not yet sure where his platoon
was at this point. I was certain that the men in the platoon
would await full dark before they advanced any farther,
thus giving our little scouting party plenty of time. Flag
Man was intrigued and excited, to say the least, over our
ability to know what was going on in people's minds. We
moved back to the forest, and again through the outer edge
of the swamp, showing Flag Man how to walk, stalk, and
erase tracks along the way. Then we finally emerged and
headed to the place where Flag Man had lost his nerve only

a few hours before. He now looked very confident and trusting of our ability.

At dusk we were well out into the field, following the edge of brush as we inched along on our bellies, becoming part of the shadows. As we reached the outer high sandbag wall, Rick deftly slipped over the top without a sound. Flag Man grabbed at my ankle and I looked around only to see a worried look on his face. I smiled at him and I could feel his trembling grip relax. I slipped over the wall and he followed close behind. Even though he made a little sound coming over, it would be nothing that even an experienced guard would pick up. I knew from the many years of doing this sort of thing that his heart must have been pounding with excitement to a point where he feared the guards would hear it in his chest. We moved now silently along the outer edge of the inner wall, the same way we had the night before. I could tell by instinct that the guards were not taking their attention off the trees and fields in front of them. This gave us the edge for they would never think of looking right under their noses.

We shifted through the shadows to the open door of the brick building. The Flag Man and I held our positions deep in the shadows as Rick moved close to the door so he could get a better look inside. There at a desk sat the leader of this whole war game. He was apparently poring over papers that lay on his desk. Rick suddenly disappeared and I pressed Flag Man deeper into the shadows as the man at the desk, arose, stretched, and walked outside. I could see the flare of his match and hear the heavy puffing as he lit a cigar. Judging from the wafts of smoke and the pungent smell, it was a large cigar and very cheap. I held onto Flag Man's trembling arm as the boss-man passed within inches of us and headed around the back of the building. With a bang, the door of an unseen latrine slammed shut.

Rick motioned to Flag Man and me and we slipped inside the building. It had a single, very weathered desk and chair, upon which was spread a series of small maps and other official papers. Rick moved to the desk and picked up a large red grease pen and began to write something on a piece of paper, while motioning to Flag Man to come over. Rick directed Flag Man's gaze down to the paper, where he had written, *SURPRISE! BOMB! BANG, YOU'RE DEAD! LOVE, FLAG MAN* and motioned to Flag Man to do the same to all the papers in his own writing. Flag Man looked like he wanted to laugh, cry, run, and scream all at the same time, but as he began to write on all of the papers a big smile began to appear on his face. Rick slipped a copy of the letter he had written into the top desk drawer, gathered up the rest, and we slipped back outside into the shadows as quickly as we entered.

We were working our way along the outer perimeter of the inner wall when we heard the door of the latrine slam again. We heard the footfalls of the boss-man as he passed the open door and headed up the ladder to the lookout platform. I looked back at Flag Man and smiled and he looked at me in amazement, slightly shaking his head in disbelief. We moved along the wall, placing the signed messages just along the top of the wall between the men. At first Flag Man was terrified, but as soon as we reached the machine gun bunker he grabbed the last message, rolled it up, and quietly slipped it between the machine gun and the tripod. We then slipped away to the outer edge of the compound by the latrines, then into the fields behind the wall. After a short rest we headed through the fields to the distant tree line, again on a route far different than we had used before.

When we finally reached the tree line we could finally talk. The first thing Flag Man wanted to know was how we knew that the boss-man would not be right out of the latrine and that he would not go back inside the building. We told him that if he was only going to urinate then he would have not used the latrine but gone around the side of the building as he always did. We also knew that he would not return because he had taken his writing pen with him when he left the desk. If he intended to return he would have left the pen on the desk. He also brought his hat, which was also an indicator of his plan. Flag Man then asked how we had known that the guards along the wall would not see us place the papers on top of the bunkers. He laughed when we told them that they were far too intent on the tree line and fields to pay much attention to what was going on right under their noses. He then sat back in a state of total disbelief over what he had accomplished.

He finally asked us where we had learned to do what we did. We would not answer him at first but told him that if he did exactly what we asked of him, then we would show him more at a later date. We briefed him on what to do and accompanied him back to the wall. We watched him slip over the top without a sound, get to the back of the latrine, then remove his boots and quietly scale the back of the building, using the latrine much like a step ladder. He quickly disappeared into the shadows to await our signal. We in turn moved back away from the wall, to the tree line, into the swamp again, and finally up behind the open field alongside the slowly stalking men. Then we moved out in front, carefully cut and dismantled the trip wires, took a flare, and retreated to the edge of the open field.

Rick and I then split up. I tied together all the trip wire lines that I had cut and created one long line. Rick headed to the back of the advancing men and I went into the compound again. I set up the flare so that it would go off right into the sandbags in front of the machine gun bunker, thus blinding the men with intense light as it went off. I then ran the line out into the open field as far as I could, and lay down in the scant brush to await the signal. At this point the waiting seemed to take forever. I worried how Rick was doing and if Flag Man would fall asleep while waiting or if he might be seen. My greatest concern was not for Rick, for he had the experience to take care of himself. My concern was focused on Flag Man. He had no experience and was a definite liability.

Suddenly a gun sounded from the rear of the advancing line, which caught me by surprise and shocked me awake. Rick had done his job and attached his string to a rifle the same way he had done the night before. I pulled the line and set off the flare, blinding the machine gunners before they could even fire. At the same time Flag Man jumped up, firing shots in the air and yelling "Charge!" Then all erupted as the men in the field began running and shooting as they charged the compound. The once-still night air was now filled with gunfire and the smell of spent gunpowder. I could see all the men on the platform with their hands in the air as Flag Man held them at bay. Cheering erupted as we watched the Flag Man lowering the flag. We slipped into the now-quiet night and disappeared into the swamp.

The next evening, Rick and I were sitting atop the platform of the now-deserted sandbagged fort. As we relaxed, I could hear the distant rise of concentric rings and I knew that Flag Man was on his way. Within fifteen minutes he was sitting with us, relaxing, and reveling in our victory. Flag Man tried to explain to us the look on the boss-man's face when he had appeared behind him and shot into the air. The second-in-command had almost fallen from the platform with the shots, and the others had dropped to the floor. They all were speechless when Flag Man had told them that none of their shots had counted during the battle. After all, the whole compound was rigged with explosives, and he proved it to them by telling them where they could find the signed notes. There was a humbled hush in the fort as his platoon members carried him triumphantly on their shoulders to the truck.

Ironically, the higher brass had been so impressed with what he was able to do that they gave him several days off. Several days off were also awarded to the rest of his platoon, and nothing but hard work for the losing side. He also now carried the nickname of Flag Man. They now wanted him to teach not only his platoon but several other platoons, including several officers. He laughed long and hard when he told us that part. Rick shook his head and laughed along with him, telling him that he had better learn some skills, then. I agreed and we told Flag Man to follow us, though we did not tell him where he was going. All we told him was that he would be working during his several days off, and learn what it meant to be a warrior.

I cannot describe the look on Flag Man's face when he first saw Grandfather. He was virtually speechless and his face ran the course of every feasible expression. Grandfather motioned to him to sit down, and then spoke to him, saying, "So you are the young Flag Man that my grandsons have been telling me about. They have made a wise choice bringing you here, for what you learn here will save your life in the wars of a distant land. So then, tell me, young man, of what tribe is your grandmother from?" I don't know who was more shocked, Rick and I or Flag Man. I had never taken the time to notice the faint native American features that were in Flag Man's face, or the very way he held himself. All I know is that Grandfather melted something in Flag Man's heart that brought him to tears.

We worked on and off with Flag Man all through the week. He adapted quickly and easily to our survival lifestyle and seemed very eager to learn the ways of the earth.

He seemed to hunger for the knowledge that Grandfather possessed, especially when it came to spiritual things. He had a natural ability in the wilderness and he learned quickly, studying many times well into the night, long after Rick and I had gone to sleep. He knew that his time with Grandfather was limited and he wanted to make the most of it.

We would go often to the edge of the field where Flag Man was teaching the men. Sometimes even Grandfather would go along and watch, nodding now and then his approval from the protection of deep brush so that only Flag Man could see.

Rick and I watched Flag Man play war game after war game and win for his platoon. His tasks became more demanding as the forts became more secure, but on every occasion he would rise above the challenges and lead his team to victory. Each time it would be he who got into the fort, yet several of his men were getting good also and the platoon began to gain quite a reputation. He seemed to love a challenge even as much as we did and would be constantly pushing his skills and argue with his superiors. The most heated arguments came over the fact that he would rarely use his boots on a raid and preferred to go barefoot as Grandfather had taught him. He would also get into a lot of trouble for getting his fatigues covered in mud. This did not sit well with the all-spit-and-polish military establishment. Not only did his skill grow but he became a natural leader, though we doubted that he would rise very high in rank because of his rebellious attitude.

Then one day Flag Man was gone without a word or a trace. We stalked into the base and to the barracks where Flag Man had lived but all familiar faces were now gone. We overheard a conversation the last time we were there, learning that a large detachment of men had shipped out overseas, and we guessed that Flag Man was one of them. We worried for his safety and we wished that he had had the time to finish all that Grandfather wanted to teach him. Rick and I often wondered what ever happened to Flag Man. He didn't know where we really lived other than that temporary outpost camp. When it came time for Rick and me to move our camp back to the winter area, we knew that we would never see the Flag Man again. It had been fun to teach him and watch him grow in the ways of his ancestors. He had not only become a friend but also a brother. I prayed so often for his safety and that someday I might get to see him again.

I never knew Flag Man's real name or to what detachment he belonged, but I tried finding him time after time without success. Flag Man, if you are out there reading this, please contact me at my school address. I really would like to talk to you and possibly see you again. If not, my prayers are with you no matter what side of life you now exist on.

CHAPTER 7

GRADUATION DAY

Rick and I had been practicing our scout skills and missions for better than eight years. We had come to understand that the consciousness and the skills of the scout take one far beyond the common concepts of survival, tracking, and awareness. It was a life-style, where wilderness became home, and survival, tracking, and awareness skills became not only a science but an art form. Survival became high speed and invisible, blending one's existence into perfect harmony with the earth and elements. It meant we could survive easily where others would only perish. Through this philosophy of survival we became children of the earth, where we needed nothing from the outside world. Wilderness became our home, our protector, our teacher, and our sanctuary. It led us into the grand realms of communication beyond that of the flesh so that truly we spoke and understood the language of the earth and all things of the earth.

Tracking became a doorway to the past, where we could not only know everything about an animal or human from its tracks, but go beyond and into the entity's very mind. We read the earth like an open book, unlocking secrets that very few could see. Tracking was not only a window to the past but a window to the animal's very soul. It was in fact our secret weapon. So too was the consciousness of awareness, the doorway to the spirit. Awareness took us beyond the flesh and into vast realms of spiritual communication. Awareness was the most important element to the scout, for without the keen awareness Grandfather demanded, we could not live the scout life. Here in the scout consciousness of awareness we became one with earth and spirit.

Rick and I continually practiced our physical skills, pushing our limits constantly to higher levels. I don't think I can remember a time when I wasn't practicing something. Relaxation was not a word in our vocabulary. Even if we had just finished a long hike or completed some other physically demanding skill, we would not rest, but sit down by the fire and work on other simpler, more sedentary skills until it was time to go to sleep. Even the periods of what would appear to be relaxation were not relaxation at all. We would be engaged in practicing the sacred silence, inner vision, body control, invisibility, communication with the earth and the spirit-that-moves-through-all-things, or penetrating the world of spirit. This whole spiritual part of our existence is what we practiced most. Even when we were involved in doing a physical skill or a workout, we were also practicing our spiritual skills.

Grandfather considered the spiritual skills to be even more important than those of the flesh. Without spiritual ability a scout would be ineffective, or mediocre at best. Countless times I watched my physical skills fail, only to transcend to the spiritual level and become victorious. It was the spirit that made us walk silently and invisibly. It allowed us to know what was moving outside of our realm of physical senses. It pushed us deeper into the level of tracking until we became that which we tracked, feeling the very entity moving within ourselves. The spirit warned us of danger and kept us safe. Through the spirit we transcended the limitations of the flesh and the spirit became our sustenance.

I was so proud to be following the way of the scout. Though I was an outside member of this small and secret medicine society of scouts, I could feel the lineage moving with my consciousness. I would in some way ensure that the way of the scout would not die. Possibly I might even pass it on to future generations. As far as I was concerned, however, I was never to be a scout. To me that was an obtainable goal, only open to those who were born into that consciousness. I marveled at Grandfather and held his skill in awe, humbled by his immense ability of flesh and spirit. I had so much to learn, so far to go, before I could ever call myself a scout and have my heart agree. I could never envision myself being even a hint of what Grandfather was. Yet, one day, all of that changed.

Rick and I had been wandering close to civilization, practicing our scout skills. It was the middle of the day and we were stalking about the houses that fringed that area of our pine wilderness. We moved about through yards, in and out of sheds, under houses, on roofs, hid in hedgerows, and stalked past dogs and people without being seen. We loved to practice in the full light of day, for that made it more difficult to hide. However, we had an advantage because we knew where to find the "dead space," the invisible places, just beyond what people saw. We also had the advantage of knowing that in familiar surroundings people were in their deepest "ruts." Our first year of scout missions to the subdivisions were a real challenge, but after so many years it became more play than challenge.

However, we found plenty of opportunity to push our skills to the limit. Rick's favorite, because he was smaller than me, was to hide in a garbage can while someone actually dumped garbage on top of him. I loved to get up into the rafters of garages or sit atop garage refrigerators or boxes and watch people pull in or drive out. We even took to deftly slipping in the back door of a house, past the dogs, and out the front or side door, unobserved by the occupants. Sometimes, especially in the waning light of day or during the early morning, we would allow ourselves to be seen for a moment. Thus we perpetuated the sightings of the Jersey Devil and other ghostly things, which many times would be the topic of discussion and gossip in the subdivision for weeks to come.

We loved to play psychological games on people. Games that could be considered scout psychological warfare but which lacked the trembling and long-lasting impact of such intense games. We would raid a backyard picnic and turn off the gas grill when no one was looking or take the cooking utensils when the chef put them down. We would replace full bottles of soda with empty ones, rearrange plates and settings, move tools to bizarre locations when people were working on things, and generally create a mild state of confusion that bordered on anger. I often wondered how many people thought that they were getting absentminded on account of our games. I remember once when Rick took almost an entire pack of cigarettes, one at a time; each time a woman lit one and put it down in the ashtry it would disappear. All this was done from under a very crowded picnic table, which tended to really up the odds of our capture. The woman looked on the ground and partly under the table several times but never saw Rick.

I also delighted in crawling under picnic tables and tying people's shoes together, or tying the corner of the tablecloth to someone's belt loop. Our raids into the towns and various subdivisions became less frequent over the years, however, because it was rare that we would find a challenge. This day was one of those rare occasions we visited the subdivision, looking for challenges. What really brought us into this particular neighborhood was a peer named Bill. Bill was a typical bully, not only physically but psychologically. He threatened kids constantly and controlled the woods out behind the development. No one was permitted into them unless they belonged to his gang. The Fringe, as they called themselves, had a little shack in the woods. It was from this shack that he would peddle drugs to kids.

He saw Bill as a threat, not only because he was dealing drugs and influencing little kids that looked up to him, but he was also keeping kids out of the woods. We saw him as a cancer, evil, an alien to the temples of creation. We wanted him out in the worst way. He was older than us but I was bigger and stronger. Yet it was not in my nature to confront someone with physical violence. That was contrary to my scout training, and a warrior was the last to pick up the lance. Rick and I decided that the best approach would be to use scout psychological warfare and drive him from the temple of this pine wilderness. We wanted to do it slowly, with as much agony and fear as possible, paying him back for all the little kids he had beaten up and kept out of the woods. We wanted the impression to be so powerful that it would haunt him for the rest of his life. Yet even more so, we just wanted him to change his ways and appreciate the woods.

Our first assault on his stronghold had come a few months earlier. We had gotten to his shack shortly before he arrived, removed the box where he kept his drugs hidden, burned the drugs, and placed a big dead rotting snake in the box. We watched him enter the shack, heard the steel box hitting the ground, followed by a horrible scream, and saw his panic-stricken run from the shack to his house. Later he returned with several of his friends, but as we had ensured, they found nothing. We could tell by his attitude from that point on that he was paranoid, and even hid his drug box in the ground several yards away from the shack. The second time we visited him, several weeks later, we burned the drugs in the box and placed them back into the ground. This really shocked him because he believed that no one could ever find them. He also became more paranoid and now kept the box buried in the ground, far back in the crawl space of his parent's house. We repeated the procedure again. At this point we suspected that he now kept the drugs in the house.

His paranoia began to backfire on his group, the Fringe. He first suspected the gang members of stealing his drugs and watching him. He even went to the extent of shoving around several of the members. One kid got punched in the mouth and needed stitches. We heard Bill tell the kid that he had better tell his parents that he fell. If he told his folks who did it he would make his life miserable. Slowly the gang dissipated and refused to hang around with him, due to his suspicion and paranoia. He then began to suspect the little kids of the neighborhood, and pushed them around even more fiercely than before. It wasn't long before everyone avoided him and many wouldn't even speak to him. Yet they still would come to him for drugs and he would push the drugs harder than ever. Now instead of smoking pot with his gang, he would smoke alone at night in his shack.

The last raid we had pulled on Bill drove him out of the woods at night. Late one night when he finished smoking his dope he wandered out of the shack to urinate and then head home. Unfortunately his plans were sped up considerably. As he was urinating I reached out with a stick and touched his penis and he reeled back, pissing all over himself. He looked up to see me standing there covered in mud and leaves, let out a shriek, turned and ran right into Rick, who grabbed him with his muddy hands and pretended to bite him on the neck, leaving big muddy splotches and handprints on him. Rick got the short end of the stick because in his panic Bill had urinated all over Rick's feet as well as his own. The last we saw was him running into the brush, unable to find the trail, pants still open.

We knew from the tracks that Bill was back frequenting his cabin, but not at night. The tracks also told us that he had become even more paranoid and that he had become an even heavier pot smoker. In fact we could not find any of his tracks that indicated any sobriety. We had worked our way through his subdivision and were now near the cabin, hiding in the bushes very close to the shack. We could tell from the smoke that poured from the roof and intermittent wafts of scent that he was intermittently smoking his dope and topping them off with cigarettes. In a way we were very angry because we had not succeeded in driving him from the woods, and his terrorism on the young children of the neighborhood had become more violent.

Every kid there walked around in a constant state of apprehension and fear.

At this point I was considering a forceful confrontation. Yet, in the final analysis, it would not produce the long-lasting impression I was seeking to achieve. Rick and I had no idea what we were going to do next, but waited to see what circumstances and opportunity would reveal to us. I guess that the real shocker came when I peered through a crack in the shack wall and found Bill involved in some bizarre ritual. On a makeshift board table he had strung out a dead squirrel, belly up. The squirrel appeared to have been killed by a gunshot to the head, though I could not be certain. On the four corners of the table were burning candles, the only real illumination in the room other than the daylight coming through the cracks. I watched him as he lifted a knife, called the name of Satan, and plunged the knife into the squirrel. That was enough for me to see and I backed away, trying to contain my rage.

Not only had he brought drugs into the temple of creation and had driven out the children, but now he was calling Satan into the woods. My soul became a smoldering battleground between my rage and the code of the scout. Finally I could not contain myself any more and I exploded into a fit of violence. The animal within me had taken over my body and my mind became primal. I bashed at the wooden slats of the shack, crushing a huge hole through the boards. I reached in and lunged at Bill, who shrieked and fell to the floor in a trembling panic. I pulled the boards from the corner of the shack, and clawing, biting, and snarling, I smashed my way through. I grabbed Bill by his sweatshirt and lifted him clean off the ground and over my head. "So you want Satan!" I screamed. "I'll show you Satan!"

I threw him hard against the wall, screaming, "I'll give

you Satan, I'll give you hell. Welcome to hell, Billy Boy.''
I did not realize the power of my voice or of my appearance, covered with mud and debris, for it shook the foun-
dations of Bill's existence even more than being thrown up
against the wall. My muscles now surged with adrenaline,
and I trembled with the power of the beast, barely on the
edge of control. I grabbed Bill again and pushed him
through the wall of the cabin, holding him hard against the
ground and pinning him beneath me. I did not realize that
I was growling, drooling, and seething spit all over him.
He was so terrified that he couldn't even struggle, but just
lay there as if dead. Rick rounded the corner and froze in
his tracks. He knew enough not to try to interfere with the
raging beast I had unleashed. When Bill saw him standing
there he began to wail out of control, babbling.

I grabbed him by the back of the sweatshirt, holding
also his long hair, and dragged him screaming all the way
to a big box at the edge of the cabin. It was a box with a
hole cut into it in the shape of a toilet seat. Here is what
Bill and his gang used as a latrine pit for years and now I
was determined to introduce him to the bowels of hell. I
kicked away the box in a fury, busting it to pieces, and
revealing the deep hole full of human feces. I screamed at
him again, ''You want hell! Well, here are the gates of
hell,'' and with that I threw him face-first into the pit. Desperately wallowing in the heap of human excrement, flies
all around, he began to scream wildly and loudly in blind
terror and panic.

Rick suddenly grabbed my arm and I was pulled back
into human consciousness. At the far edge of the trail we
saw a group of people gathered and several policemen. The
baying of hounds could be heard coming up behind us and
instantly we knew we were in trouble. The day we had
chosen to raid Bill's shack was the same day and time the

police were going to raid Bill's shack. Realizing the danger
of being caught was now becoming reality, I slammed back
through the shack, motioning to Rick to follow me. I
grabbed the body of the squirrel, kicked out the back wall,
and retreated into the underbrush. A few yards away we
slipped into the thick cover of the swamp, the dogs closing
in fast. We slipped into the water, moved a few yards along
the bank downstream, and then buried ourselves in the deep
mud. Only our eyes and noses were exposed.

First came a German shepherd, who crossed the swamp
and kept running up the other bank away from where we
lay. He continued on. It was obvious that he was not scent-
trained, otherwise he would have stopped at the bridge.
Unfortunately the two bloodhounds were scent-trained,
one better than the other. The one who was not made it
across the small stream before he realized he had lost the
scent; the other stopped directly at the spot where we had
entered the water. Police closed in on the dog, stopping just
a few yards from the deep mud pit we were hiding in. Their
guns were drawn, and one officer had a scope rifle, which
he aimed at the distant brush, only to bring it down when
he saw the German shepherd returning. It was obvious that
these guys wanted to play for keeps. I began to grow concerned that if we were caught, they might think we were
part of Bill's gang.

From what I could see three policemen were now at the
edge of the creek with the three dogs. There may have been
more but I could not tell from my position and I was far
too close to move, especially because of the dogs. One
officer turned to the other and said, "Looks like they went
off downstream. Bud and I'll take the dogs, you stay here
and wait for the detectives."

The other man asked, "Did they catch the ringleader?"

"Yes," came the reply, "but they didn't find the drugs."

"Well, who the hell are we looking for now?"

"I don't know. Someone said they thought they saw someone running, and the kid keeps babbling about being beaten up by monsters. He didn't even run from us, but kept pointing to the swamp and babbling. He's a mess anyway. He's as stoned as all hell and covered in shit."

A different voice now joined the conversation as a man walked up to the group, saying, "Apparently we are off on a wild-goose chase. It was one of the known gang members that said someone was beating up the kid. I say he was so stoned that he got out of control and beat holes in the shack with an axe or something. Looks like he also fell in the s——hole when he tried to take a crap."

"You just can't trust these a——holes, especially when they're stoned," another officer commented.

A new man in street clothes now joined the group and said in an authoritative way, "These idiots would believe a moving bush was a Martian. The captain thinks that the kid might really have been beat up by pushers looking for their money, but I doubt it. The dogs stopped right here and don't look to be interested in anything else. Let's just have the dogs check downstream a bit to satisfy the captain, then we'll see if we can find the stash."

The two hounds and their trainers combed both sides of the stream, until they hit the thick mud farther down from us. They passed us back and forth, several times within inches of my nose, but the dogs never picked us up. Within half an hour the men and all the dogs had gone back toward the cabin. We slid into the water, went downstream a bit, recamouflaged ourselves, and headed back to the shack through the thickest, most inpenetrable brush we could find. We were curious to see if the police had found anything, and if they were still looking for other people. From our position we could not only see the shack clearly but also several of the police cars. In back of one of the police cars we could see Bill, wrapped up in some kind of plastic, apparently an attempt by the police to keep the feces off the car. He looked dazed and very upset.

We watched him talking to an officer who was standing back from the car. From his overexaggerated hand movements we knew he was describing the attack in all of its horrid detail. Our attention was drawn back to the shack where the police were tearing things apart. The man with the commanding voice called the men off the search and told everyone the search was over. He said, "Well, damn it! We haven't found anything, so I guess we are going to have to let the a——hole go."

They all began to walk away and I could feel the shiver of disappointment run through me. Without thinking, and in spite of the close proximity of the dogs and men, I slithered forward, to the original hiding place where Bill had kept his drugs. I hoped that after such a long time he might have used the place again.

I dug down into the soil. The closest officer was only about fifteen feet from me but looking the other way. The German shepherd was at his side. I still dug down, determination becoming more powerful than my fear of being caught. Suddenly I struck the box, and the audible click caused the officer to turn around and look directly at me. He glanced back and forth but did not see me at all. I continued to unearth the box, opened it quietly, and saw the stash of drugs. Bill had made the fatal mistake of using the same hiding place again, and now his rut would prove his doom. As I looked at the box of drugs I became torn between giving it to the police and just letting it alone. Part of me said that I had disobeyed the scout law and unleashed my rage without enough cause. The other part of me thought of all of the little kids that Bill had terrorized or turned on to drugs.

I gave Rick the signal to back off and hide. As soon as I could sense that he was well into the swamp, I hurled the box in a high arc above me. I had been trained by Grandfather to throw weapons, use spears, shoot bows, and even launch atlatls from any position without making a sound. It paid off beautifully. The box crashed against the side of the roof and then hit the ground. It appeared to the men that the box of drugs had been in a hiding place in the outside rafters and had somehow jarred loose. Several men ran to the box. One officer held a bag of pot high in the air so that the chief could see it, and within half an hour everyone had vacated the woods. Bill was well on his way to punishment. Rick and I slipped into the swamp, followed it a long ways from the shack, then moved back to the trail networks that would take us to Grandfather's camp.

All the way back I felt so very guilty for what I had done. Not only guilty for throwing poor Bill around the shack and dumping him into the latrine pit, but also for virtually giving the police his stash of drugs. If I just hadn't lost my head through rage and allowed the animal within to emerge, things might be far different for Bill right now. No, the cops might not have found the drugs without me, but they might have just scared him enough so that he would stop peddling his drugs. However, part of me sincerely doubted that he would have ever gone straight. After all, we had been trying for a few months, and only succeeded in scaring him a bit, a scare that he soon got over. I was simply confused, for I did not know what would have been the right thing to do. Both sides held a good argument for being the right thing. I just wished that I had left well enough alone and stopped trying to play vigilante.

Essentially, what I had become was the judge, jury, and executioner. A role that I would not have played if the raging beast had not been in control of my mind. It further troubled me because my heart would not answer one way or another. It was as if my inner vision had completely shut down to teach me a lesson, a lesson that I had to figure out with my own mind and emotion. One thing was for certain, I felt very guilty for what I had done and I know that I would have felt just as guilty for not doing anything at all. The whole concept of right and wrong troubled me so much that I could not think of anything else. The only thing that I was truly happy about was the fact that, at least for a while, Bill would not be keeping kids out of the woods or turning them on to drugs. Yet I had little faith in the legal system, for I had seen so many criminals let go with nothing more than a slap on the wrist. No, I didn't want to see Bill do hard time, but enough of a punishment to break his cycle.

I then began to wonder what choice Bill really had. I should not have taken my rage out on Bill, but hate rather what he was doing. It was not really his fault. Though Bill did not go to the same school as Rick and I, it was obvious that he had nothing much to do. There was no adventure or excitement in his life, nor did he know where to find it outside of dealing and doing drugs. No one had taken the time to teach him a better way. I thought to myself that possibly Rick and I should have taken a different approach to the problem and tried to reason with him, yet I doubted it would have done much good. The more I thought about it, the more it upset and confused me. I wondered to myself if Grandfather would be angry at me for doing what I had done, especially because I had unleashed the primal self for an offense rather than a defense. I knew that by using the animal as an offense violated the laws of the scout.

By the time we reached Grandfather's camp it was full dark. We could see a small fire burning in the sacred area, with Grandfather sitting nearby. I could tell by his body language that he awaited us. Humbly, more like a whipped puppy than a warrior scout, I sat down by the fire. Grandfather looked at me long and hard, searching my soul with his piercing gaze. He then asked, "Tell me, Grandson, what troubles you so deeply on such a beautiful night."

I realized then that Grandfather had not been watching what Rick and I were doing on the raid. I began, slowly at first, telling Grandfather the whole story of the raid, fumbling with words and emotions all the way. Watching him carefully to see if I could find any look of disapproval or condemnation on his face. There was just the usual masked smile.

I told him, beyond the details of the raid, what I was feeling and how confused I was. This was the only time that Grandfather changed his expression, to one of confusion. Grandfather spoke then, saying, "Yes, I have taught you that you must not release the beast through the vehicle of rage. Nor should you use that beast for aggression. It should only be used in situations where there is a dire need, an intense struggle of life and death, where you are left with no other choice. The animal blinded your sense of reason temporarily and also blinded your senses. That is why you failed to see the police coming to the shack. Yet you were still in control. You did not really hurt this boy named Bill, you only frightened and humiliated him. The only injury inflicted was to his ego, his pride, and his arrogance.

"I have also taught you that the animal within could be used when it threatened the life of a loved one," Grandfather continued. "Were not the children that were being hurt also your children? Did he not violate our Mother

Earth, and threaten her with harm? In so doing you had every right to release the beast, for your family had been threatened and was in danger. The only wrong you committed was to hate him rather than his actions. As far as the drug box is concerned, you know that you have taken the right path. Did you not say that you could not scare him away from his wrongs? If the drugs were not found he would have nothing to face and would go back to his old ways, but in a more secretive way. You may have saved his life by giving those who defend the law the drug box.'' He paused for a moment, then said, ''Prepare for sacred ceremony.''

Rick and I were a little baffled by his statement. We could see no need for a ceremony. It was not the time of year to honor any entities or actions, as was custom. It was just an ordinary night as far as we knew. Nonetheless, without any questions we began to prepare. As I built up the fire, took out the pipes and the drums, and placed them in their proper places, all I could think about was what the ceremony was going to be about. So too did I think about Bill and what he must be going through now. I wished that there could have been a better way. Possibly, I thought, the ceremony might be for Bill and all that he had to face. Possibly, it was Grandfather's way of sending him love, compassion, and peace. After all, Grandfather always said that we should pray for our enemy and send them love. I satisfied myself then that the impending ceremony must be for Bill.

Rick and I sat alone at the far side of the fire. Rick played the drum softly as I sat holding Grandfather's pipe. Grandfather entered the circle wearing a loincloth, a beaded neck bag that I made for him, and his red, faded headband made out of dyed buckskin. He held in his hand a small parfleche, the type used to hold feathers or other items that had to be protected. He placed the parfleche before him on the ground and then slowly took the pipe from me. He then called upon the Creator, and honored the directions and the earth. He then called the spirits with his sacred song, inviting them to join in this sacred circle. There was nothing about the ceremony that we hadn't seen before, until he called the spirits. Not only was the song a little different than we had heard before, but so was the feeling. We could feel the spirits' presence, a very powerful presence, that made us shake to our very core. I could feel them deeply scrutinize me, I could see the flickering shadows moving, and the deft flow of silent footfalls. The walk of the scout.

There was no doubt in my mind that these were not just any spirits, but the spirits of scouts. That was the difference in his sacred "calling of the spirits," for I recognized the word for "scout" in the song. I felt uneasy and self-conscious, knowing that they were out there. I could feel them, hear them, and vaguely see them sitting there, and judging from Rick's demeanor, so could he. Suddenly it hit me that something was strange about this gathering. Though I could not clearly see, in the physical reality, I could sense that they were all wearing the red headbands, just like Grandfather's. Until this time Grandfather had said nothing of his red headband. We had assumed that it was just his choice of color.

Grandfather put the pipe down carefully, acknowledging individually the spirits that had gathered there. He then took two red headbands out of the parfleche, and holding them in his outstretched hands, he implored all who were present to take notice and bless these sacred items. Finally Grandfather spoke to us, saying, "These are the symbol of the scout. When one has proven himself above all others to possess the skill, knowledge, and spirit of the scout, he transcends his old ways and joins the sacred brotherhood.

These are a symbol of those who love the earth and will protect the earth with their lives if need be. They are only worn by the scout. Those who have chosen to live the way of the scout, who protect the people, the earth, and the spirit.''

Grandfather paused for a long moment, holding the red headbands to the heavens. Finally for the first time I realized the significance of Grandfather's red headband, and the awesome responsibility that it held. Grandfather continued, talking both to us and to the unseen who surrounded us, saying, ''The scout is a circle of all circles. He walks in both flesh and spirit. He listens, watches, and understands all things beyond the flesh, and it is in this world beyond the flesh that he is also a scout. The scout follows a higher law, a law that is not understood or heard by common man. The scout is the protector of the flesh and the spirit in all things. The scout is directed by the Creator, the earth, and his life will never be his own. To be a scout is to live the greater vision. To be a scout is to be one with all things of earth and spirit.

''Grandsons! You have proven beyond my dreams and visions that you can walk this path. You have passed the test of physical and spiritual skill, and have transcended the self for the protection of others. You have been constantly striving to grow and understand, and you have withstood the test of time and sacrifice.'' Grandfather walked behind us. I could feel the headband being tied around my head as tears flowed freely down my cheeks. I felt humbled and, under the intensity of the onlooking spirits, I did not feel like I deserved such an honor.

Grandfather then said, ''The red is the symbol of the earth's blood, your blood, and the spiritual blood which surrounds. It shows the common man that the scout has skill beyond his imagination, for the scout cannot be seen even when wearing the red band about his head. Welcome to the world of the scout. Now go to your sacred areas and give thanks.'' Tears filled Grandfather's eyes as he walked into the night.

As I walked back into the depths of my sacred area by the swamp I could hear faint drumming coming from far off. Then as I began to pray, more drums joined in, all around me. The drumming was faint yet so powerful that I could feel it rock my very soul. I stood, arms outstretched to the sky, trembling as tears ran down my face, and crying out my oath and vision to the Creator and the earth. I was both humbled and elated, unable to fathom the depth of what had just happened to me. I had become a scout. I had achieved that impossible vision, so unexpected and profound. I felt the rapture of belonging to a greater brotherhood. Yet I was saddened by the thought that Rick and I might be the tradition's end. Unless Rick and I could pass it on it might die with us. I understood now why Grandfather had cried when tying on the headbands. He had fulfilled his vision, and now passed the responsibility on to us.

Within six months, Rick and Grandfather were gone. In the flesh I would never see them again. Yet in all the things that Grandfather ever taught me, in all the things that we experienced, nothing had a more profound and lasting effect on my life than the night Grandfather placed the red headband on my head. I can still feel his tears falling onto my back as he placed the final knot. I vowed never to let the way of the scout die.

CHAPTER 8

The Airport

Primary rules with Grandfather concerning the actions of the scout were to never break the law and to never hurt anyone. Yet sometimes I would bend those rules a bit to fit a certain situation. I guessed that getting in and out without being seen and doing no damage would not really be breaking the law. After all, what people didn't know couldn't be all that bad. If I had been caught I would have been breaking the law of trespass, but then again, I thought I would have to be caught. Right or wrong, my reasoning tended to suit my purposes. Sometimes I would just claim ignorance, or something that seemed to satisfy my logic. Like the time Rick and I got onto the military base. I knew that there were ''No Tres-passing'' signs along the highway. But we didn't come from the highway; we came from the deep woods, where there were no signs. At least, that is what I would have told anyone who might have caught me.

Several years after Grandfather and Rick had left and taken their spiritual journey to the other side of life, I was wandering in the West. I don't think there has been a day in my life that I have not been practicing my scout skills or thinking of new scout missions to try. I am a creature of opportunity where scout raids are concerned and I was always looking for opportunities to press my scout skills harder than ever before. In essence, once you become a scout, you live in the consciousness of the scout for the rest of your life. You are a different animal with different ways of seeing things as compared to normal folk. Life becomes an adventure, filled with excitement, if you know how to look at it through the eyes of the scout. This day was no exception.

I was trying to get around a very large city, as was typ-ical of me in my years of wandering. I always avoided cities and towns at all costs, even if I had to go miles out of my way to get around them. Yet unfortunately, there is hardly anyplace I could go without encountering somewhere along my path a large town or city. It was typical that people would put cities at the shortest distance between two wil-derness areas. Towns and cities did not disgust me alto-gether, however, for there were times that I would use them to practice my scout skills. They became playgrounds of adventure, where raids could be had anytime. Cities al-lowed me to push my skills right to the edge, for most peo-ple of the city are closed off and blind to everything about them. A good scout in a city could accomplish anything.

I was getting around this particular city in my usual way, by moving at night and through the streets of the outlying suburbs. I was taking my time in this journey, for scouting opportunities abounded along the way. I loved nothing more than to leave in my wake vast confusion, stories of monsters and ghosts, and people scratching their heads in disbelief. As I worked my way through the last subdivision, the sound of landing airplanes and jets alerted me to the city airport. I had never used a large airport as a scout playground before and I figured this one would afford a great opportunity. I knew there had been a rash of hijacking in the past few years and most airports were on the alert. The fear of terrorists and hijackers had beefed up security tremendously. This could be a real test of my skill.

The outer perimeter of the airport was easy enough to get to since not many houses were around. The city had placed this airport far enough away so as not to be right in the heart of the city and subdivisions. I don't know whether it was because they would eventually want to expand or if they didn't want complaints of jet noise. Whatever the reason, it made it easy for me to get to the outer fence. For that matter anyone could get to the outer fence unnoticed, even a brass band. Once at the fence, I decided that it would be a better test of skill if I went in closest to the terminal. After all, that was where the security would be the heaviest. I found a small hill that looked down onto the terminal area and afforded good cover and a good view of everything. I decided to camp there for a few days. I wanted to observe the personality of the terminal, its guards, the workers, and, most important, the awareness level and routines.

I had originally thought that it would take me two or more days to scope out the airport and learn all the routines but, much to my disappointment, it took me but one full day. I had figured that because it was such a major airport, near one of the largest cities, the security would be top rate. Looking back now over all the raids I pulled off, even in the most secure compounds, nothing is what I consider to be top rate. Even to this day. Everything remains very vulnerable and unchallenging. Possibly to the ordinary person this airport had top security standards, but to a scout, every modern security is a joke. I knew of movie stars and rock and roll stars who had better security than most government installations, and I could waltz in and out of their yards and homes as if I were on a Sunday stroll. The most difficult security to beat would be that of a top-security prison. But given time I knew that too could be beaten.

After reviewing all that I had seen of the security, the awareness levels, and the ruts and routines of the airport, I decided to make several smaller raids rather than one big one. The reason was simple: the airport was so big and there was so much to do, one raid could not possibly accomplish it all. I decided first to scout out the big hangars where most of the repair work was being done on the commercial airlines and alongside which were parked several military fighter jets. I figured, given the fact that some sort of military presence was there, that it would have a lot of security. I awaited full dark before I began my scouting expedition, camouflaging myself with charcoal I took from an old burned building near where I was camped. I always felt it best to blend camouflage to shadow. It was the universal scout camouflage, after all.

I carefully moved along the brush lines and old hedgerows to the vast parking lot located right behind the main hangar. I moved along the outermost row of cars, which had been parked there for a long time, judging from the grime settled on them. I thought they would not be moved very soon and so were probably well entrenched into the security guard's mental rut. I knew he looked toward them, but he didn't really see them. At best he would be attuned to abrupt movements, people walking, or the sound of cars being broken into, not for me belly crawling along the top curb behind them. Oddly, the lot was fenced in only on three sides. The fourth side looked out onto a vast field and I guess they didn't think anyone would enter from that direction. After all, the field was in clear view from the guard shack, thus in their minds it must be secure. Who would even think of entering the airport through the wilderness, anyway?

As soon as I had crawled along the line of cars I was at the chain link fence that separated the parking lot from the hangar area. Fortunately for me, but not for them, there was a slight oversight in the construction of the fence. First of all it was not touching the ground and second it did not compensate for the dips in the natural landscape. There was also a nice little rim of high grass along the fence, which the mowers could not reach. This afforded me ample cover on my short crawl along the fence to the nearest dip in the landscape. Within a few moments I was under the fence and out of sight. Making my approach to the hangar even easier was the amount of old and new machinery, vehicles, and piled oil drums that lay between the fence and the hangar.

Given the poorly lit state of the area behind the hangar and the randomly parked and piled equipment, I walked to the hangar rather than crawling or stalking. There was just no need to. If there had been guard dogs then I would have had no other choice but to move quietly, but there were no guard dogs and I just walked with the same confidence I would have had if I owned the place. Before I approached the hangar I had to lie in wait for the guard to punch his time card out behind the hangar. As was typical of his rut, he never looked around but just got right out of the car, went directly to the time clock, punched his card, then went back to the car and off he drove to the other end of the airport. According to routine, it would be nearly four hours before he returned.

As soon as he left, I headed directly to the back door of the hangar, using the noise of his departing patrol car to mask any noise I might make. Even under the worst of circumstances, though, I didn't make noise when using the scout walk. Conveniently, a bathroom window next to the back door was left slightly ajar, no doubt to air it out. I could hear the sound of workers in the hangar but I knew that it was just a skeleton cleaning crew, and I would hear them walk to the bathroom. I could also get a clear view of the hangar area directly in front of the bathroom door. Only the front part of the hangar was illuminated, leaving the back completely in darkness, including the bathroom. As soon as I was inside, and after using the urinal, I slipped into the inner darkness of the hangar complex.

Two large aircraft were out in front of the hangar. One of them was being cleaned by the crew. The other was locked up tight. One large jet airliner was also in the hangar, doors open, with various machinery, ladders, and equipment lying all around. I decided then that my first mission would be to get on the airliner in the hangar. I had never been through such an airplane, other than when I was a passenger heading to a police tracking case, and I was determined to explore every inch of its interior. I began with the luggage compartments and moved from far up in the nose almost all the way back to the tail. Then it was up into the main cabin, where I tried out the chairs, looked through the galley areas, and played with the intercom, which was not working. I then went into the cockpit and tried out all three positions and looked at the various gauges, dials, switches, and gadgets strewn across, above, and below the dashboard, being careful not to touch anything.

I then climbed out through the forward door onto some scaffolding, which got me up onto the wing. I stalked across the wing in full view of the work crew, knowing that they couldn't see me because the spotlight blinded them in that direction, and onto another scaffolding, which terminated at a raised hydraulic bucket. I entered the bucket then gently pushed the lever, which slowly lowered the bucket to the ground. The roar of cleaning equipment drowned out the slight hissing sound the descending bucket made. I then explored the landing gear, the wheels, and the landing gear compartments, wondering if anyone could stow away up in one of these things. Finally, getting bored with the ease with which I was able to get onto the plane, I decided to explore the hangar. That proved to be even less exciting. Then I decided to see if I could get close to the cleaning crew.

The plane they were working on was parked outside in an intensely floodlit area. Here too were all manner of vehicles and equipment lying about in no definite order. It appeared to be equipment used to service and clean the aircraft, but most of it was not being used. Judging from the activity, all major work had been done and now they were just in the process of cleaning the interior. As far as I could see from my vantage point inside the shadows of the hangar, just two people were inside the main cabin and a third was on the ground. No one else was in sight. I was near the center of the huge open doorway, leaning on a forklift, watching the routines unfold. Suddenly, the man on the ground turned and walked directly toward me. I froze in place, for I figured that he would just walk right by me in the dark and head to the bathroom. At least his walk told me that he had to go.

He switched on a flashlight, which startled me. His beam swept right over me then onto a fuse box on the wall. Before I could react, he stepped to the box and threw the lever. It felt as if a thousand flashbulbs fired at once, such was the assault on my eyes. I did not move, but froze bolt upright next to the forklift. Through squinted eyes I watched him walk right by me without even taking a second look at the forklift. The sound of his footfalls stopped and I heard the bathroom door slam shut. Just as I was about to move, car headlights appeared from somewhere behind me and the other two workers walked down a gangplank from the plane and into the far end of the hangar. The car parked directly out front and only about ten yards from me. The driver got out and joined the men at the far end of the hangar. I could see them opening bags and hear them pouring drinks. I looked around me and realized that I was standing virtually in the open. Nothing was around me but the forklift and I was on their side of it, to make matters worse.

I heard the bathroom door slam and the sound of footfalls heading to the men at the far end of the hangar. As they sat at the table, backs toward me, I slipped out the front door to the aircraft they had been cleaning. I knew from the angle of the gangplank that they could not see the plane, or at least the part of the plane that held the gangplank. I paused by the front wheel of the aircraft, scanning the surrounding area for any more workers, guards, or oncoming vehicles. The arrival of the security guard did not take me by surprise, for as a scout I learned to expect and prepare for anything, but its arrival did break the airport's routine. The more I live in the scout consciousness the more powerful becomes the concept of having no routines. Yet routines and ruts are just a small but important part of the whole story.

Once satisfied that all was reasonably safe, I moved to the gangway, slipped through the rail, and in a low crouch ascended the stairs. I first explored the cockpit area, made even more vivid than the one before by the back lighting of the main cabin area. I then explored the main cabin, taking a break and glancing through a magazine while reclining in one of the chairs. From my vantage point at the windows to the rear of the cabin I could see that the workers in the hangar were finishing up their food, and two were having a cigarette outside the hangar. This didn't bother me too much because they were still quite some distance away and out of sight of the gangplank. I did realize, however, that even though the workers did not yet pose a problem I had very little time. I knew I could always slip out the back door and drop to the ground if they came aboard.

I was just completing my inspection of the rear of the aircraft when I heard several sets of footfalls ascending the gangway. I turned immediately to the rear door, only to find that it was closed. I was trapped by my own stupid mistake. If I tried to open the door it would only alert the oncoming workers to my presence, and with the security guard about I might get shot.

Fighting off panic, I crawled back into the galley area to try to find a place to hide. To my amazement there was an open doorway leading into the belly of the aircraft. I guessed that it must have had something to do with movement of food storage boxes, for there were no steps or ladders. Without a second thought I slipped down through the opening and landed on the lower deck without a sound. I paused for a long moment to listen for the workers returning to their tasks.

I listened to the patrol car drive off, watching out the

open cargo hatch as its lights disappeared, and heard the last worker climb the steps to the cabin. I slid out the hatch to hang at arms' length, then made the final drop to the ground, where I paused for a moment, moved to the large landing wheel, then to the nose wheel, then back inside the now-dark hangar. The hangar and the airplanes no longer posed any sort of a challenge, so I decided to see if I could press my skill a little more and play with the workers' minds. I figured that the best place to start would be at the table where they had taken their break, since most of their personal items were still there. I searched through the lunch bags, and found that they still contained food, so I began to swap some of the contents with one another. This way all of their food would be mixed up.

I then grabbed their jackets and headed to the aircraft that was parked in the hangar. Using the scaffolding I climbed up on the aircraft wing, and, using the second scaffolding, onto the top of the plane. I left one of the jackets hanging from the tail fin, which was no easy task. The top of the tail fin was well out of reach and I had to throw the jacket up until it caught, hoping that no one would hear the sound of the jacket being thrown. I then took the other two jackets, stuffed them carefully with trash, and headed back to the jet that was being cleaned. I climbed beneath the gangway and wrenched myself up and around so that I could peer inside the main cabin and locate the workers. They were all working diligently in the back of the plane, so I slipped inside and propped the stuffed jackets into the pilots' seats. To all immediate appearances they would look like two people were sitting there.

Still not satisfied with all that I had accomplished, I went looking for something else to do. I worked my way out on the gangway, moved around and beneath it, and slid to the ground. At that moment I noticed that the gangway

was the only way in and out of the aircraft. Finding the
wheel brakes I silently opened them and gently, impercep-
tibly pushed the gangway back from the aircraft about
twenty feet. A longer distance than they could ever hope
to jump. I then locked the brakes and slipped back into the
hangar, where I decided to wait and watch the antics. I
knew that they would not try to jump to the gangway, and
dropping the distance from the belly of the aircraft to the
tarmac would turn most people off. I thought it might be
fun to watch and see if they could figure it all out.

One of the problems with scout psychological tactics
was that I rarely got to stay around and learn the outcome
of a mission. Often I could not take the chance of staying
so close to the action, for that would put me in danger of
being caught. Once something was discovered out of place
or wrong, it would only put the people concerned on alert.
Oftentimes I had to read of my success from the tracks that
were left behind, long after the incident was over, or I
would hear it secondhand in gossip someplace. However, I
thought the large hangar and good cover of machinery and
supplies would afford me a relatively safe place to observe
all that was going on. If they did get crazy with fear and
began to search, it would be easy for me to get away unobserved.

It did not take long before the first worker discovered
the problem. He was on his way outside to have a cigarette,
which was already in his mouth but unlit. The shock of
seeing the gangway far back from the doorway caused the
cigarette to drop out of his mouth and fall to the ground.
He yelled to the other workers, who came running. They
all cautiously peered outside, like little children looking
around a doorway to see if the bogeyman was there. They
argued with each other, accusations flew, one man accused
the other of not locking the wheels, another said that the

plane might have rolled. This went on for a good quarter
hour, the arguments rising and falling like the tide. Then,
first one man, then all three began calling for help, though
they knew it was futile, since no one was around and the
guard was not due back on his rounds for quite some time.

They stopped calling out after a while and sat down to
wait. One man sat on the deck, feet hanging out the door,
and the other two men eventually sat back in the cabin
seats. I could see them looking out the windows once in a
while waiting for the guard to pass. It was during this time
that they discovered the stuffed jackets in the pilot seats.
Accusations flew wildly and arguments escalated as each
man denied responsibility for the stuffed jackets. The arguments fell off immediately at the approach of the patrol
car. The men began yelling to the guard, and the car
swerved from its intended route and headed over to the
airplane. The guard got out of the car and looked at the
men in astonishment as they accused him of pushing back
the gangway. One man also threw a stuffed jacket at him,
laughing and feigning anger.

The guard pushed the gangway back to the door and
the men immediately scampered down. I watched them
talking for a long time, then suddenly turn and look toward
the hangar. One of the men climbed up into the cargo area
of the plane and with a flashlight began to search it. It was
apparent now that the guard and the other two men were
suspicious but confused, and they walked directly to the
hangar with purpose in their step. I climbed a steel ladder
that was permanently affixed to the wall and walked out on
a huge upper beam that spanned the entire hangar. No
sooner had I gotten to the top of the beam and lain down
than the blinding lights of the hangar were switched on. I
could clearly hear one of the men on the phone as the two

others sheepishly looked around below. I could tell that they did not want to be heroes and were wary of everything.

Just then, one of the men cried out and pointed to the jacket that hung on the edge of the plane's tail rudder. Unfortunately it was not far below where I lay. I worried that the men might think that it had been dropped from the beam above and that might give away my hiding place. I began to do the slow scout belly crawl across the top of the beam. The width of the beam was barely wider than my body and I had to make sure that I did not let any part of me hang over. Fortunately it was from this beam that the front row of lights were hung and the glare would most certainly block my outline from view. The lights also cast the beam into deep shadow, which was also to my advantage. Just as I approached the center point of the hangar another patrol car pulled up and three security guards got out, flashlights in hand, and began to talk to the original guard.

I had no choice other than to keep moving because there was nothing between me and the ladder except for open beam. By the time I had reached the far wall above the table where the workers had originally taken a break, the security guards had fanned out throughout the hangar, searching every possible hiding place, or so they thought. Another car, unmarked, showed up and two men got out, one in uniform and one in plainclothes. They talked to the original guard, who pointed to the outside aircraft, showed him the stuffed jacket, and then pointed to the tail of the hangared aircraft. The search continued out back of the hangar though several men stayed inside. One clearly pointed to the ladder on the wall and swept his flashlight beam right by me. It was painfully apparent that the man was going to climb to the beam.

As he headed to the ladder, talking to the man in plainclothes, I stood on the beam. Making sure that the people below had affixed their attention on the ladder, I stepped off the beam and onto a wall brace that consisted of a small angled piece of metal, about two inches wide, and that ran the entire upper length of the wall. I watched over my shoulder as the man ascended the ladder, apparently very apprehensive of the height. It seemed that it would take him forever to make it to the top. I got as far out on the little wall brace that I could, till it terminated at a thick column. There I froze motionless alongside the column, blending my body into conformity with the wall. The flashlight beam swept by me several times, but did not stop. I could hear the man climbing down and I slowly returned to the high beam before the group turned around. The scout spirits were certainly with me at that point.

I could hear the men talking as they gathered below me. At first the conversation was lively, but as other men joined the ones underneath the beam, the conversation abruptly ended. One of the men that had come in from the back said that there was no sign of anything wrong. Finally the man in plainclothes said, ''Looks like the first shift is playing practical jokes on you guys. Let's not let it get out of hand again. I don't mind practical jokes but when my men have to be called in, that involves some valuable security time wasted. Got it? You tell first shift when and if you see them to knock it off.''

The response was more of a disgruntled acknowledgment rather than an agreement. I lay up in the rafters until all but the workers had gone. Judging from the workers' conversation, they did not believe the first shift was playing any practical jokes. They began to suspect that the security staff were the ones playing the jokes, and discussed that possibility as they walked back to the plane.

I crawled back along the top of the beam and stopped just above the jacket hanging on top of the aircraft's tail. I shifted around to the underside of the I beam, hung as far down as I possibly could, and with my outstretched toes I lifted the jacket from the tail. I slowly hoisted myself back up on the beam, being careful not to drop the jacket. Though I could have easily kicked the jacket off the tail and to the ground, I didn't want to take the outside chance of having the workers hear it hit. I moved down the ladder slowly, turning upside down as I reached the overhang of the hangar to see where the workers were, as I didn't want my body to be in view before my head knew what was going on. For practice I decided to go the rest of the way down the ladder upside down, holding the precious jacket in my teeth.

Moving through the hangar was a little more difficult, in that the men had purposely left the lights on, no doubt out of fear. I watched the workers time and again peering out from the plane's cockpit or through the door just to keep an eye on things. I pressed my luck and took the jacket back out to the plane and, folding it neatly, placed it on the bottom step of the gangway. That would really get them thinking. I decided then that I had bigger and better things to do and retreated to behind the hangar where I could relax for a while and plan out my next move. Parts of this hangar mission were exciting, but I was looking for more. I knew that best would be to run a raid on the airport security headquarters. After all, they were rather smug when dealing with the workers, possibly the fat one in plainclothes needed to be taught a lesson.

Normally I should have waited till the following evening to begin raiding the security headquarters, but I did not want to chance this shift not being back in for a few days. The night was still very young, which would give me plenty of time to get in and out with a lot of time to spare. The security headquarters were in a small building right next to the main overseas terminal, connected by a breeze-way. It housed not only the airport security but also the customs personnel, which added a little more difficulty to the scouting mission. Next to the security offices was a series of fenced compounds and buildings used for quarantine and for holding various bulk items shipped in from overseas and awaiting inspection. Of course these compounds were the most heavily guarded of the airport.

From the hangar building there were two ways to the security building. One was to go out the way I came into the airport and work my way around the outside fence, till I came to the terminal building complex. This would be a long and tedious route and no doubt eat up precious time and energy. Though a little more risky, the other approach was to go directly to it from the hangar area. Unfortunately this route would take me out into the open and across two of the runways. Not only did this pose the problem of being seen—that is, if someone were looking and seeing—but I would also have to time it so that any landing aircraft would not see me or worse yet, run me over in my attempt to cross the runway. Also, due to the previous raid, all security personnel would be a bit more aware.

I worked my way from the hangar and across the concrete aprons and into the first wide field. This field was nothing more than lawn, probably twice the width of a football field and nearly a mile long. The only way I could go across this first field was to crawl diagonally. Any other direction would take me far away from my destination. Nearly the entire distance had to be covered on my belly to minimize my outline, especially with the presence of rows of runway lights along each side of the grass fields. The lights were spaced in such a way, however, that they did not overlap but created a faint shadow, which I followed. Adding to this advantage were several small gully-like depressions that I could use as a path. By using the slight gullies and working with the shadows I could not be seen at all, even with approaching headlights.

I followed one of these natural drainage gullies right to the edge of the first runway and lay back ten yards from its edge. Even though the hour was late planes were still landing, but with no regularity. Also, several times patrol cars or other airport vehicles would travel up the runways and turn off far ahead to enter some unknown building complex. I decided that the best way across the runway was to wait until a plane landed, then just as it passed, scamper across the runway. I had no idea of the power of one of these planes since I had been far back in the middle of the field when the last one had passed. Even being many yards away I still had to plug my ears and close my eyes from the noise and flying debris.

I watched a big plane make its approach and final descent. I plugged my ears and readied my body in such a way that I could spring out into the runway and get across just as it passed. I could feel the tremendous shocking surge of pressure as the wing passed over me and I stood to run. I took a few steps and was blown right down on the runway by the after-draft. I was almost deafened by the sound as I removed my hands from my ears to break my fall. I actually staggered to the other side and fell down into the grass, so unlike the flowing gazellelike motion I had been envisioning. I struggled to find a depression in the grass so I could sink into it, but the second field stretched out like a lawn before me without even the slightest ripple in the ground. Lights on this grass strip were even more intense because it was the median between both runways. I was very vulnerable to say the least.

I slithered along on my belly, flattening myself as close to the ground as possible. Several airport vehicles passed by but I could not tell if they were security or some other type of airport vehicle. Fortunately none of them hinted at slowing down. My mind wanted me to get up and run, but my scout instincts held me fast to the ground and at a dead-slow speed. Even though it took only about half an hour to cross the center grass strip it felt like it had taken all night. When I walk this close to the edge of being caught, time seems to distort very badly. In one instance a few minutes could seem like hours and in another a few hours could feel like minutes. I never knew which way my mind was going to react to the concept of time. When I experienced this time distortion I found myself looking at the position of the stars to mark my relative position in time.

When I reached the second runway, the one used for planes taking off, I did not want to make the same mistake as I had in crossing the first. I wanted to make sure that the plane was well past me before I made the run. Good thing, because as soon as I bolted across the runway in a low crouch, a scorching hot blast of exhaust hit me, nearly knocking me off my feet again. Fortunately for me there was a rather deep gully running through the final grass field, alongside the runway. I hit that just in time to see the oncoming lights of a big airport truck. This truck had huge spotlights and crawled along at a slow pace, probably inspecting the runway. It drew slowly past me and stopped on the side of the grass strip momentarily, for what reason I do not know, but then proceeded again at a faster pace.

Now between me and the security building was nothing more than a huge blacktop area, large enough to allow planes to get by and still leave enough room for other vehicles to park. The area was about the length of a football field, and it terminated at several rows of parked cars. This parking area contained several patrol cars, several airport trucks, a few sedans with government license plates, and many private vehicles. From my position I could see very distinctly two large poles at either end of the security building, each holding a surveillance camera. I could also clearly see that they were moving back and forth in a strange sequence. The one on the right moved faster than the one on the left. Getting across this lot was going to be difficult at best.

At least one thing was in my favor. The blacktop near me was not illuminated all that well, although the area by the cars and other vehicles was lit up like daylight. I would have to move across the dark side of the blacktop at a run, timing my approach so that both cameras were facing in opposite directions from each other, and hope that once committed to the run no one exited the building and no vehicle drove up. If that happened I would be caught for sure. I knew from experience that in scout missions there were times I would have to take risks, but all risks had to be calculated in my favor. This risk was equal as far as I was concerned, fifty-fifty chance that I might make it or get caught. I had to lie there for a long time, watching the cadence of the cameras, the ebb and flow of traffic and people. Planning the perfect time to move and then just allow my body to react.

It seemed to be all over even before it had begun. As soon as the cameras came together I began my run through the darkness and without breaking stride hit the illuminated pavement when the cameras were at their highest arc. I was behind the bumper of a pickup truck before the cameras had even come together again. Then watching the faster camera from low and behind the rear wheel of the pickup truck I made another move that brought me up to the vehicles parked along the front of the security building. All had gone well, that is, until a security guard came out of

the building and headed to the parked cars. I had no idea
which car he was going to go to, and had to wait for the
last moment of his commitment before I could make a
move.

As luck would have it, he had gotten into the car next
to the one I lay in front of, and I hardly had to move at
all. I watched him fumbling around in his front seat, putting
his things away, and rolling his window down partway. The
car then started and idled for a while, then suddenly to my
surprise the engine went dead. I heard the car door open,
slam shut again, and the sound of footfalls trailing away
from the car. I glanced at the camera, saw it swinging away
from me, dodged around the car, reached in the window,
and took the keys. I then bolted to the building and slipped
behind the ornamental bushes that lay out front and next to
the wall. My position could not have been better. Not only
were the bushes low and impossible for most people to hide
in, thus removing them from suspicion, but I had created a
diversion by removing the keys. Everyone would be focused on the patrol car.

As I expected, the guard came out of the building and
headed back to the car, carrying with him an attaché case,
no doubt what he had forgotten in the first place. He got
in the car and paused for a long time, almost in a state of
frozen animation, where I could not tell what he was doing.
I could then see him going through the motions of looking
around for the keys, getting out of the car and looking at
the ground, fumbling through his pockets, looking back into
the car with his flashlight, then heading back to the building
in a huff. This process of going and coming to the car was
repeated two more times; each time he searched the route
to the car with his flashlight. The last time he entered the
building I could clearly hear someone yelling. The word

that stood out in my mind was "incompetent." I knew the voice, for it belonged to the plainclothesman that I had seen earlier at the hangar.

The officer and the man in plainclothes exited the building, walking with arrogant purpose. I watched the officer transfer his things to another patrol car and as he got into that car I heard the man in plainclothes say, "Now get your a—— over to the hangar and tell those a——holes to knock off the games. Get the keys back and tell them that you will arrest them if this keeps up!"

The car drove away as the man in plainclothes walked back to the steps, where he was met by another uniformed officer. I was very close to the steps and could hear a cigarette lighter flick and smell tobacco smoke. They began to get locked into a conversation that bordered on rampant complaining so I decided to see how close I could get to them. I slid silently along the brush, under the open steel stairs, and directly beneath them.

Amid the heat of the conversation above, I reached up and gently pulled the lace on the plainclothesman's shoe. I did not expect that he would notice so I did the same to the other man. Backing away I crawled along the hedge while they still sat there, and disappeared behind their building. I was appalled at the lack of awareness, but I shouldn't have been. As Grandfather told me so often, "A man is in his deepest rut where he is most familiar." Again and again Grandfather was right. I wondered if I could have stood up and walked away without them seeing me. Even if they did see me they probably wouldn't have believed what they were seeing. How many loinclothed, barefooted, muddy bodies do you see on any given day at a major metropolitan airport?

Working my way around the back of the building I found a ladder that was permanently affixed to the wall and which led to the roof. I decided that it might be fun to see if I could get onto the roof and stand above the men on the stairs without them knowing. Even though it was not much of a test of skill, I gave it a shot anyway. Part of the scout's game is to see how much you can get away with to observe the actions and reactions of people, much as you would observe any other animal. By observing people in this way you know what you are capable of, what they see and do not see. With no hesitation and walking in full upright position I stood directly above them, listening to their conversation, which was getting very interesting.

By this time I knew that the uniformed officer was named John and he called the plainclothesman Chief. I also knew that the officer in the patrol car that had just taken off was named Lou. What stunned me was when the chief asked John if Lou suspected him of sleeping with his wife yet. John just chuckled and said to the captain that the stupid bastard doesn't even know that his wife is sleeping with anyone. I backed away from that conversation as they stood and walked into the building. I watched them through the skylights for a while, but could not hear any more conversation. Searching for more adventure I walked to the rear of the building and looked down upon the back parking lot. This lot was very unlike the front lot. It was poorly lit and unguarded by either man or camera. What a joke, I thought. Do these people expect that terrorists would only come in from one way?

I climbed back down the ladder and explored around the building. I noticed that its front entrance was larger than its back entrance. Through the side window next to the front door I could clearly see another security guard. I assumed he would be the one to let people in and to stand guard over the parking lot. He never looked up from his desk in all the time I was there. At this point in my mission

I was a little upset over the lack of challenge in this situation and began to grope for ideas. My first idea was to get up to the side window and see what the guard in the window was looking at. It turned out to be the latest issue of *Playboy*. No wonder he was so absorbed. On the wall behind him I could clearly see the TV monitors for the outside cameras. Of course he was not looking at them.

I decided to move into the rear parking lot to see what else I might be able to do or find. Interestingly, the first vehicle I came to was a late-model gray sedan with an official crest painted on the side. Around the crest were the words *Chief of Airport Security*. Delightful, I thought, how convenient. I decided to avenge the chief's mocking and belittling attitude toward Lou. Creeping up to the garbage can that sat alongside the back steps, I carefully pulled out all the garbage and carried it to the chief's car. I then dragged it under his car, reached up and pulled out the distributor wire, and stuffed all the garbage up into the engine compartment. It was so much trash that I had a hard time fitting it all.

I then beat a slow retreat back out the front of the building, to the hedges and then on to the patrol car whose keys I had stolen. Watching the cameras sweep away, I slipped into the car through the open window to explore its interior. It had the usual police equipment, a shotgun, mounted radio, fire extinguisher, flares, and a huge flashlight. On the seat sat a hand-held radio, a clipboard, and a pen. I grabbed the pen and clipboard and wrote, "Dear Lou, John is in love with your wife. She is cheating on you. Love, the Chief." I then tore off the paper, stabbed the stolen keys through it, and pushed the keys into the ignition. I then grabbed the hand-held radio and slipped out of the car as soon as the cameras swept away. I made my retreat to the

opposite side of the steps, where the darkest shadows were
to be found.

Between the security headquarters and the main terminal were about a hundred yards of poorly lit parking lot,
which ran along the covered walkway connecting the two
buildings. The entire area was strangely deserted, with the
only workers in sight at the far end of the terminal unloading baggage. As I began to move away from the building
I noticed that a golf cart sat in the first parking spot. I
touched the control knob and it moved ahead with a quiet
whir. I got a jolt from the thought of riding in the cart and
without any hesitation I jumped into the cart and drove it
to the other building. I looked to the far end of the terminal
where they were unloading baggage to see if anyone had
noticed, but no one broke routine or even looked my way.
I decided then that I would take the long route out, which
required that I pass through the entire length of the loading
area. That would surely test my skills.

I moved in and out of loading cars and trolleys at the
deserted end of the terminal. Some of the carts had baggage
still inside while others were empty. Only once in my romp
through the maze of baggage cars did I encounter a security
guard as he drove by quickly in a golf cart similar to the
one I had used. That far end of the terminal proved no real
challenge at all. Without any hesitation or concern I entered
the first open door I could find and entered a maze of conveyor belts, loading platforms, and all manner of machinery. Now midway through the terminal I could see all the
activity in the working part of the loading area. Bags moved
by quickly on belts that wound around the outer perimeter
of the loading area and through various openings in the
walls, no doubt moving the bags to their appointed pickup
places. I was very close to the outermost belt where it

passed through the darkened area where I stood, and I was tempted to rearrange some baggage. But I knew that it would be breaking Grandfather's rules and the rules of the scout. I left well enough alone.

As I moved dangerously close to this main working area I spotted a catwalk high up in the rafters. I decided that the best way around this area would be above it. I climbed the wall silently, like an unnoticed fly, using fuse boxes, conduits, and bolts that stuck through the wall, much like free-climbing a rock face. Just as I was approaching the catwalk, fully exposed to the floor below, the lights in that part of the terminal came on and just as suddenly all the conveyor belts started moving. The room below me hummed with activity. Loading carts came and went, baggage moved by quickly, while workers were consumed with the task at hand. Little did they know that a figure was moving in the shadows high above them, toward the catwalk.

Not one of the workers or customs officers that walked about watching the baggage looked up. From my shadowy position on the catwalk I could get a full view of the ordered mayhem that stretched endlessly below me. Very near the catwalk a high conveyor belt moved by, carrying luggage to the upper levels of the terminal. I could not resist. I walked out on the catwalk, silently jumped on the conveyor belt, and rode it to the far end of the terminal. There, just before it disappeared through the wall, I grabbed hold of a support beam and made my way out to the catwalk again. Just as I was trying to figure out how I would get back to my camp area, the lights in that far portion of the terminal went out, leaving just the center portion illuminated. All work was now being done there.

I silently climbed down the ladder while looking over my shoulder. Anytime someone looked my way I froze, but there was no way they could see me in the darkened room.

Finally at the ground, I slipped through the bay door, around the building, and stopped at the fence that stretched clear around the outer part of the airport. I followed along the fence, still within the airport proper, crouching low to conform to the height of the uncut brush and hedgerows that grew on the other side of the fence. Here was nothing but open bushy fields and the high, stepped towers of the landing lights. I made my way all the way to the smallest tower, which was nothing more than a column of lights supported across two poles. I could see the distant patch of woods and knoll where I had my camp, realizing that from here it was not more than a short walk away. Here too the fence ended and did not start again for several hundred yards.

I pulled the hand-held radio out of my loincloth belt and flipped it on. Feigning a distressed voice as if in trouble, I called "Lou. Lou! Come in, Lou!" A voice responded, saying, "This is Lou. Over." I responded, "Lou. The captain tells me that John is making love to your wife and that you are too stupid to find out. Over!" There was a silence for a long time. Then suddenly a voice came over the speaker loud and clear. It was the captain, asking, "Who the hell are you?" I immediately responded, "This is the Bogeyman of the Airport. Lou, your wife is cheating. Captain, if you want your radio back it is on top of the first light tower. Good night, kids. Great airport security!" I left with the sound of obscenities being shouted over the radio and disappeared into the woods.

I watched for hours as cars raced to and from the main terminal, the hangar, and parts unknown. They searched the fences and outer fields with powerful lights but never got out of their cars. I thought to myself how unaware these people were, yet entrusted with passenger safety. Virtually anyone that knew how to tiptoe could have walked right into that place and run little risk of being caught, far less even seen. I wondered how many other places that were said to be secure were as big a joke as this one, and I satisfied my curiosity many times in the ensuing years.

CHAPTER 9

CHEMICAL TRUCK

Certainly it was Grandfather's primary rule that on a scouting mission we could not damage any property, hurt anyone, or break the law, but that was during practice. A scout's primary mission was to get into a place, observe, possibly dabble in a little psychological warfare, and then get out without being observed. A scout that was seen was disgraced and was considered "bad medicine," avoided by the scout society or even banished from that society altogether. However, even Grandfather admitted more than once that there were times when a scout had to become a warrior and pick up the lance. It was at these

rare times, when things could not be settled with psychological warfare, or through less martial means, that the
scout could break the primary rules, especially when the
scout's or his loved ones' lives were in danger.

A scout's loved ones expanded well beyond his immediate spouse and family and embraced the whole tribe.
A true scout would even love those beyond his family,
even, in many cases, his enemies. The earth, and all things
of the earth, were also part of his flesh. The true scout first
learned tolerance, so he loved everyone and everything. He
would love his enemy but despise their actions. He would
never let anger, hatred, or violence rule his mind, emotions,
and heart. That is why the scout rarely killed, for all things,
all people, were part of his own flesh. Killing was always
a last resort and was typically followed by a great sense of
mourning. The scout would mourn his fallen enemy even
as if that enemy were of his own immediate family. To hurt
the enemy would also be inflicting pain on oneself.

Even though the scout was master of wolverine fighting,
knife fighting, and the use of all weapons, and constantly
kept his body fit through grueling daily workouts, fighting
was a skill he was reluctant to use. More than practicing
these skills to engage ultimately in warfare, the scout used
the skills to build his confidence, push his body, and teach
himself discipline. With Grandfather, Rick and I could be
assured of three things every day: a lesson in philosophy,
a lesson in awareness, and a grueling physical workout.
Without fail, these three areas were included in our daily
activities. Yet, despite our mastery of fighting techniques
and martial skills, we would always turn away from a fight,
no matter how badly we were beaten or pushed around.
The fight was only for when we had no other choice and
our lives were threatened.

These basic codes of scout honor were driven into our

very soul so that they became an important part of our consciousness. That is why it became so very hard to deal with confrontation, and we avoided it at nearly all cost, even to the point of personal humiliation by our peers. According to Grandfather, we should be known as the peacemakers, not the warriors. That peacemaking attitude also effectively increased the depth of our disguise. Yet the peacemaker attitude, the saintly tolerance, was that which set the scout apart. Peace was one of the most cherished possessions. Grandfather warned us so often that the demons of anger or rage, hatred and malice would undermine the code of scout conduct. That rage could also preclude any rational thought, and thus rage would fuel the fires of hatred, and cause us to hurt someone.

So many times during scout missions I had to fight back the demons of rage and hatred, and to see things as they really were. Many times I could almost taste the justification in lashing out at someone like an uncontrolled raging beast, and feel no remorse for my actions. At such times the internal battles became far more vicious than anything that could have ever taken place physically. I knew that if I had ever done something in the consciousness of rage, Grandfather would never have forgiven me, nor forgiven himself for teaching me such a deadly art. It would prove to him that I had no self-control, and self-control was a mark of a good scout. As I grew older, however, I found it much easier to control my rage and hatred. I satisfied myself instead with becoming more artistic and effective with my psychological warfare and that usually appeased the beast within.

Grandfather believed, as I have come to believe, that anger, rage, and hatred, in fact negative emotion in general, is a liability to the scout. These negative emotions hinder clear thinking, exhaust the body, and otherwise obstruct all related action. They can become a demon that not only produces some deadly mistakes but can also hurt the scout himself. We learned long ago that we could use someone's anger against him for our own victory. So many times Rick and I would try to get the other fired up with the demon of anger, knowing full well that the anger would not empower, but only destroy the one who allowed it to consume him. Every time I failed in a mission, it was either directly or indirectly because of anger. Fortunately I was able to see my errors myself, and subsequently correct them.

Sometimes the situation would merit that some of the scout rules and code of ethics be broken, or bent slightly. Especially when all other approaches had failed. However, such an extreme approach was never fueled by rage or malice, but by the knowledge that all other ways had been tried and had failed. Then it was time to take extreme measures of psychological warfare or outright aggression. My first real encounter with having to make that kind of choice came nearly two full years after Grandfather and Rick had gone. Looking back on the situation now, I don't think I could have handled it in any other way, given the circumstances surrounding the mission. Even though I did not really harm anyone physically, or at least permanently, I still wish that it could have been different.

Even within the same month that Grandfather had left the Pine Barrens a war between me and a certain individual had begun. I had wandered out to one of our outpost camps, only to find that the sacred ground had been defiled by illegally dumped chemicals. There were several dump locations, all showing the same tire pattern, and each several days apart. In the hot sun the outpost camp reeked so badly with the vapors of caustic chemicals that it caused the eyes to burn and water, breathing to be painful, and queasiness to occur. Many of the trees were wilted and dying, and the small stream that ran nearby had discolored vegetation along its banks and bloated bodies of dead fish, frogs, and turtles floating on its surface or drifting morbidly along its tiny currents.

Of our outpost camps, this was not one of the more important, but like the rest of the wilderness it was still sacred ground to me, still the flesh of my mother. I could feel the anger boil within me, and I vowed to the spirits of the earth that I would somehow revenge this senseless poisoning and death. This truck driver knew exactly what he was doing; it was evident in the way he dumped the toxic solution and the way he had tried to cover up his tracks. He had also varied his pattern of dumping, as was evident by the tracks, so that it was random, never following any pattern of a certain hour or a certain spacing of days. So too had he chosen the actual dump site so that thick vegetation would conceal the runoff marks of the chemicals and the soil would allow the fastest seepage into the subsoil.

Studying the tires and relative size of the truck I knew that I had seen it before on the highways, and had found other evidence in the Pine Barrens of its old dump sites. The owner of the truck had definitely designed and built the truck to undertake such a task as secret dumping. It was the body and wheelbase of a six-wheel-drive army vehicle, capable of going far back into the Pine Barrens and needing no trails. The original military body of the truck had been removed and it was replaced by a tank such as oil companies use for home oil delivery. The times I did see the truck race past me along trails in the past, it was painted a flat army green so as not to be detectable in the woods, and in all cases the license plates were covered over by mud or removed altogether.

I had encountered the driver of the truck on one occasion only. He had broken down with a flat front tire along one of the back roads of the Pine Barrens and I watched him as he changed the flat. He was a burly man with a hot temper. He would curse and beat anything that interfered with his tire-changing. He continually drank beer, which was always at hand in a homemade cooler that sat next to the driver's seat. His arms were huge and strong, depicting a life of hard physical labor and his tracks indicated some kind of heavy lifting. He seemed never to smile or be at peace. He exuded anger and evil and I could feel it on a much deeper level than just through the mind and physical body. To put it bluntly, he was scary.

He was so belligerent and scary, in fact, that I did not even think of pulling any kind of raid on him when he was changing his tire. It was not only the feeling that surrounded him that made me apprehensive but also the fact that across his back windshield was a gun rack with a twelve-gauge shotgun, and with him was a rather evil-looking dog, part shepherd and part Doberman pinscher, I would suspect. I had no doubt that the man would not hesitate to send his dog after me or to shoot me and leave me lying in the Pine Barrens. However, I did watch his every move as he changed the tire. Though he was far more aware than most, mainly because of his fear of being caught, he was still out of place in the woods and I could tell that the concept of wilderness scared him.

My first real raid on this illegal chemical dumper was during one of his dumping episodes. He had driven into the woods late one night and I had heard him crashing through the trees from quite some distance away. I had purposely camped near the place where I had found the evidence of the last several dumpings, and I figured that he would likely use the area again. As soon as I heard the trees crashing and the thunderous engine revving, I immediately got to work camouflaging my body. At the time I had no idea what I was going to do, in that I was concerned about his attitude, his dog, and his gun. Whatever it was, I had to be sure that I made no mistakes. There was no doubt in my mind that any confrontation between us would probably result in my death. It would be a different story if he had no gun, however. There was no doubt in my mind that if we came face to face I could easily beat him, given all of my years of working out and martial training.

I found him quite near to the original dumping sites, though a little farther into the lowland areas. I could see from his chosen position that there were going to be several more dumping runs. Anticipating the dog's probable presence, I had expected my initial approach would be rather slow and labored, so I was surprised at how quickly and easily I was able to accomplish it. I got into a well-concealed position quite close to the truck so that I could observe what was taking place and from there plan my raid. I was thrilled that the dog, though vicious, was not very aware of the woods around him. In fact, he appeared to be downright inept. He never once paid any attention to the faint noises of deer and other animals moving through the forest. He growled only once when he heard a sound that was close at hand. His growling stopped abruptly when the man violently kicked him in the head. It was clear that the dog was very abused, judging from the way he cowered around the man.

The man was leaning up against the rear bumper of the truck, watching the chemicals slowly run away, and having a beer. Several other beer cans were lying around just where he had thrown them. He was constantly watching the flow of chemicals and adjusting the valves so as to permit a gentle runoff and adequate time for the ground to suck up the liquid. I noted also that he had positioned the truck so as to be upwind from the caustic vapors, which smelled much like turpentine mixed with some other paint thinner. The dog was out of sight, having now moved to near the driver's door, and lying almost asleep on the ground. I moved in on the truck to get closer to the man but I initially made a bad choice and found myself downwind of the chemical. My eyes teared violently and I almost coughed out loud.

I had to take the longer route now along the front of the truck, which would bring me very close to the sleeping dog. Nonetheless this journey went very quickly, and I hardly lost any time at all. I was still perplexed as to what I was going to do to the truck and the man. As I approached the front of the truck I decided, though reluctantly because of the dog, that I would get up under the engine and see if I could keep the truck from starting. I was not concerned that it was a diesel engine, for I had learned some things from watching my father work on all manner of machinery. I thought that if I could just detain the truck and keep the man from driving off then surely someone would find him, and he would pay the penalty for illegal dumping.

I got up under the truck easily enough, but then came the problem of working on the engine without the dog hearing it. I reached up and grabbed the thick wire of the starter motor, slowly and carefully cutting through it with a large flake of flint. It took the better part of an hour to get all the way through and move onto something else. I then took the copper fuel line and bent it in several places, knowing that if he ever did get the starter motor to work he would not be able to repair the copper tubing that easily. That would really keep him stuck in the woods. As I slipped out from under the truck I thought that I should go out and get

the police, but I worried that he might be paying off the
police. I had known it to occur before and I just didn't
want to take the chance. I thought it best that I attempt to
further scare him out.

I worked my way around the back of the truck, trying
to stay as close as possible to its side. Fortunately for me,
he had parked the truck virtually on the heavy brush on
that side and he would not be able to walk around it that
easily, nor for that matter would the dog. The first thing I
encountered as I approached the bumper was his discarded
beer can lying a few inches in front of me. I could tell the
strength of his grip by the slight dents his fingers had made
in the can. I thought back to the countless long hours Rick
and I had studied cans, crushed cigarettes, and all manner
of other things that people touched and used. At that time
I could not understand why Grandfather had us learn these
things and study people so closely. Those lessons of awareness had become important to me even before my first scout
mission.

Gently picking up the beer can and moving with it far
behind the truck, I located an area where the chemicals had
formed a small puddle. There I filled the beer can, holding
my breath as much as possible and sucking in air while
looking away from the toxic fumes. After filling the beer
can nearly three-quarters of the way full, I belly crawled
back to the truck's side, slipped under, and moved into
position under the back bumper. The man put his current
beer can down on the bumper and moved toward the valves
to adjust their flow again, just as he had been doing
throughout the night. I quickly switched his can of beer on
the bumper with the beer can containing the chemicals. I
thought it would be a grand lesson for him in poetic justice.
He makes the earth and the animals drink the vile chemicals
and I make him drink those same chemicals.

I had just gotten away from the truck and was settling into cover when the man began to turn off the valves and prepare to leave. Without a pause in his motion he grabbed the beer can and took a big drink. The action of lifting the beer can was done so quickly and with the confidence of a seasoned beer guzzler that he never had time to smell the fumes. Immediately he began choking, coughing, and nearly vomiting. He crawled on the ground on all fours, spewing and coughing all the way to the front of the truck. I could tell from his violent reaction that he didn't swallow any of the chemical, just took it in his mouth. He then dragged himself up into the truck, grabbed a jug of water from the floor, and kept washing out his mouth. He dried his forehead and face repeatedly with his shirt.

At one time the dog came up to him to see what was wrong, but the man kicked him hard on the chin, sending him running away with a yelp. Tail between his legs he now stood trembling by the man. Grabbing a flashlight, the man kicked at the dog again and headed to the back of the truck, cursing the whole way. I could see him searching the place where the beer can had sat on the bumper and the area of the tank above. From his actions he must have assumed that somehow the tank had leaked into his beer, but he could not find the origin of the leak. It hadn't crossed his mind yet that anyone was around. Returning to the cab of the truck, taking another long drink of water, and then jumping inside, he tried to start the truck. Nothing happened. The only sound was that of his temper exploding and his curse words flowing.

He got out of the truck, virtually shaking with rage. He opened the hood and looked inside the engine compartment. I watched the flashlight moving slowly back and forth as he tested wires and tugged at hoses. He also banged the battery several times with the end of the flashlight. Back again inside the truck he attempted to start it again, but to no avail. Still fuming and nearly out of control he went back to the engine compartment. It took only a few seconds this time for him to see the cut wire. He let out a string of screaming curse words and banged on the hood of the truck with his fist. He yelled, "I'll teach you bastards to f—— around with me!" He was so upset that he nearly tripped as he headed back to the cab. Without any hesitation he grabbed his shotgun and began to point it at the woods with a menacing display of insanity. He was intent on shooting anything that moved.

Unfortunately, the dog chose that moment to walk up to the truck. The man lashed out at him and began kicking him brutally and repeatedly, to a point where the dog could hardly get off the ground to get away. The man cursed at the dog as he kicked, screaming, "You stupid, good-for-nothing idiot! People come right in here and all you do is sleep." The man kicked wildly again and the dog began to bolt for the thicket. The man raised his gun, leveled it off, and shot at the dog. Most of the shot hit the ground next to the running dog, but I could tell by the wincing whimper that the dog took some of the shot in the rear thigh. The man now began to talk to himself, his voice rising and falling with rage, nearly babbling instead of talking. This enraged conversation lasted quite a long time as he searched all the way around the truck for other damage.

I watched the antics of the man trying desperately to repair his truck. I stayed as long as I could but the oncoming light of dawn was making it difficult to stay in my position. He had stripped, rejoined, and taped the wire earlier on, and now was in the process of putting together pieces of hosing to replace the crimped fuel lines. All this while he was so enraged that he looked like he was going to have a stroke at any time. As I moved back from the truck and out of sight I could clearly hear the engine turning over and firing up. Within moments I could hear the sound of him driving off as small trees crashed around him. I hoped that this would be the last I saw of him.

On the way back to camp I encountered his battered and wounded dog, lying under a tree, curled up in pain. As I approached him he let out a convincing snarl, but as soon as I began to speak softly to him he began to calm. It took him a while to transcend his suspicion of me and it was not until I finished caring for his leg that he seemed friendly. I nearly had to carry him all the way back to my camp and it took nearly ten days of healing before he could walk without any signs of pain. I could not believe that anyone could have been so cruel to an animal. No wonder the man had shown no remorse for dumping the chemicals. There was no doubt in my mind now that he would have done the same to me, or worse, if he had ever found me. I was happy that the dog was no longer with him, and happier still when I found him a good home with a local family that lived in the woods.

Within a month the man was back dumping in the Pine Barrens again. I tried time after time to scare him off with all manner of scout psychological warfare but nothing even came close to working. Instead of showing any fear, he lashed out with aggression and gunfire. Once a shot hit so close to where I stood that bark fragments splattered all over me. The more I tried to drive him out, the more determined he seemed. It was a war that I was not winning or even drawing. I was just so frustrated, and I did not know what to do next to get him to stop. Even trying to get the police involved did nothing. They just used the excuse that they could not assign a man to the woods for days at a time, waiting for the truck to come. Yet his killing of the Pine Barrens with his dumping was growing more frequent.

With me, the whole affair was becoming unbearable. I had to struggle constantly with anger and hatred over this unchecked dumping. It also seemed to me that with all the Pine Barrens areas to choose from, he always chose my area to dump in. That was only an assumption on my part, for I had no idea what he did on the nights he was not in my area. In addition, his dumping pattern was getting closer and closer to the old Medicine Cabin and I knew if I ever caught him there, gun or not, there would be a physical confrontation. With my increasing bouts of anger and frustration over the whole thing I began to feel myself moving toward the inevitable. I struggled with the thought of physical confrontation almost as much as I struggled with the anger. I tried to seek clarity through the sweat lodge, prayer, and vision quest, but those avenues were of no help. They simply confirmed what I already knew, and that was to follow my heart.

I decided that the only option I had left was to somehow destroy his truck, or to render it inoperable anytime it came into the Pine Barrens. I felt that if it began to cost him money and became a real chore to fix the truck, then I might eventually drive him out. However, I began to imagine that he might not stop dumping but go to another part of the Pine Barrens altogether. Then I would never know if he had stopped dumping or not. I realized that I had reached the point where I had no other choice than to physically confront him, but even that did not sit well with me. I just did not want to hurt him or anyone else. As angry as I was with him, the thought of a physical attack was against the scout rules, against my personal rules. Yes, the life of the earth, my flesh, was threatened and I could justify physical violence in that way, but still I could not accept that kind of confrontation. There had to be another way.

I began to become consumed with what course of action I would take. As the days slipped by I knew that it would just be a matter of time before he came back into the Pine Barrens to dump his deadly load again. I still had nothing concrete as to what I was going to do. The menace of the toxic dumping and the man's arrogance even began to seep into my dreams, causing me restless nights of broken sleep. I had to constantly check my involvement so it did not become an obsession, for obsession, like anger or hatred, would feed on itself and grow stronger. Obsession unchecked would become my reality, and obsessive reality would lead to self-destruction. Obsession could consume one's very mind and body. Thus, my obsession would cause me to lose this important battle, and possibly my life if I was not careful.

One morning I awoke from a nightmare. Grandfather's voice still sounded in my head. As clearly as if he were talking to me he said, ". . . and then let nature punish those who defile her." I knew that those words had very little to do with any dream but were born of spiritual reality, an answer to the question burning inside me as to what to do with the man dumping the toxic chemicals. Without any hesitation I jumped out of my shelter and ran all the way home. I fumbled around our basement and found a long piece of chain that I had found in the public dump, and also two of my padlocks, then ran all the way back to my camp area. I set about cleaning up the locks and oiling them so that they would make very little sound when closing. I also oiled the chain and wrapped old cloth through it several times so that it would make no sound when I moved it.

The dream had come just in time. For no sooner had

the sun gone down than I could hear the truck coming. The man was getting more secure with his operation now and did not take the precautions he once did. To me his actions were blatantly obvious and I could not understand why the police did not pick him up. I found out after the fact that the police had been trying to catch him for years, but because their vehicles could not follow him into the woods, and because of his erratic dumping schedule, they could not catch him in the act. It always baffled me why something so obvious would go unpunished, but I also knew that the laws were such that the police could make no mistakes in his arrest or he would get off. Having now worked with the police so often in criminal tracking I can understand how severely their hands were tied.

I took my time camouflaging my body, for the repeated raids on the truck had really piqued the man's awareness. I could take no chances on shoddy camouflage. I then camouflaged the chain and the locks in the same way, and wrapped them up in a buckskin bag so tightly that they would not make a sound. I then headed out to where I had heard the truck stop. I would not allow myself the indulgence of hurrying, for I had the whole night before me and to hurry at this point, even at the beginning of the raid, would only put me in danger. My slow travel was at odds with the excitement that grew within me. I wanted to get there and get on with my plan, but my training spoke otherwise. This internal battle followed me all the way to within sight of the truck.

I decided to come from the least-expected direction. No one would expect someone to stalk them through toxic chemical sludge. Not even this man, as paranoid as he was. I had in the past come from all manner of directions, other then the place where the chemicals were being dumped. I stalked all the way around his truck, stopping every so often to watch him and to define his weakness. As I began to get closer to the running chemical sound I grew concerned, for the sound was more of a plopping than a steady flow of liquid. I was upwind from the truck so my nose was of no use. I had to be careful, for I had been burned by his chemicals before and I wanted to make sure that I was not going to belly crawl through them.

As soon as I came even with the far back side of the truck, I knew why the sound had been so different. It was not toxic chemicals that he was dumping, but cesspool sludge. I don't know how long this sludge had sat in his tank but when I inadvertently crawled into it, it reeked of human waste and felt the consistency of warm, lumpy mud. I had to fight back my gag reflex, which was so severe that I don't know why he did not hear me approaching. I tried to roll out of the waste but soon found that it was like a mushroom-shaped puddle that fanned out in an ever-increasing delta behind the truck. Much of my body and face were covered in its rancid ooze, and I was now locked into taking the direction through the septic slick. If I had changed course and come from a different direction at this point, he would surely smell me coming. It was the longest belly crawl I had ever done in my life.

As I got closer to the truck the sound of the continuous glopping, splattering, and bubbling increased dramatically. So too did the depth of the septic muck in which I was crawling. I could no longer feel the ground beneath me, but instead nearly floated on this thick carpet of ooze. I decided at that point to follow the full flow of the stream, and come up under the truck by using the steady stream of sludge to mask my approach and my sound. The closer I got, the thicker and warmer became the ooze. I wondered how many days this tank had sat in the hot sun, and I worried what diseases I might pick up from latterly bathing in it.

Such as it was, I had at least become accustomed to the stench. My gagging did not occur that often now.

Finally I made it to where the outermost stream of ooze hit the ground on its journey from the high rear nozzle of the truck. Through the splatter and spray of the vile glop, I could see the man standing back from the truck and to the far side. It was apparent that he did not want to go back to the nozzle area until all the sludge had been dumped. I kept going forward, keeping the flow of ooze between me and the man, but staying so close to the flow that part of my shoulder and body were fully in its course. It was very difficult to see him through the haze of splattering and spraying sewage. I could not wipe my eyes, for that movement would certainly alert him to my presence. As the sewage sprayed in my face, and the vile smell nearly gagged me, I made it all the way up to the truck. I did not care if the sewage sickened me, for I would gladly sicken and die, more than gladly crawl through vile sludge, for the earth.

I slowly moved up to the front end of the truck and out to the passenger door, which was on the opposite side of the truck from the man. Chemical Man, as I began to call him, just sat on a tree stump back from the truck and upwind from the sludge, watching his handiwork run out into the landscape. I realized from his position that he had been looking at me the whole time but never saw me. Even if he did see something move, the last thing he would have thought of was a human. I reached in through the open window of the truck and carefully pulled the shotgun off the rear rack. It had been my primary objective to get the gun away from him in case he flew into a violent rage again. I moved back under the truck and dismantled the shotgun completely. Each part I buried in a different location under the truck, completely covering all tracks of digging.

I then slithered back to the rear of the truck, listening for any sound of the man moving. It was quite difficult to hear anything above the constant gurgling and hissing of the draining truck. I took the chain out of my sewage-soaked bag and wrapped it around the rear axle of the truck, then secured it with the padlock, leaving the end coiled loosely inside the rear wheel. No sooner did I get the chain coiled than I heard Chemical Man start the truck, and I began to grow concerned that he was going to drive off. Yet I didn't think that he would, since the sewage was still dripping from the valve, though at a much slower rate. I suddenly heard the sound of some kind of pumping device running, and the sewage began hissing and spitting from the rear of the truck, giving off a tremendous spray.

I watched Chemical Man now walk back to his original location to watch the remainder of the tank's contents drain out. I took the opportunity to move again to the cab and remove as many of his tools as I possibly could, and with the covering sounds of the spray I cast them out into the forest as far as I could. Even though one of his wrenches made quite a racket when I accidentally hit a thick patch of brush, he never even looked up, such was the sound of the running engine and pumping sewage. I moved again to the rear of the truck, where my chain was, and began to explore for the pumping mechanism. It did not take me long to find that the pump was nothing more than an in-line apparatus, not an engine-drive like I first assumed. It dawned on me that he did not start the engine to run the pump, but to keep his battery from running down while the pump was running.

The drainage pipe of the truck came from just forward of the tank's centerline, and ran externally back to the rear. The pump was located just where the drainage pipe emerged from the tank. I could feel the wires connected to its rear side, though the connection was not a professional job. I assumed that Chemical Man had installed this pump on his own, judging from the poor welding and makeshift wiring. I first uncoiled the chain so that it lay along the outside edge of the truck, and covered it with pine needles and sand for camouflage. Then, without hesitating because the tank sounded like it was nearing empty, I reached up under the pump and pulled out the wires. The pump went dead and the sewage spray died off to a dribble.

I deftly moved to the rear of the tire, and waited. Chemical Man did not at first notice that the pump had died, but soon he was on his way to the truck. I could hear him tapping the side of the tank to see if in fact it was empty, but the sound told him that there was still some sludge left. He then went into the cab of the truck and stayed there for quite a while, apparently playing with the pump switch or fuses. Finally the engine was turned off and I could see the beam of the flashlight emerge from the corner of the front wheel. I froze against the truck as he crawled under and shined the light on the pump. He worked his way up under the chassis and felt around for the wiring. Listening to a string of curse words, I could tell that he had found the pulled wires, but I do not think at this point that he suspected it was done by anyone. The wires had been so poorly attached in the first place he probably thought they had come loose with the vibration.

He kicked out from under the truck grumbling to himself, reached in his pocket, and pulled out a small pocketknife. He went back again under the truck and while lying on his back and holding the flashlight in his mouth he began to strip the wires. I slipped around the outside of the rear tire and gently lifted the chain that lay beneath his left leg. Very carefully I pulled the chain down so that just the very end was near his ankle. As slowly and carefully as possible I lay the end of the chain over his high boot, brought up the other end, then slipped the padlock through and locked it without a sound. I then backed away from the truck, and headed to where Chemical Man had originally been sitting while he watched the dumping process.

He worked on the wiring for about ten minutes before he began to emerge from underneath. He stood all the way up without noticing the tight chain around his boot. I simply said, speaking in a rather calm voice, "Haven't you done enough damage to my woods?" He turned on the flashlight and let out a gasp, dropping it to the ground where it went out. I could hear him fumbling with the light, tapping it as he tried to get it to light. I slipped away into the brush and waited. The light came on again and he scanned the area, erratically and frantically moving the beam at first, but then just sweeping. I watched him as he turned the light back to the area where I sat, then suddenly he bolted for the cab. He took two quick steps, the chain went tight, and he fell hard to the ground. I could hear him cussing and grappling as it sank into his drunken consciousness that he was trapped.

He was belligerent as he stood, infuriated at the chain around his ankle. He bellowed, "When I find you I'm going to kill you!" I said nothing but just lay and watched. I could see him yanking at the chain in a frenzy, then trying to take off his boot. After a while he cut away his boot with his little pocketknife, then finally slipped out of the lower part, which now looked like a shoe. He tried to work the chain down over his ankle but it was just too tight. Now even more enraged he tried to get into the cab of the truck, but the chain would not even reach the edge of the door. He groped frantically for some tools that were lodged between the cab and the tank, but they too were far out of reach. He finally boiled over in a frenzy of rage, kicking and screaming obscenities like a little kid throwing a temper tantrum.

Finally he began to calm down and I chuckled out loud. There was no doubt that he heard me for he began to curse me out, telling me to come out and fight like a man. I answered him simply, saying, ''The wilderness will be what you're going to fight now, my friend. I have nothing to do with it. You have been killing the earth for a long time now. It is time that the earth starts killing you.'' I did not show myself or say another word to him. I just slipped back into the muck where he could not see or hear me and moved out into the deeper forest. I had a real tough time washing all of the sewage from me. I did not want to pollute the waterways so I had to haul buckets of water and wash off while standing in a knee-deep hole. The sun had broken the horizon by the time I had gotten cleaned up and back to camp.

I slept for a few hours and then headed back to the truck. I had no worries about anyone finding him, for in that case he would surely have a lot of explaining to do. I approached the truck slowly, taking care to note any changes. Once satisfied that all was the same, I got into position where I could closely view the situation. Already the pounding heat of the day was turning the sandy ground into an anvil. The constant drone and buzz of flies around the sewage and the choking smell had enveloped the entire scene. The ground around the truck was all torn up from Chemical Man's struggle to free himself through the rest of the night and well into the morning. He now lay asleep, leaning up against the rear tire. His face appeared so contorted with pain, and his lips were parched. I decided to go in for a closer look.

Knowing that he could not get anywhere near the cab, I stalked around to the passenger side and went through his truck. Being careful not to awaken him, I found out where he lived and where he worked by the information he carried with him. He had a picture on his dashboard of himself and what looked to be his wife and two children, apparently in their early teens. I wondered to myself how he could ever explain to his children that he was destroying the earth and possibly killing his grandchildren in the process. I wondered if he even knew the far-reaching impact of what he was doing, or was he just trying to take any job that would feed his family. Looking further through his truck I found his wallet. In it was probably more money than I had seen in any one place in my life and also the registration for a late-model Cadillac, in his name.

There was no doubt in my mind now that he was not doing this just to keep his family alive. I put everything back the way it was, satisfied to know his real name and where he lived. That gave me a lot of bargaining power. I then returned to my vantage point and watched him slip in and out of tormented sleep for a good part of the day. Once he awoke with a jolt, looked around to determine where he was, tugged at the chain almost to see if it was still real, and then slipped back to sleep. I felt tormented myself, watching him there baking in the sun. No matter what he had done, nothing deserves to suffer. Yet I was torn between letting him go back about his business of killing my wilderness or teaching him a lesson. I certainly was not going to allow him to die, just to let nature be the judge.

I headed back to my camp and camouflaged up again, so that not even my own mother would have known who I was. I then grabbed a wooden bowl and a water bladder and headed back to the truck. When I arrived I saw him standing at the rear of the truck, head lowered, kicking at the dirt. The ground around him said that he had been awake for quite some time but there was no new evidence of any struggle since the night before. His body language and attitude had certainly also changed. He no longer held himself in his typical arrogant manner, but now looked like a whipped puppy. His actions were not unlike a man who had been condemned to die. I watched him for a long time. I thought that I even heard a hushed sniffle coming from him, so he might have been crying. I felt so bad for him again.

I whistled and he turned with a start. He looked directly at me with a shocked expression on his face; he was startled not only by my whistle, but also by my camouflage. Within moments he regained his composure and his sheepishness turned to arrogance. He lunged toward me grabbing, but the chain pulled tight and he fell to the ground cursing. I didn't say a word to him, but just sat down on the ground and stared at him, or rather through him. He cursed at me venomously, telling me that if he got free of the chain he would beat me to death. I reached out my hand to him and he grabbed it hard. The consciousness of the wolverine and the animal within, combined with all the years of working out, cutting wood, and other physical activity, suddenly surged into my hand. Slowly I began squeezing, smiling as he looked at me in utter disbelief. I felt his bones beginning to crush together as he let out a cry of pain. I let him go without a word.

I then rose from the ground and pretended that I was going to walk away. He cried out, "Please, my God, please don't leave me here to die." I turned and smiled at him again, without saying a word. I walked over to a nearby bush where I lifted out the bowl and water bladder. He watched longingly as I poured and took a long drink. It was not to tease him, but to show him that it was not poison. Still without a word I filled the bowl and placed it on the ground in front of him. He lifted it and gobbled the water like a man that had just crossed Death Valley. As he put the bowl on the ground I refilled it and he drank again, though this time much slower. He then looked at me and asked, "What are you going to do to me? Are you going to leave me here to die? I have a family." I said nothing but let him stew in his words.

He asked again, and this time I answered him. "I don't know what I am going to do. To punish you for destroying this sacred land with your vile chemicals and now human waste, I should let the land have its way with you. You should lie here alongside your own sewage. Or then again, I might leave you chained here and go call for the police. After all, the truck is registered in your name, the crime is obvious, and I wonder what your wife and kids are going to say. I wonder what your neighbors are going to say when they throw you in jail. Possibly I should just do both; leave you here to suffer until you are nearly dead, and then call the police. Then I would be sure that you will never dump in these sacred forests again."

I watched the horrified look on his face as I related all the options I had concerning his predicament. He begged me again to please let him go and said that he would never dump again. He confessed to me that he had done it all because of greed. He made a good living in his regular job but he had wanted more. I asked him then, "At the cost of killing your grandchildren?" He looked dumbfounded, and I answered his unspoken question, saying, "You have killed so many areas of the Pine Barrens. Your children cannot camp here anymore, the waters now run vile, and your grandchildren will never even be able to swim in the streams or wander in these woods. You have stolen that freedom from them. The legacy you leave them is not success, but a land raped and defiled."

I watched the tears beginning to well up in his eyes. I

could tell that they were from his heart, for it was the first time that he had ever thought about the full impact of what he was doing. I spoke to him again, this time with a sense of love and compassion in my voice. I said, "All of this for greed? Don't you realize that the choices you make today will affect your children and grandchildren tomorrow? Instead of killing the earth you should be saving it. If you want your children to live successfully, then give them a pure world to become successful in. I know who you are and where you live. You have destroyed my home, these sacred lands. I should be angry, but right now all I feel is pity. I don't think that you will be returning to your old ways."

I stood slowly and looked at him long and hard. He looked back at me sheepishly; the sense of sorrow exuded from his every pore. He began to ask again, "What will you do with me—?" But I cut him short and said, "I, unlike you, trust people. In my heart I know that you have seen what scars you have left on the earth, and I know that your heart will tell you to do what is right." I reached in the little pouch on my loincloth belt, grabbed the key, and tossed it to him. He looked at it lying in his hands in utter disbelief. I then said, "The stream is clean just up from your truck. Get yourself cleaned up before you leave, and hurry, 'cause your wife and kids will be worried." I then just turned and slipped away.

CHAPTER 10

ALIEN KILLER

They told me he was a veteran with a dishonorable discharge, now a soldier of fortune who had returned only a few months back from some small drug war in South America. They said that he was an expert survivalist who could live off the land indefinitely, using no tools or weapons. He was a sniper, a tracker, and a master of camouflage and disguise. He was said to be one of the best at escape, evasion, and resistance. A black belt, a known hired assassin, and extremely dangerous. The way that the police and sheriff's deputies were describing this guy he could have been a modern-day superhero, capable of leaping tall buildings in a single bound. Judging from the fear in their voices as they filled in the details, they sort of held him in awe. I only giggled when they listed all of his vicious credentials.

Well, our action hero was on the run in the wilderness and had now been gone for the better part of two weeks. Rumor had it that he was going to head up to Canada and that he'd vowed to never be taken alive. He had killed two known drug dealers, and in a fit of rage he had killed his young girlfriend and her infant son. He was considered, of course, very armed and dangerous. He had successfully eluded police and other law enforcement officials, and no one had even found a track. Not even the dogs could trace him from where he had discarded his pickup truck, for it had rained for days before they had even found the truck. They told me that the heavy rains had washed away all scent, and probably all tracks. They simply said that they could not see what good I was going to be able to do.

I guess they figured that he was long since gone from this part of the country and was well on his way to Canada, for they gave me just two deputies as backup. Each of them shouldered a heavy pack, heavy clothing, a heavy hunting rifle, and side arms as we left that first morning and headed into the wilderness. They had looked at me long and hard when I showed up to meet them with just a pair of wool pants, moccasins, and a buckskin shirt on. One of them asked me if I was planning to pick up my pack someplace in the woods. I could tell that these two men had respect for me because I had come so highly recommended, but still there was a reserved skepticism in their manner. We were not into the bush two hours when they began to complain that I was moving too fast. Within four hours I had left them far behind.

I knew nothing of the man I was tracking other than

the horror stories I had been told. At best, I knew that these stories were just that, hearsay inflated out of fear. From what I had seen in watching military training exercises, and having trained military groups on and off, it was easy enough to judge what route he was likely to have taken. Without any hesitation, and after losing the liability of my excess baggage—my backup team—I headed right to the area where any escaping prisoner would surely go. I had located his trail not five hours after I had first entered the wilderness, and I arrived at his first camp area within the next two hours. From all indications of his tracks, he was more aware than most people, but inept as far as I was concerned. His camp was a disgrace. So many mistakes for such a colorful and frightening fighting machine.

To save time, I foraged along the way so that I would not have to stop and prepare a meal. I took water whenever I crossed a spring, thirsty or not. My camps were nothing more than quickly made debris huts, and I slept in catnaps. As I got to know his trail, his habits, and his level of skill and awareness, I began to take shortcuts across his trails, knowing exactly where I would intersect his next trail. This allowed me to make up considerable time and take just a few hours to do what he had done in days. Slowly but surely I was closing the gap between us. At one point I saw he had become confused, for he nearly wandered in a huge circle before he realized his mistake. Apparently he was trying to get around a ridge and misguessed the distance; at least, that was how it appeared to me. So too, I inferred from his direction and actions that he was not heading toward Canada at all. It was possible that he was actually heading to Mexico.

The longer I stayed on his trail, the more convinced I was that my assumption was right. He was heading to Mexico. Though it was a longer distance to Mexico than to

Canada, he was probably using this fact as an evasive technique. Everyone would most certainly expect him to go to Canada. But winter was coming, and coming hard. It was already late fall and the landscape had been battered by snow squalls, freezing rains, and high winds. To survive in the wilderness area of Canada at this time of the year would take Grandfather's skill and knowledge. This man was far from that level. No wonder he was making the trek to Mexico. Not only would the authorities not be looking for him there but it would be a much easier climate to survive in. I also began to assume that he might have friends waiting for him there, since the stories had said he was involved in some drug wars.

By the third day I knew that I was only a day behind him. His pattern was to travel three days and rest a full day. Mine was not to rest, but not to get burned out either. His tracks showed his confident attitude, and I could also clearly see that he was following a map and compass course. His awareness level was even worse than I first thought, for several times he had jumped off the trail just as backpackers or outfitters on horseback would come into view. It was obvious that he knew little of the voices of nature through the language of concentric rings. He was only mildly aware of tracks, and practically unaware of everything else. He was just a good camper as far as I could see, and even here he left a lot to be desired. Most of all, I could see that his supposedly superhuman strength and stealth were not superhuman at all. Just a little above average.

I should have known better. What society considers a good woodsman and survivalist, Grandfather considered inept. Yes, in the modern world he would have been considered great, an expert, and very deadly, but to a scout he was an alien. He did not belong in the wilderness, he knew it and I knew it. Without his modern technology, his weaponry, and his high-tech camping gear he could not survive, and I was certain of that fact. To me he was like a scuba diver, an alien to his own planet. Without the umbilical cord of the backpack that reached back to society he would be no better off than a scuba diver out of air. No wonder there was so much apprehension in his track patterns. It was so obvious why he guarded his backpack as if it were made of solid gold. He knew full well that if he made any mistakes he would certainly be dead.

I caught up to him by the evening of the sixth day. I could just see his little fire nestled deep in a thicket alongside a stream. He was smart enough to build his fires after dark and keep them shielded from the air by putting them beneath a rock overhang. But the faint glow was unmistakable. I knew from his pattern that this was going to be the place he rested for the next day. The camp area was well chosen to escape detection, he had running water and several springs nearby, and the surrounding landscape was such that he could see someone coming from a long way off. There was no doubt that he was settling in and no doubt about his intended way out when he did leave. I could also easily guess his emergency escape routes. Looked like the only thing he had not planned for was me.

I camouflaged myself, using the charcoal and ash from an old, abandoned camp area. Normally it would have infuriated me that someone had left a camp area with a mound of ash unburied, but I thanked whomever it was that left this one for me. I was lucky to have a totally moonless sky, and no snow had yet accumulated on the ground, so I did not have to take much care in covering my tracks. I had no real plan as to what I was going to do, other than to observe the Alien Killer, as I now called him. I was

unarmed, and for all I knew, my backup deputies were lost
someplace many days behind me, or possibly crushed under
the weight of their packs. I knew, however, that knowledge
was more than half the battle when dealing with this kind
of situation, so I was determined to gather all the information I possibly could.

I checked the tracks that went down off the ridge trail,
and nowhere was there any indication that he suspected
anyone of following him. That was in my favor. I had been
shot in the back while tracking a killer once before because
I had failed to notice that he suspected someone was following him, and I was not about to make that mistake
again. I took the most open route to Alien Killer's camp
area, fully exposed to him. Not a tuft of grass or a rock
blocked his view of me and I was dead certain that if he
saw me I would surely be killed. This was not a time for
any mistakes, sloppiness, or chances. I had little respect for
his skills and less respect for him, but he was more aware
than most and that was a critical factor. I could not allow
complacency or overconfidence to enter my consciousness
at all.

I easily got to within ten yards of him, taking cover in
a small thicket that blocked his camp from the open area
through which I had come. I watched him sitting by the
fire, his camouflage-pattern tent pitched near the river and
his pack and rifle close by. The whole layout of his camp
was wrong. Not only was it not that well hidden, but putting
the tent so close to the water was against all camping prin-
ciples. Yes, he was better than most, but his camping style
indicated blatantly his lack of refined skill. I watched him
go in and out of acute awareness as the night would periodically erupt with sounds of animals moving. Several
times he stood quickly and grabbed his gun, ready to fire
at anything that might approach. His time was split between

reacting to the sounds and periodically studying a map that he kept in the pants pocket of his fatigues.

I stayed there until he finally went to sleep. He pulled his pack, gun, and everything else inside his tent, but did not zip up the door. I suspected this was so he could stay aware of what was going on outside and could make a moment's escape if need be. He also seemed to sleep with his clothing and boots on, though I could not be sure, but probably also to facilitate a quick retreat. As he slipped off to sleep, no doubt exhausted from his trek, I thoroughly explored his camp area proper. I found that he was eating dehydrated foods and was treating his water with Halazone tablets. That answered my question why he had not yet become sickened from the poor sources of water that he was drinking. He also had overlooked an important part of his equipment when he retired. He had left the bottle of water purification tablets next to the rock where he sat. As I left camp I took them with me without a second thought.

Now I was certain of several things. First, if he continued to get water where he had been, he would certainly come down with an intestinal distress that could prove to be his undoing. Second, if he was using those tablets so he would not have to search out better water supplies, then he would now have to slow his trek so as to find better water. But the biggest issue in my mind would come up when he discovered the tablets missing. Would he notice that they were gone right away, would he assume that they were in his pack and not find out until later, and ultimately would he think that he had just misplaced them or that someone had taken them? I figured that he would just think that he had misplaced them, especially if he did not find them missing until his next camp. Before I left his camp I had dumped out his canteen of treated water and replaced it with water from a near-stagnant pool just downstream of his camp.

After hiding the tablets, I then went to his probable route of travel out of this little valley. On a high trail that looked down a sheer rock wall, I set a bent-branch trip wire. It was time-consuming to make the trap the exact way I wanted it, but it would certainly do its job. Unless he closely inspected it after it had sprung, he would not know this was a trap at all, but probably a bent branch that had come free naturally. It was late by the time I settled in for the night and I wanted to get plenty of sleep for the next day's trek. I wanted to make damn sure that he was more tired than me. Though I had learned to work with extreme fatigue many times before, this was a life-or-death struggle and I needed to stay in top condition.

I awoke abruptly to the sound of footfalls very near to where I slept. My shelter was nothing more than a deep pile of forest litter piled into an opening between two boulders. I could just see outside through a small opening I had purposely left for my eyes. It was full light and the horrible realization that I had slept late overwhelmed me. I also knew that someone was wandering quite close to me and I froze motionless. Though I was well hidden and my shelter looked just like any natural accumulation of debris, I could take no chances. The footfalls continued to get closer and closer to the opening between the boulders. Finally Alien Killer showed himself, walking slowly past the opening, glancing in briefly as he passed. In his hand he held a small, pistol-type crossbow, and he was obviously hunting. It was also obvious that he brought along the crossbow for just such an occasion. He could not take the chance of firing a gun and having someone hear him.

He moved on as quietly as he could in his heavy, military, lug-sole boots. I almost laughed out loud as I watched him disappear around the rock. I listened as the concentric rings of nature moved away from me and disappeared back in the direction of his camp. Once I was sure that the animals were telling me that he was back in his camp, I moved out. The voices of nature had told me that there was now considerable activity in his camp area so I knew that I had to hurry. I got to the place where I could look down and see him; his entire camp had been packed up and he was now on the move. As soon as he disappeared along the outer side of the ridge trail, I moved down to his camp for inspection. It was apparent from the way he covered the fire area and his tracks that he would not be back. He had broken his routine for some reason. Yet there was no indication in his tracks that he thought anyone was following him, or that anything out of the ordinary was going on.

His route took him right to the very trail I had predicted he would take out of this little valley. He carefully picked his way along, sticking close to the cover beside the trail just as I had imagined he would. He was determined not to be seen by aircraft or anyone else, always leaving himself a way out. I worked my way high above him and onto an open ridge, moving with the large boulders and talus, again the least-expected route of travel. No one would believe that anyone could follow there, especially in the open talus areas. There was little cover and too much chance of starting a landslide. I eventually worked my way well out in front of him and to a place where I could get a clear view of the trap area. I wanted to make sure that the trap did its job, and that afterward he had no suspicion that he had actually tripped a man-made trap.

He moved along the edge of the tiny trail with extreme caution, being careful not to jar loose any overhanging talus, or come too close to the edge of the cliff. He never saw my trap but blundered right into it as expected. He hit the trigger branch, which in turn released the branch, which swept across the slope. Rocks, talus, and rotting logs began giving way and sliding toward him. He held onto the sweep branch just as I expected he would, the only way he would not go over the cliff. So too did he let go of his rifle, and it careened over the edge, hitting boulders and shattering bits of gun stock and scope all the way down. Eventually in the final long fall it smashed on a huge flat rock and the stock broke from the rifle barrel completely. There was no doubt in my mind that the rifle was inoperable.

As soon as the landslide stopped Alien Killer hoisted himself back up to the trail and looked around for his rifle. It took him a while but he finally spotted it far down the slope. Taking his binoculars out of his pack he looked long and hard at the rifle and I could tell that he was torn between retrieving it and just going on. It was obvious that his training had gotten the better of him, but I could not understand why. One part of him should have wanted to get out of there because of the landslide and the possibility of alerting people to his whereabouts. The other part of him wanted to see if he could salvage the rifle and if not, to bury it so no one would find it and figure his location and ultimate destination. He chose the latter and began to work his way around and down the treacherous slope.

I watched his progress. Once, the rocks gave way and he hurled down the slope in a deadly slide, bouncing off several anchored boulders, which jarred his body quite hard. When he arose from that fall his walk had a definite limp. The limp definitely indicated a knee and ankle injury to the right leg, which was his dominant side. This would severely handicap him in what routes and how fast he could travel. I watched as he first picked up the rifle barrel, then the shattered and broken stock, and finally the clip. He sat for a long time on the slope attempting to put the rifle back together. Even from my distant vantage point I could see clearly a bend in the barrel. I knew there was no way that he could ever use that gun. He then went about burying the rifle, and I marked the position of its burial with a prominent landmark. We might need that rifle later for conviction purposes.

He now limped on, moving diagonally back up the slope to the end of the trail beyond the talus slope. I could tell that the injury was aggravating him to no end, and I could see his temper flare now and then. Yet he still stayed close to the various brush tangles and boulders to prevent detection. By the time he got back on the trail just where it crested the low ridge, he was clearly exhausted. I watched him take a long drink from his canteen. The sound the canteen made as he put it down beside him told me that it was nearly empty and he would soon need more water. Fortunately for me the landscape indicated that the nearest water was quite some distance away. This would certainly put him on the edge of extreme thirst and increase the difficulty of his journey. It would also give the polluted water time to work on his system.

I followed him well into the day. His pace got slower and slower and he had run out of water long before. The wilderness was beginning to beat him up and he was losing his arrogant confidence. My philosophy of following him was quite simple. I would allow him to get way ahead of me, listening to the voices of nature telling me his position. Then I would take the quickest route there, cutting miles off his trail. He was getting very weary and I was fresh and well rested. He finally made camp late in the afternoon, again near a small stream. I watched him as he filled his canteen and then groped around in his pack for the water purification tablets. He nearly had taken the entire pack apart before he would accept the fact that the tablets were gone. Yet he must have assumed that he had either lost them along the way or left them back at his last camp. No paranoia appeared to arise in his actions.

I knew from the personality of the stream that no close springs would be along it. It ran slowly and no doubt would be filled with more microorganisms. I watched as he washed his face, removed his pants, and soaked his leg in the stream for a long time. From my position I could see that his knee was bloody and his ankle discolored, though it was not really that bad. Just enough to slow him down and humble him, I thought. As the day slipped into night I watched him take water from the stream and boil it on a little propane stove he had. As it boiled I watched him take some toilet paper from his pack and quickly hobble to the other side of a big boulder. He did not dig a small hole as was his normal practice, but as soon as he lowered his pants I could hear the sputtering sounds of diarrhea. The bad water had now done its job.

I watched him return to camp and pull several vials out of a first-aid kit. No doubt he came prepared with some diarrhea medication and an antibiotic. I figured correctly. He did not realize he was surrounded by several wild medicinal plants which would work far better than anything he carried in his pack. The limitations of his knowledge were becoming dramatically apparent. Still, I had to give him credit; he was one of the best I had seen coming from society. Most would have considered him an expert, but what society considered an expert and my interpretation of an expert were vast oceans apart. I saw all his actions revolving around his backpack, that lifeline. He treated it like his most cherished possession, never leaving it out of sight for very long.

I found a camp and settled in early, even before full dark. I didn't want to sleep in, and I wanted to be near his

camp before he awoke the next morning. My plan, though
not fully formed in my mind, was to do to Alien Killer
something similar to what I had done to Chemical Man,
though I was not going to be so easy on Alien Killer. I
don't know what made me despise him so much. Part of it
was because he killed people, especially a helpless child,
but the other part was that the general public thought his
skills were so damn good. I got so tired of hearing how
good someone was in the wilderness only to find that they
had little skill, and were still aliens to the earth, kept alive
by their high-tech camping gear and firearms. All my life
I was a purist, feeling that to truly be a child of the earth
one had to enter the wild places with nothing, naked, and
flourish no matter what the topography or weather condition. Everyone else had to bring everything in with them.

I was awake and at Alien Killer's camp well before first
light. I settled into position to watch his movements as he
awoke. I knew now that all he had in the way of protection
was a handgun, the crossbow, and a large, military-type
hunting knife. The hunting rifle had been my biggest concern, for he could use it to kill me at incredible distances.
This way he could only kill me if I was close to him and
that was only if he could see me. That seemed unlikely
unless I made a blatant mistake. I watched him slowly
crawl out of his tent and immediately head to his latrine
area. Judging from the ground around it, the medication
had not yet taken effect and he was still locked in the grip
of diarrhea. I could also see that his injured leg had stiff-
ened up on him and was getting worse. He no longer boiled
his water; I watched him take a cup of water directly from
the stream and drink it without hesitation.

I watched him go through the slow process of packing
up his camp. He got everything in order, checked his pistol,
and began to erase the indications of his camp. The job he

did was worse than the last, and I could tell that it was rushed. Before he even finished covering the fire, he hobbled quickly to his backpack, removed the toilet paper, and quickly hobbled around the boulder. Without hesitation I slipped deftly into his camp and took his backpack, being careful not to step on any soft ground. I was well up on the rocky hillside when he returned and discovered his backpack missing. He quickly drew his gun and looked about, head and body following the barrel of his pistol in classic military style. He glanced around all the typical hiding areas carefully, but never gave my true location a thought. I then watched him search the ground for telltale tracks, but he abandoned it with disgust and backed away into the brush on full alert.

All he had now were his pistol, his knife, map and compass, and whatever else he carried in his pockets. His actions were those of a man running out of time. I could sense the confusion and apprehension in his movements. I could also see him fighting back terror. He now moved deep into the bushy landscape, refusing to enter any open area. He eventually moved into the forest and attempted to put distance between himself and whoever was out there stalking him. I followed him my usual way, watching as he tried to cover his trail, reversed course, backtracked, and used the waterways as much as possible just in case bloodhounds were involved. His movements through the woods were damaging and exhausting to his body. He did not move fluidly, and he treated the landscape like an enemy instead of a place of security.

I did nothing for the next two full days and nights except follow him and watch the wilderness persecute his very soul. He had not eaten a thing; though he tried to kill a rabbit with a stick and catch a fish with his bare hands, he was not successful. He drank from every stream and waterway he could find, trying desperately to replace the water in his body that the diarrhea was taking away. The nights had been very cold and he slept hardly at all, shivering beneath a thin covering of leaves that he had piled up. At least he had the right idea, but he did not know how much debris was needed for a proper shelter. His only relief came from the fires he built at night, made with the waterproof matches he carried in his top pocket. He no longer took care in covering his camp area or his night fires. I could tell that he was losing confidence and beginning to make mistakes born of fear.

Beginning now the third day he was without his gear, the temperature began to climb. He had to rest frequently from the dehydration, and soon, in the full heat of the day, he decided to rest near a little stream. There he drank long and hard, for it was the first water he had come to since the morning. He made his next major mistake when he took off his shirt and went back to the water to wash his face and upper body. Quickly and deftly I slipped up from behind, grabbed the shirt, and disappeared into the thick underbrush. I found it ironic and unexpected how long it took him to realize that his shirt was missing. I would have thought that because it held his map, compass, and matches he would have protected it as well as he had his backpack. I assumed that he again felt safe, probably thinking he had outdistanced and outsmarted his pursuers.

I watched him walk over to where the shirt had been, look on the branch it had hung from, and then look at the ground beneath, figuring it had fallen. Immediately he grabbed his pistol and sank to the ground like a man who had just been shot at. He scanned the landscape as he backed up against the underbrush where I lay. It was then that I noticed his knife sheath was empty. He had left it lying by the water after he had washed, and forgotten to take it with him when he went for his shirt. He then hobbled quickly into the underbrush and I could hear him running through the thickets. I entered the little stream that was just a few yards from me, moved upstream, and easily took his knife. No sooner had I moved back downstream and into the thick brush alongside than he reemerged from the thicket. Cautiously he went directly to the stream bank where he had washed.

Still watching the landscape intently, he squatted as if he were going to pick up the knife but when he looked down it was gone. He let out a gasp and then ran blindly, as best he could on the injured leg, into the thicket again. I listened to his running, panting, and crashing slowly disappear deep into the forest. All he had left now were his pants, his boots, his blessed pistol, and a military-style undershirt. I knew now that it would only be a matter of time before he succumbed to the wilderness, and so did he. I felt that for the first time in his violent life he must have realized that he was not so great in the wilderness after all. He wasn't even a great warrior, for he had made far too many assumptions and mistakes. One of the scout laws was that you never underestimate your enemy. He felt that he was the best; thus, to him, his enemy was not that good.

His movements were nearly panicked, yet he still struggled to hold on to some sort of control. I could tell from his actions that he had been hunted before, but those who hunted him must have done it in a far different way. This was alien to him, and I knew that it frightened him, especially because he didn't know who was doing the stalking. The scouts always loved to use this fear of the unknown as a powerful weapon against their enemies. I knew at this point that the wilderness would certainly do its part in persecuting him, I had to do mine and get the pistol away from him, and, for that matter, whatever else I could take.

I wanted him fully exposed to the elements he thought he was lord over. I wanted him to feel his frailty, like the child he had so mercilessly killed. I wanted him to taste his vulnerability.

It did not take very long for me to get exactly the opportunity I needed. He had traveled through that night and all the next morning. He was obviously trying to put distance between himself and whatever stalked him. The day was hot again for the time of year and the exhaustion of the night's travel, the diarrhea, and the heat had gotten the better of him. He had no other choice than to lie down and rest. He looked blankly at the surrounding landscape, trying to find any sign of anything or anyone moving out of the ordinary. Satisfied that no one was about, he headed downhill to a stream that had been barely visible in the distance. When he reached the stream he nearly collapsed as he drank. Slowly he began to strip off his clothing, constantly staying as much on the alert as he could. His leg looked painfully swollen and very discolored. I could tell that he was going to enter the stream to both cool off and soak his leg. He piled his clothing neatly on the bank and sank into the water.

Even though his gun lay on top of his clothing and was in easy reach of him, it took very little effort or stealth at all to take them. I simply waited for him to fully submerge, then moved out and grabbed the clothing and the gun, and moved back into cover with ease. When he reemerged from the water and wiped his eyes, he saw that the clothing and gun were gone. He let out a horrified gasp as he stood and nervously looked around. He was right where I wanted him to be. Naked and fully exposed to nature in all of his splendid vulnerability. There was no doubt in his mind that someone was around—and close—but he had no idea where. He called out venomously, but I did not respond.

His only response was an increasing wind sifting through the pines, a wind that foretold an oncoming storm.

Now my job was finished and all I had to do was wait for nature to finish the sentencing. I was sure that it would not take long. I knew of many people who had his skills, veterans of wars that lived in the wilderness. These were guys who had given their all for their country, and on their own they learned how to survive. They had become children of the earth, but only by first abandoning their old ways of thinking. They knew not to be arrogant, nor to abuse the wilderness. Theirs was a consciousness of submission to the powers of wilderness, never a struggle but a surrender to her laws. Alien Killer was an embarrassment to them all, and now even to himself. His arrogance, and his belief that he was superior to the lowly beasts of the earth, were now being fully challenged and beaten. All he had left were his frailty, his vulnerability, and his struggle.

I continued following him through the next two agonizing days. Bone-chilling weather had moved in, with intermittent snow squalls and high winds. The days were gray, damp, and bleak, and the nights were so cold that ice began to form on the fringes of the waterways. The cloudiness caused Alien Killer to lose his bearings altogether, and now he was hopelessly lost. He was naked, freezing, starving, and badly beaten up. I watched his arrogance melt away as he realized that he was so close to a slow and agonizing end. When he finally reached the point where he could barely walk, I let him see me, standing high above him on a rocky outcropping. He must have thought that he was hallucinating, for he shook his head as though to see if I would disappear. He finally called out to me but I just disappeared into the rocks.

Finally late that last evening of his punishment, he collapsed. He babbled as I moved him into my shelter, yet he never regained consciousness. He slept for nearly the next twenty hours. When he finally awoke I gave him a hot herbal tea drink, one that would not only give him the much-needed moisture but would also drive away his diarrhea. He did not try to communicate with me in any way at first, but just took what I offered him like a feral puppy that had been saved from death. The next day he slowly began to regain his strength and I could see the fiery arrogance working back into his eyes. He first asked me where my camp and other gear were located, probably with the thought of eventually killing me and taking my gear. His expression dropped as soon as I told him that I had nothing.

He slept again for a long time, but this time in the morning I was gone. He searched around as he emerged from the shelter but found no food, water, or equipment. He looked horrified again. I let him see me far along the trail, and he cried out to me. "Wait, wait," he said, trying to get me to stop. I allowed him to come close, but not too close. He asked me, now out of breath, "What are you going to do with me?" I told him that I was going to do nothing. I wanted to get on with what I was doing and he could fend for himself. I also stated that everyone knew that he was supposed to be the great survivalist, so he should start surviving. As I walked away he limped after me begging, "Please don't leave me here. I'll die." I paid no attention but just kept going on, keeping far ahead of him, but not out of sight.

This went on for two more full days. I would forage something at night, pretend I had finished it, and go on, allowing him to finish the food. This kept him alive, but at subsistence level. I also pushed myself to make sure I could slip away and get some sleep before moving back onto the trail. He would eventually go to sleep in a bed of leaves when he gave up trying to find me. I also made sure that he saw me drinking only at the springs so that he would know where to find good water. There was no doubt in my mind that he would continue following me, for if he ever lost me he would surely die. I have no idea if he knew exactly where we were going or not, but my trek took me straight back to where I had originally begun the search.

On the last day, I walked up on my two backup deputies and nearly scared the hell out of them. One actually fell over the log he was sitting on and accidentally fired off his shotgun. They looked at me with their mouths open, nearly unable to speak. Finally one said, "We almost gave up 'cause we thought you were dead or something. Possibly even killed by that madman." I smiled as Alien Killer began hobbling toward us at the fastest pace he could muster, crying out, "Please don't shoot me. Don't shoot me! I give up."

The two men looked at me a little dumbfounded, unable to comprehend the strange image of a man hobbling toward them fully naked. I smiled and said, "Here's your expert survivalist and outdoorsman." I then told them where to find all of his things, and began to walk away. One of the deputies called after me, but I didn't stop. I walked back out into the wilderness, which was pure once again, and decided to stay for the winter.

CHAPTER 11

THE CITY

Cities, towns, and even subdivisions always literally terrorize me. I avoid them at all costs, and rarely enter them unless there is no other choice. They are chaotic and confusing, filled with ceaseless noise, traffic, and blind rushing. Pollution fills the air and the streets. Nature here is obscured or removed altogether. Concrete, glass, chrome, and tar create an imitation world, far removed from anything real or natural. It is a world of people caught up in the "American Dream," chasing the false gods of the flesh to hollow goals of wealth, power, and possibly fame. Along the wayside are the homeless, the

bums, and the poor. Broken people and broken lives, living on cold and impersonal streets where no one cares and no one helps. It is a world of high-power deals, violent crimes, killing, glitter, and filth. It is man at his worst.

The city to me was like the wilderness is to most other people. I was an alien, totally out of place and out of touch with its reality. To me it was the most vicious and terrorizing jungle on earth. I could not see how anyone could survive in it for very long. Yet, in a strange way, it intrigued me. I wondered often through my life how the street people, the homeless, and the hobos survived. Surely they had their own way of getting around and living off the city. I wondered what the street life was like, what one would have to know to stay safe, and what laws of this jungle were similar to the laws of nature. I had remembered Grandfather telling us about the time he had spent stalking a city and teaching some homeless people. It intrigued me when I heard him tell of his adventures and what he had learned. It seemed to me that stalking the city was a tremendous learning experience for him.

By far, the most terrorizing city of them all had to be New York City, and it was literally on my doorstep. As the crow flies it was only about hundred miles from the Pine Barrens, but throughout my childhood I rarely ever went there. Anytime my folks asked me if I wanted to go with them to see a museum, I turned them down flatly. The only museum that I would ever go to was the Museum of Natural History, and that was rarely. I loved the museum but I hated what I had to pass through to get to it. I loved the showcases of animals and artifacts, but I hated the sterility of the building itself and the crowds of people wandering about. At times I actually felt like I was going to suffocate, and once I remember getting so upset I threw up on the floor of its grand entryway. During the same trip, I first saw

Central Park, for that is where my dad took me after I got sick, so that I could get a breath of fresh air.

I was in my early twenties and between wilderness excursions when I began to consider the city and the people of the streets again, this time with a certain seriousness and curiosity. I felt that I had to live in that wilderness at least once in my life and learn all that I could about its ways. I wanted to know what Grandfather had learned about the city and to experience firsthand that which I so loathed. If nothing else, I would come away from the experience appreciating the purity of wilderness and the freedom of my life that much more. I began to ask my parents and their friends who actually worked in the city all about its personality. Within the span of a month I knew about the hobos and homeless of the Bowery, Central Park, and many other areas. I knew of Harlem, Greenwich Village, and many tourist attractions.

Even armed with all my newfound insights and information about the city, it took me a long time to work up the courage to go. At times I felt I would rather face a firing squad. I left for the city on a bus one day in mid-November. I took no money with me, nor any other supplies, just the old clothing that I wore. I decided not to wear my buckskins because that would only make me stand out. After years of going barefoot or wearing moccasins, my brother's tennis shoes felt like huge lead weights. Wearing clothing other than a buckskin was uncomfortable and I must admit that I felt strangely self-conscious, as if I was wearing a uniform of some sort. I chose to go into the city during the late fall and winter months because that would be the most trying time for a street person.

As the bus began to approach the Lincoln Tunnel, which ran into the city, I could feel my heart leap into my throat and I began to feel queasy. I struggled inside: one part of me wanted to go on to explore and learn, and the other part wanted to ask the bus driver to stop so I could jump out. As the bus passed into the Lincoln Tunnel I could feel my heart pounding in my chest, I began to sweat profusely, and my mouth went dry. Some of the passengers on the bus began to look at me strangely, as if I were diseased or something. It might also have been because of the way I was dressed. Everything I wore was old, tattered, and taken from an old Salvation Army box. I figured my outfit would blend in nicely but apparently not on the bus. On the bus, only my brother's sneakers seemed acceptable. For once I could fully imagine what Grandfather must have felt when he first encountered a city.

The bus reached its final destination, the Port Authority Terminal, shortly after 9:00 P.M. I had chosen the later arrival time because I wanted the cover of darkness and I thought that the city would be quieter. Was I in for a shock. The bus terminal literally bulged with people. I wandered about in a daze, trying to find my way out of the terminal. Everyone was going every which way, rushing, but seeming to go nowhere. It took me nearly half an hour to move through the crowds and find the doors to the street. In that short time I had been propositioned, panhandled, and closely scrutinized by the police. Just before I went through the doors to get to the street I found a five-dollar bill, just lying behind a garbage can. At first I didn't want to keep it, but my fear got the better of me and I tucked it in my pants.

I emerged onto the street and was met with a crush of people coming and going, pushing and shoving, and the sound of blaring horns, revving engines, and people shouting. Everywhere there seemed madness, a blinding rush and confusion of people, cars, buses, taxis, and even police on horseback. I had to struggle to get to the side of a building where I could get out of the way of the crushing crowds. I watched both in horror and morbid fascination as people rushed by. I was astounded by the impersonal and hostile attitude of everyone I saw. No one would look directly into my eyes, but looked away every time I looked at them. I made the mistake of making eye contact with a police officer and he looked back at me, arrogance written all over him. I looked at him more, trying to figure out what he was looking at. Suddenly he and another officer began to approach me. I smiled at them as they came up to me.

The officer I had been looking at grabbed me and threw me hard up against the wall. He screamed at me, saying, "What the f—— are you, some kind of faggot or something?" I was dazed, and could hardly speak, fumbling any words that came out. He didn't give me a chance to speak, but asked abusively, "What the f—— are you doing loitering around here? You hitting people up for money, faggot, or do you just want a boyfriend?" I tried to tell him that I just got into the city and I didn't know my way around but he would not listen. I then asked him which way should I go to get to the Museum of Natural History, trying to be as friendly as I could be. He threw me up against the wall again and shouted, "It's closed, —— hole!" He laughed and began to walk off with the other officer, who turned to me and said, "You had better get your a——out of here before we get back."

I left immediately, moving through people at a slow fox run. I shifted with the tides and waves of people, darted across intersections and down streets until I found a thinning in the crowds. I then began to ask people in what direction I could find Central Park. Most would not even look at, far less answer me. I finally heard one guy say "North" as he rushed off but I had no idea which way north was. I couldn't see the stars, the winds blowing through the city buildings couldn't be trusted, and I could not smell the direction of the water, the pollution of bus fumes and auto exhaust was so thick. I looked up and down the streets trying to see if there was any break in the buildings and frenzy, but there was no end. I knew if I walked long enough in one direction I would have to come to some place where I could get my bearings, but that might take me miles from where I wanted to go.

Finally, I spotted an old woman who was moving slower than the crowds and seemed out of context compared to the normal frenzy of motion. She was pushing a shopping cart full of clothing, boxes, and newspapers. I knew instantly that she was what they called a bag lady. I went directly to her and asked her to help me find Central Park. She looked at me wistfully for a long time without saying a word. I wondered if mine was the first kind voice she had heard in a long time. She finally sighed, told me to go two blocks up, hit Forty-second Street, make a left on Broadway, and follow it to the park. She went on without another word. I thanked her, but she never responded. I watched her as she approached a garbage can and began to root through the contents. I headed on up the street.

I now walked at a slower pace, a little more relaxed now that I knew where I was going. I began to study the personalities of the city and its people. They seemed to rush along in their own little worlds, cut off from everything around them, wrapped in fear, and afraid to communicate. I saw seas of unhappy, contorted faces, wrought in tension and worry. I watched subculture after subculture emerge and disappear. The city had layers of activity and social structure, worlds within worlds. There were the worlds of the panhandlers, the drug pushers, the drunks, the businesspeople, the entertainers, the hookers, the gays, the taxi drivers, the police, the opera-goers, the rich, the poor, and so many countless others, each stuck in their own world, each out of touch with the others.

Within a block I was on Forty-second Street, and was almost shocked by what stretched before me. This street was lit up brighter than all the rest, appearing almost as bright as daylight. I walked through another sea of people, past porn shops, hookers soliciting boldly, marquees advertising sex shows, pimps, pushers, all mixed in with the constant rush of every other imaginable type of person. I walked on as fast as I could, gathering in as much information as I possibly could without being obvious. I did not want a repeat of my earlier incident with the police, and some of these people would surely cut my throat without a second thought. I could see the Broadway street sign far ahead, and without looking back on this modern Sodom and Gomorrah, I turned onto Broadway and walked north.

Within a few steps I had entered another world. Here people were dressed in the finest clothes, limos sped by or dropped off people in front of theaters, and the pace was slightly slower. Finer stores now replaced the porn shops and sex theaters, and the hustling and panhandling were less obvious. I watched these people too, play the game, feigning laughter, and all the while deep inside they seemed to be empty. I could not understand the draw of this city or why people would put up with the facades, the hostilities, the rush, and the shallowness of life here. I wondered to myself as I walked if any of these people had ever seen the wilderness and if they had, how they could ever come back to this place. It was all so confusing, rushed, and overwhelming.

I finally reached Central Park and disappeared into its security. Though many people were about, the pace was leisurely and I was in vaguely familiar surroundings. Here at least, where the city merged with manicured nature, I had a better chance. A secure feeling immediately embraced me. I could move in this environment without being noticed, and though the concentric rings of nature were muffled here, they still spoke to me, telling me where all things could be found. In a way, being in Central Park would mean living not really on the street, but in a more familiar environment that would make survival easier. However, I wanted to spend my first several weeks here, using it as a starting point from which to get to know the city.

I searched a long time for the right place to make my camp. It seemed that some of the homeless people had taken up refuge in the naturally sheltered areas but their camps were not permanent. They were cardboard structures at best; some just slept on the ground covered with newspapers, blankets, coats, and anything else they could find. It seemed that at nearly every garbage can someone was foraging, and deep in the inner recesses, along quiet and seldom-used paths, prowlers and stalkers moved, no doubt awaiting an unsuspecting victim. In the span of a few hours I had already witnessed three muggings and countless drug deals. As time passed I was growing desperate for a place to camp. I had to make camp fully, gathering everything I needed and camouflaging it, before first light. At least now, as I pressed deeper into the park, the number of people lessened and the sounds of the city streets outside of the park grew strangely quiet.

I pushed on to the far edge of the swamp on the west side and looked over the concrete guardrail to see if I could find some landmark or street sign that would indicate my location. As soon as I looked out onto the road I found, to my surprise, that I was directly across from the Museum of Natural History. It was like seeing an old friend in a hostile place. I felt relieved and somehow I knew that my camp area would be close to this place. In what seemed to be no time at all I found a huge assortment of boulders and cliffs, which were a natural part of the landscape. Between two of the boulders I found a huge crevice that was large enough to accommodate me. Accumulated in this crevice was a huge pile of leaves and other debris that had never been cleaned out. It was an ideal place to spend the night. I burrowed in and went to sleep.

I awoke to the thunderous, abrasive sound of traffic noise and the movement of people. I could just see the sun high above me and I knew that it must be noon. I did not move until I checked out my surroundings; though I had long since trained myself to awaken at the slightest sound out of context with the surrounding noises, I could not fully trust the effects the city might have on my perceptions and training. Satisfied that everything was quiet around me I set out to explore the area and see if I could find another camp area, though this one was fine enough. I marveled at the amount of animals and plants that lived in the protection of the park. It would be all too easy to forage and hunt, but that was strictly against the rules I had laid out for myself at the onset of the trip. My first order of business was to find food, and water, but I was not going to forage garbage cans and dumpsters.

I stumbled across a restaurant not far from my camp and there found a hose coiled alongside the delivery entrance. I moved quietly to the hose, turned on the faucet, and drank, deep in the shrubbery and out of sight of everyone. I then set about finding fresh food that the restaurant was throwing out. This also did not take much time. I watched the kitchen help pile bags of food outside on the platform, ready to be taken to the dumpster, and within a few moments I stalked up, took some food, and retired back into the garden thicket to feast. My first real meal in the city was of baked potato, steak that was still warm, string beans, shrimp cocktail, and a slice of apple pie. It seemed to be a meal someone had ordered and returned because the steak was underdone. However, it was cooked exactly the way I would have ordered it. My compliments to the chef.

I was so full that I could fell my stomach bulge. As I sauntered back to my camp, staying off the trails and mostly out of sight, I watched the homeless and destitute foraging the garbage cans quite close to the restaurant. I was surprised that no one ventured behind it to where the good food was. I climbed a tall sycamore tree to watch the restaurant for a while, wondering why the homeless did not go there. The answer became painfully apparent when I watched a homeless man forcefully chased away by irate kitchen help. I could not understand why. After all, the food was to be thrown out anyway. Had these people no compassion for the starving homeless? Or did they just want these people to stay away and out of sight so that the wealthy clientele did not have to see them?

I slowly walked back to my camp, depressed over the lack of compassion I had seen, not only at the restaurant but in all parts of the city I had been thus far. As the day grew to a close I began to build my camp. I first dug into the soft ground in the crevice, where it naturally sloped back in under the larger boulder and made a natural overhang. I dug the pit about three feet deep and long and wide enough to easily accommodate my body. I then filled the pit with the most luxurious forest debris I could find, and covered over the top with thick branches and sticks that I had collected from the unkept areas of the park. Over this I put back the dirt and landscaped the whole thing so it looked natural. Finally I made a camouflaged door plug to conceal the entrance into my scout pit. Even to a trained tracker nothing would look out of place. I finished up long before first light.

For the next several weeks I explored the areas around the park and in the surrounding city communities. I watched the various worlds, the subcultures, of people living and operating within their realities. I learned the movements and personalities of muggers, the homeless, the various levels of businessmen and -women, the hard laborers, the street gangs, the pushers and drug dealers, the pimps, and the police. I watched them carefully, observing what drew their attention and what did not, their level of awareness, and what they were aware of. I defined their routines and ruts so that I could easily move around them in any city environment as adeptly as I was able to move in the wilderness. I tested various scout skills and techniques on them, only to find that I rarely had to modify anything. It became apparent almost immediately that the scout skills of wilderness were also applicable as skills of the city.

Once I learned the routines and deep ruts, I could establish my movements around people, seeking the invisibility of dead space. I learned how to move in the city out of the context of the immediate situation, though not so out of context that the flow of living would be disrupted, thus drawing attention to myself. Being of context in the city, as in the wilderness, was a scout art. The scout observes a routine, finds the weak point in that routine, and then enters the weak point and moves with it, thus becoming invisible to everyone. This dead space exists in both nature and the city. Even those people walking alone at night, fearful of attack or robbery, frightened and hypervigilant, still had countless dead spaces in which I could operate. Even those who stalked had this dead space. It is this use of dead space, this philosophy of being out of context, that creates invisibility. This was why I could so easily take food from the back of restaurants when everyone else could not.

I also learned to move anywhere and at any time within the city superstructure. I could move in and out of buildings, day or night, without being observed. I could slip past the finest security systems and guards with ease. All it took was to find that hole in their awareness, or in the system itself. I explored construction sites, museums, police headquarters, tourist attractions, and skyscrapers, whether they were open or not. I would even move across the rooftops of Harlem, watching the gangs below or even gathered on the roofs on which I stalked, without leaving a trace. I learned here in the city the same way I learned in the wilderness, through careful observation and strict application of the skills and philosophy of the scout. The city no longer terrified me, but became a vast playground, filled with excitement and adventure. Though not as powerful as the scouting experiences of wilderness, it was exciting nonetheless.

My first real friendship was with an old homeless man everyone called Johnny Popa. Ours was not just a friendship but an equal sharing of knowledge; yet to me he became like a Grandfather. What Grandfather was to the wilderness, Johnny Popa was to the city. He became my mentor, guru, and companion, always eager to learn and equally eager to teach anyone that would listen. He was like a father figure to everyone, especially to runaway kids that came to the city thinking they could start a new life. Johnny would eventually turn them onto the right path, and most who came under his wing would eventually go back home. What astounded me the most was Johnny's philosophy of life. In a way he was saying the same things Grandfather had, only in the context of the city instead of wilderness. The circumstances I met him under were rather bizarre and unexpected, especially for a man that possessed so much knowledge and potential.

I was stalking the subway late one night, watching the interplay between people—the dance of mugger and potential victim, the movements of drug dealers, and the general, diminished ebb and flow of life. I saw a man out of the corner of my eye moving about almost invisibly. I watched his actions for a long time, astonished that he could move with the city similar to the way I did. His actions riveted my attention to him and I watched for a long time. He looked so very old, but not feeble. Most of all the expression on his face was not the usual one, contorted from unhappiness and pain, that I saw on most faces of destitution. His face exuded radiance, peace, and happiness. His eyes held a sparkle of depth of understanding just as Grandfather's had, and like Grandfather's they seemed to look right into the very soul.

I slipped up to him, hoping that he would talk to me. I found through past experience that street people were a little reluctant to talk to anyone at first and they would have to get to know and trust you before they would open up. I actually trembled inside, fumbling with the right words to open the conversation, as I watched him foraging a garbage can. Suddenly, and I don't know why, I remembered the five-dollar bill I had found at the bus terminal long ago. I tapped him on the shoulder and he looked up at me smiling. I handed him the five-dollar bill and said, "Why don't you get yourself a good meal tonight?"

His expression changed dramatically to one full of pride as he eyed me up and down. He then said, "I don't need your money. I am a free man, unlike most out there who sold their souls to the gods of business and success. I worship no god of business, nor is my soul imprisoned by the laws of society."

I was hammered by his statement and set back. My act of compassion had been turned against me. I had no idea where my words came from, but they flowed out of me. I said "So you're a free man? Are you not imprisoned by your need for that garbage can, the city streets, and the castoffs of society? Are you not living on the wastes of that same system you so despise, thus becoming part of that system, like the rats of the city sewers? You too are shackled by those same rules that apply to others who work for the false gods of the flesh. You may have no person or corporation as a boss, but your boss is the routine in your life dictated by this throw-away society in which you live. If society dies, then like everyone in it, you would die. You are not a free man. I am the only truly free man that I know of."

He looked at me long and hard, jaw slack in amazement over what I said. He looked confused and taken aback by my statement. He finally said, "Where does such a young man come up with such profound knowledge?"

That became my opening and we walked and talked all through that night. I told him about my life in the wilderness and the teachings of Grandfather. I talked to him about my wanderings and my vision, and of the things I knew would surely transpire if society did not change its ways. I also told him what I was doing in the city and of the scout skills. He told me of his life. Of how the city was his wilderness and what his vision was. I was amazed. He had held a Ph.D. in engineering and had been employed by a large firm in the city. The city cost him his family, his sanity, and his dreams. He had realized that his job was leading nowhere. He had decided long ago, thirty-four years in fact, that he wanted to help people, so he took to the city streets.

It quickly became apparent to me what his vision in life

now was. He had tried to work within the cumbersome bureaucratic system that was in charge of helping the homeless and especially the runaways, but he had been restricted. Finally, in what I could only call a visionary experience, he decided that the only way to help these runaway kids was from inside their own world. So he took to the streets and began working his magic, not only with the runaways, but also with any homeless people, both individuals and families. He was like a father figure who would help guide their lives back to the mainstream of society, or, for those who did not want to abandon street life, he taught them how to live. I was amazed at his conviction and dedication to his vision and how he truly sacrificed all comforts and even himself to help others.

I began to show Johnny my world. I taught him how to forage the various plants in the park for medication and as dietary supplements. At the same time I taught him how to become a caretaker, knowing how and when to forage so as not delete the plants. When I eventually showed him my scout-pit shelter he was amazed and as excited as a child. I built him an identical pit farther up between the same rocks that I used. We joked that it was like a two-bedroom apartment—best of all, rent and landlord free. I also taught him how to move like a scout and out of context with the flow of the city. Thus he was soon able to gather food from behind the various restaurants just as I did. Though he still relied on society's castoffs, at least it was no longer the rotted garbage of the subways.

He also showed me his world and introduced me to many of the street people. He taught me the ways of the city, and how to move about in his manner. I watched him as he worked with people, especially the runaway kids, and how he worked miracles with them. He was able to reach kids that no one else could reach and send them back with a new philosophy of life. It was amazing how closely he resembled Grandfather in his actions and mannerisms. I knew without a doubt that this man was not only working in the flesh, but was a healer of spirits. A true shaman of the city streets. I learned much from him, both physically and spiritually. I realized that though on the surface it appeared that we were teaching each other, he was doing more of the teaching than I was.

My most powerful lesson from Johnny came when I brought him a young black boy that I had snatched from death. I had been wandering through the upper part of Central Park late one night when I was halted by a violent commotion not far ahead of me. I stalked to where I could get a good view of what was going on and to my horror I found a twelve-year-old black boy being held by an older black man. Two other men, one with a club and the other with a knife, were taking turns beating, cutting, and hitting the kid, who was now nearly unconscious. I had made it a personal law, even before I came to the city, that I would not get involved with anything. I would not allow myself to become a vigilante, for I wanted to remain invisible, and not disrupt the flow of this concrete jungle. Many times I had watched people being robbed at gunpoint, purses being snatched, drug deals taking place, and all manner of other violent criminal activity, and all I could do was to stand back and watch. It became an internal struggle not to intervene.

This was far different. A boy's life was on the line and my promise was only good until the point where my intervention could actually save someone's life. There was no doubt in my heart that this young man was going to die, and die painfully, unless I did something. For the first time since I had come to the city, the primal self thundered into my body, and the animal was released. I rushed down to the scene of the beating, grabbed the stick from the man, and, using the scout stick-fighting technique, beat him several times across the head and knocked him unconscious. With the stick I also broke the knife out of the other man's hand, smashing his forearm with a blow that sent his bone through his flesh. I then sent him into the world of the unconscious with a blow to the head. Both men were taken down before the third had a chance to drop the boy to the ground and react.

The man who had held the boy was a big man, apparently powerful. He lunged at me and I dropped the stick purposely while sidestepping his forward motion. He looked around, grinning confidently now that I had lost the stick. He lunged again and I grabbed both of his hands, crushed his fingers with the fury of the beast, wrenched his arms around till I could feel them break from the shoulder sockets, then smashed his face with my forehead. He joined his brothers in the land of the unconscious. I picked up the boy from the ground and carried him into the safety of the thicket, just as other gang members were arriving. I made sure that he was well hidden, and went back to see what the gang was going to do, the beast still raging within me. I was in a rage over the beating and slicing of the child's flesh. I doubted that he would live and I wanted to make them pay.

By the time I stalked back to the bushes, some of the gang members were helping their fallen heroes up off the ground. One big guy dressed in pimplike clothing seemed to be directing the operation now. He screamed at the three that they were supposed to kill the kid, not let him get away. He held a gun menacingly, and directed other members of the gang to fan out and search. As I expected, they took the easy routes along trails and I knew that the boy would be safe. As the last of the beaten men were helped away, only the leader remained, waiting for his searching men to return with the boy. He still held his gun defiantly. I grabbed a strong stick from the underbrush and with all the force of the raging animal, I threw it at the leader. The stick hit the gun hand squarely on the wrist with such power that the gun fired and then went flying into the underbrush. I ran at the leader and hit him with a powerful blow that sent him off his feet and collapsing into a muddy ditch, out cold.

Leaving behind the shouting and searching gang members, I carried the boy back to my camp area. I thought that if he wasn't dead he would surely be dying. Fortunately for both of us I found Johnny sitting just outside our shelter area and brought the boy to him. I watched in amazement as Johnny went to work. We stopped his bleeding and Johnny asked me to carry the boy and come with him. We went out to the street and Johnny hailed a cab, a twenty-dollar bill in his outstretched hand. We jumped into the cab, and the driver sped off without getting any instructions at all from Johnny or me. The driver and Johnny seemed to be a team of some sort or at least knew each other. Johnny and I worked on the boy to keep his bleeding at a minimum and I had no time to think about the interplay between the cab driver and Johnny again.

The cab came to a screeching halt in front of a well-kept stone building, and with the cab driver's help we took the young boy directly into the building. The cab driver knocked on a door and it opened to a doctor's office. The doctor came out immediately and helped us get the boy on the table. As the doctor worked on the boy he asked Johnny in a rather knowing way, "Gang beating?"

Johnny only nodded at him, then asked, "What are his chances?"

"He's bad," the doctor replied, "but not as bad as some you've brought me. He'll make it."

"Keep him in the room until he is well, and let me know as soon as he can talk," Johnny responded.

The doctor smiled and said, "I'll put it on your bill, no charge." "He's a wanted boy," Johnny then said. "They'll kill him, no doubt."

The doctor chuckled and said, "I know the routine, Johnny."

We left quickly, not a word exchanged between us. The cab dropped us back off at the park and the driver did not ask for any money, and Johnny never offered it to him. Obviously a lot was going on that was deep and unspoken. When we arrived back at the camp, Johnny told me of this part of his operation. He said that he had developed a network to get runaways away from pimps and gangs and off the streets. He had brought many kids to the doctor over the years, and they were all part of this loose network of people who wanted to help. Johnny went on to explain to me that he would try to get to the kids when they had enough of the harshness and cruelty of the city streets. He would watch the kids closely as they tried and failed, then he would move in and work his magic. He went on to tell me that his job had become more difficult since the gangs had moved into sections of the park and had become more violent.

I listened to the beauty of his vision unfolding before me. I had never realized that there was this network so committed to helping, and helping anonymously. Johnny was a shining light in this dungeon of darkness, committed selflessly to his vision of saving these kids while forgoing all creature comforts. I knew that Johnny did not approve of violence, but I had to tell him what I had done to save the kid from a slow and painful death. He simply smiled at me and said, "He who lives by the sword dies by the sword. Sometimes the ugliness of this city has to be met with the same ugliness. I can tell that you're upset because of what you had to do, but I don't think you had a choice in the matter. I know their kind and if you had attacked them any less aggressively and viciously then the boy would have died, and quite possibly so would you."

He was right, I had no choice and I knew that nothing less than the animal aggression would have stopped them. I was angry over how the gangs had taken over that part of the park, to a point where even the homeless were afraid to go there. It was then that I told Johnny that I could rid the park of gangs faster than the police could. He looked at me with a slight smile on his face that seemed to mock my immature and uninformed statement, then said, "You don't know what you are up against. These gangs rule the streets and the penalty for interference is death. How could you ever believe that you could clear these people out of the parks?" I went on to tell him of the scout concept of psychological warfare, the various man traps, and all manner of other things I had used these techniques for. That caught his interest and he listened attentively to my plan.

Johnny set out with me early in the morning of the next day to begin our scout psychological warfare on the gangs, pushers, and muggers of the park. I assured him at the onset that none of the things I did would really hurt anyone badly, but they would certainly shake them up physically and terrorize them mentally. I began by identifying all the routes in and out of the park, the hiding areas, and their escape routes. I showed him the tracks in the ground and how these tracks indicated the intentions of every maker. He seemed to understand, intrigued by what I could read in the earth. I then found an area that a potential mugger had checked out several times during the past few nights. It was near one of the park's small footpaths, one frequented by many people at night. I then disclosed how this man was planning to mug his victim.

Johnny watched with great interest as I rigged a spiked-whip-stick trip wire. He had no idea what the trap was going to accomplish, for he did not see the whip-stick mechanism. While making all traps that first night I had him stay way back from where I was working so that he would not disrupt the natural landscape. He knew the city but was only beginning to know the way of the woods. I rigged several other traps throughout this heavy crime area, but never traps that innocent victims would blunder into. To spring one of these traps you would have to be involved in some criminal activity, for the traps and their locations were designed for the movements of someone with criminal intent. I finished setting all my traps by middle evening, spacing each to fit into the scheduled movements of those I wanted to trap. That way, Johnny and I could be hiding nearby and see the traps in action.

I didn't know a better way to show Johnny the success of scout psychological warfare and the effectiveness of traps, other than to let him watch firsthand. We sat far back from the spring trip that I had set for the mugger, and as expected he came early and would thus be the recipient of my first trap. This mugger's game was to hide in the bushes around the time that the theaters let out, and thus prey on those people who walked back through the park to get to their apartments. He showed up right on time and soon disappeared behind the bush to wait. Several people passed by him, but he did not make a move. He must have figured that these folks were not good targets, being either too young and without much cash, or too strong. He did spot the undercover police officer coming, however, and retired deep into the brush until the undercover officer had long since passed. I knew that the officer was carrying a gun because of his walk and I wondered how the mugger knew.

I nudged Johnny as a middle-aged couple strolled onto the scene and began to pass the mugger. I could tell from the mugger's physical motion that these people were his target. As I expected him to do, he crouched down, waited for them to pass, then began to slip out of the bushes to get behind them. As soon as he took the obscure path he hit the trigger, and the stick let go with a whipping sound. The sharp spike caught him right below the knee and stuck him. I had purposely kept the spike short so it would not puncture too deep, but the snap stick was strong and could deliver a powerful wallop. I had to nudge Johnny as he stifled a laugh. The man rolled on the ground holding his knee in agony: his knife fell to the path and slid. The couple took one look at the knife and trotted away, crying for help. The mugger kept trying to get up and run away but his knee was too stunned. In what seemed a matter of moments two police officers and the undercover man were on him, and soon on their way out of the park with him.

Johnny was amazed by the trap's effectiveness and dumbfounded by the end of the night over what I had accomplished. He watched gangs enter a small clearing through a small grove of trees and spring a trap that dumped tar on the second man in line. He watched a drug dealer step into a pit trap and get his ankle badly sprained in the process. I explained to Johnny that this was the rolling log pit trap. Once the foot breaks through the upper surface of the pit the logs inside roll in such a way as to give the ankle a bad sprain. I also told him that I could have set it for a break. He watched another drug dealer step into a leg-hold snare, which detained him in screaming pain long enough for the police to apprehend him. Throughout the night we watched trip wires, deadfalls, rolling snares, keeper traps, and pit traps work their magic. What amazed him even more was that none of the people trapped had been hurt permanently.

He watched me as I lay in wait beside a little lowland drainage area that connected to a small lake. I had covered myself in mud and awaited a prostitute to walk by. I grabbed her by the ankles and with a frightening growl dragged her into the mud, then I deftly disappeared. She crawled out of the mud screaming and disappeared probably faster than she ever ran in her life. He was amazed when we stumbled across a mugging in progress and I knocked the knife from the mugger's hand with a stick, just as I had done with the leader of the gang. He was even more amazed when I ran down a purse snatcher and dragged him to the ground. I pretended to bite viciously while still totally covered in mud. The night for Johnny was one victorious adventure after another, culminating in the final act of scout warfare.

The grand finale was simple. I lured a gang into the thickest forested and brushy area of the park, causing them initially to try to chase me down. I then effectively took them out one at a time. I took the knife out of one guy's hand and made him strip off all his clothes and run away through the park. Another gang member I tied to a tree with his belt and told him that if he moved he would pull a string that would fire a gun that was pointed at the back of his head. The third guy I literally just frightened so badly that he could not scream, but panicked and ran from the woods, with me biting at his back. I lured the leader into another scout leg-hold trap, then I proceeded to stake him out to the ground spread eagle, using his own clothing, cut into strips, to tie him. Johnny, watching from the far end of the thicket, was laughing out of control when I was finally finished.

He told me afterward that, even having witnessed all the preparations being made and the traps being set, he would never have believed in a million years that it would work out the way it did. He was amazed how the criminal's nature could be so effectively used against him, and how powerful this game of scout psychological warfare really was. For nearly the next full month we trapped, stalked, terrorized, and intimidated all the criminal elements of the park, to a point where on any given night all was quiet. We wondered what the police must have thought about the severe drop-off in crime in that section of the park. Yet despite the results around us, our little game never even made a dent in the bigger crime picture. We knew without a doubt that it would only be a matter of time before they would be back into the park again. If I had planned to live there I could have probably kept them out forever, but I planned to go back to the wilderness soon.

I took Johnny home with me for Christmas and introduced him to my parents. We spent a few great days together; I was able to show him my wilderness, the Pine Barrens, and show him also all the things I had made and collected through the years. My folks treated him as if he were one of the family, for they were well used to me bringing home strays both animal and human. I could tell that soon after our few days together Johnny was getting anxious to get back to his work. He told me that the holidays were always the hardest time on the kids, and he had to be there for them. I accompanied him back and stayed with him until mid-February, and we continued to teach each other. Johnny went on to become what I would guess to be the first urban scout. I reluctantly left the city, now savvy of its ways, and had Johnny to thank for much of what I learned. More than anything else, Johnny taught me the self-sacrifice of a vision, and that truly the light of love and compassion can dwell even in the darkest jungles of the city.

I kept in touch with Johnny over the years as much as I possibly could. He still worked tirelessly in his efforts to save the kids, and still lived the spartan life of the street people, even through his last few years of failing health. Johnny passed away in 1987 of pneumonia at the age of seventy-nine. His quiet work still lives on through all of the lives he has touched and saved. And to those who now follow his vision—Gus, Bill, Sally, and Fred—may the Great Spirit bless you, that you may always be a shining light in the darkness.

CHAPTER 12

THE SCOUT CONSCIOUSNESS

The scout is a different kind of animal from most other humans. He lives a life on the edge of adventure, sees and hears things that most would never dream possible, and life to him is filled with endless excitement and adventure. Age has no bearing on the life of the scout, for with age he gains wisdom, and it is through wisdom that he becomes a master. Once one reaches the consciousness of the scout, he or she is always a scout, for the scout mind becomes the only reality, the only way to live. The scout's realm does not exist only in the flesh; the physical is only a starting point that leads to a spiritual existence. With age, the scout finds that he almost always operates in the spiritual, rarely entering the world of flesh. For a scout has become master when he transcends the limitations of the flesh and thus exists in the duality of flesh and spirit equally.

The scout looks at everyday life in society, and people in general, differently than most people could ever imagine. The structure of society, the games, and the routine of ordinary life, become a playground. People's lives, actions, and reactions, become a source of intense study. A trained scout can just glance at someone, scrutinizing subtle detail, and gain a glimpse into the person's very soul. People's actions, how they dress, how they react, what they observe and miss, how they tie their shoes—all give the scout an intense and accurate picture of that person. Coupled with the scout's depth of understanding of tracking, he knows more about that person than most could even dream possible. If people only knew what a scout gathers at a glance they would be embarrassed, for the scout's observation skills penetrate deep.

After living much of my life in the consciousness of the scout and observing people carefully, I have come to several conclusions. I cannot understand how people can live their lives playing the games of society and worshiping the false gods of the flesh, while passionately seeking the prisons of safety, security, and comfort, which are nothing more than euphemisms for death. Thoreau wrote that "most men live lives of quiet desperation," and I might also add, "desperate mediocrity." To the scout, each day is filled with adventure, excitement, intensity, and play. Life is a huge playground, waiting for the scout to break routine and move out of context, becoming invisible to everyone. Wilderness becomes his home, and the life of society becomes his wilderness.

The scout is the ultimate warrior. A man who can go out with nothing and survive lavishly. A man who has pushed his flesh and skill to perfection so that no place, no one, and no security are safe from his watchful eye and ability to move in and out without being observed. To the scout, even the most highly aware person in society is still living in a vacuum. No one can see the scout, touch the scout, or understand his ways. Whether in the deep recesses of wilderness or in the confines of the most intense city environment, the scout is equally powerful. A modern-day team of scouts would become the most deadly fighting force on earth, for they would need nothing of communication or supply lines. Yet the scout rarely deals with war; instead he is a peacemaker, always the last to pick up the lance. He believes in love and compassion, even for his enemies.

The classic skills of survival, tracking, and awareness are powerful but the art form and science of the scout brings these areas to an unbelievable level of proficiency. I tell my students that if life on this planet turns to mass war and starvation, where people hunt people to survive, then the skills of survival, tracking, and awareness will give you a chance of living through it, but the skills of the scout will ensure that you will survive, and survive lavishly. For a good scout can survive in any environment with nothing, entering any area naked and then turning it into a Garden of Eden. The scout can easily exist where most people would die. What most call hell, the scout calls home. And his skills are so powerful that he can exist right under the noses of his enemy, unobserved. The scouts thus become a myth, the myth of the shadow people, the ghosts, and the invisible, which they were so often called. That which is not seen or understood by people then becomes a myth.

Modern man cannot conceive of the intense skills that

a scout possesses. These skills are too farfetched, nearly impossible, to his mind. But so too are the skills of tracking and survival. People of modern society do not believe that anyone can enter the wilderness naked and survive, or follow tracks across solid rock. Yet this skepticism soon diminishes as I watch the numerous S.W.A.T. teams, elite military groups, and common students I have trained stand wide-eyed and openmouthed over the skills of the scout, and what they too have learned to accomplish. Thus the myth is dispelled, and the skills and philosophy of the scout become reality.

For many years now I have taught the ''way of the scout'' to countless students. I feared that if I died the way of the scout would die with me. Though the Scout Class is an advanced course of study and experience in my Tracker School, and demands several prerequisite classes, through it I have successfully passed on this basic consciousness and skill to many. The class became the beginning for these students, the beginning of looking at and existing in life differently. They now live life as I live life, as Grandfather lived life, and as the ancient scout societies lived life, on the edge of excitement and adventure. I am proud that throughout the world, I have scouts that are following this ancient tradition, leaving society to scratch its head in wonder and confusion.

My scouts have gotten in and out of extreme and highly secure situations without even the slightest hint of detection. My scouts who live in the cities watch the criminal elements and can move with ease throughout even the most intense gang wars. My desk is flooded by letters from my scouts, telling of their exploits and adventures, of what they have been able to accomplish. This makes my heart soar, for I had had my doubts about teaching the Scout Class. In essence all I could do was give these people the basic skills and philosophy; they had to have the passion and commitment to practice these skills to mastery and excellence on their own. I have to laugh at the power of this loose network of scouts, for with just a phone call I could send a scout in and out of any situation to gather information or to deliver the psychological warfare they so love to administer.

My modern scouts truly follow the philosophy of ancient scout life. They are a group of individuals who come together as a whole, bound by a code of honor, and living on the edge. To the scouts of old, and to those of today, I am honored that you are keeping this philosophy alive. You are the answer to so many of my prayers, that these skills are not lost to the fleshy coffins of modern life. To you I dedicate this book. Sorry for blowing your cover.

Santa Fe Community
College Library
6401 Richards Ave.
Santa Fe, NM 87508

If you would like to go further and discover more
about the wilderness with Tom Brown, please write
for information to:

The Tracker
Tom Brown, Tracker, Inc.
P.O. Box 173
Asbury, New Jersey 08802-0173
(908) 479-4681
www.trackerschool.com
Tracking, Nature, Wilderness Survival School